T0267156

Acclaim for

A BRIEF HISTORY OF THE WORLD IN 47 BORDERS

"Totally fascinating and hugely entertaining. This book is a nerd's paradise without borders—but with jokes. Jonn Elledge has such a gift for looking at complicated bits of the world, then telling you all about them in a way that feels like an incredibly fun and interesting conversation in the pub."
—Marina Hyde, author of *What Just Happened?*

"A fascinating and often very funny history of one of our great current preoccupations: borders."
—Tom Holland, author and host of *The Rest Is History* podcast

"Full of stories you thought you understood and those even the nerds in your life will never have known, this clever, confounding history will help you see the world from a new angle—if you can ever put it down."
—Patrick Maguire, author of *Left Out*

"By turns surprising, funny, bleak, ridiculous, or all four of those at once, *A Brief History of the World in 47 Borders* unknots some of the weird historical and geographical tangles we've managed to get ourselves into."
—Gideon Defoe, author of *An Atlas of Extinct Countries*

"A brilliant account of how these lines on a map shape lives, destinies and economies. You'll never look at a map in the same way again."
—Stephen Bush, *Financial Times* columnist

"All borders are artificial and every nation is an invention. Jonn Elledge provides a witty grand tour of the fascinating, disturbing and downright bizarre decisions that made the world what it is today."
—Dorian Lynskey, author of *The Ministry of Truth*

"Somehow, Jonn Elledge turns geo-political history into a funny, fascinating and revealing insight not only into the world today but into the frailty and determination of the human spirit. Packed with 'I never knew that' information (the sort that you read out to anyone in the room with you), *A Brief History of the World in 47 Borders* shows us that history doesn't repeat itself, but it plays out in weird ways right under our noses. He's such a lovely writer. A delight from start to finish."
—Miranda Sawyer, author of *Out of Time*

"This is brilliant fun, explaining the modern world in enjoyably bite-size chapters. It's exactly the book you hope it will be."
—Rob Hutton, author of *The Illusionist*

"Delightful. You'll learn more in one book than you did in years of school."
—Charlotte Ivers, *Sunday Times* columnist

"Jonn Elledge is a wonderfully lively writer—warm, funny and sharply political, all at once. This makes him the perfect guide for a survey of the world's borders, which are revealed, under his quizzical gaze, to be deadly serious and utterly absurd."
—Phil Tinline, author of *The Death of Consensus*

"With the wit—and often the tone—of Douglas Adams telling us about the tragic absurdities of the galaxy, Jonn Elledge is our guide to the lines that have divided us since we decided to stop following the caribou to plant crops and pay tax. Why are some borders straight and some crinkly? Why is Israel in the Eurovision Song Contest? Why does Northern Ireland exist? The answers are here."
—Matthew Sweet, author of *Operation Chaos*

"Full of fascinating stories."
—Greg Jenner, author and host of *You're Dead to Me* podcast

A BRIEF HISTORY OF THE WORLD IN 47 BORDERS

Suprising Stories Behind the Lines on Our Maps

JONN ELLEDGE

NEW YORK

A Brief History of the World in 47 Borders: *Surprising Stories Behind the Lines on Our Maps*
Copyright © 2024 by Jonn Elledge
Maps copyright © 2024 by Tim Peters

Originally published in the UK as *A History of the World in 47 Borders: The Stories Behind the Lines on Our Maps* by Wildfire, an imprint of Headline Publishing Group. First published in North America in revised form by The Experiment, LLC.

All rights reserved. Except for brief passages quoted in newspaper, magazine, radio, television, or online reviews, no portion of this book may be reproduced, distributed, or transmitted in any form or by any means, electronic or mechanical, including photocopying, recording, or information storage or retrieval system, without the prior written permission of the publisher.

The Experiment, LLC | 220 East 23rd Street, Suite 600 | New York, NY 10010-4658
theexperimentpublishing.com

THE EXPERIMENT and its colophon are registered trademarks of The Experiment, LLC. Many of the designations used by manufacturers and sellers to distinguish their products are claimed as trademarks. Where those designations appear in this book and The Experiment was aware of a trademark claim, the designations have been capitalized.

The Experiment's books are available at special discounts when purchased in bulk for premiums and sales promotions as well as for fundraising or educational use. For details, contact us at info@theexperimentpublishing.com.

Library of Congress Cataloging-in-Publication Data

Names: Elledge, Jonn, author.
Title: A brief history of the world in 47 borders : surprising stories behind the lines on our maps / Jonn Elledge.
Other titles: History of the world in 47 borders | Brief history of the world in forty-seven borders
Description: New York, NY : The Experiment, [2024] | Includes index. | Summary: "A fascinating history of the world told through the lines people have drawn on maps"-- Provided by publisher.
Identifiers: LCCN 2024034124 (print) | LCCN 2024034125 (ebook) | ISBN 9781891011573 | ISBN 9781891011580 (ebook)
Subjects: LCSH: Boundaries--Social aspects. | Cartography--History. | Human territoriality. | Cultural pluralism--History. | Borderlands--Political science. | Historical geography--Maps. | Human geography--Maps. | Discoveries in geography--History.
Classification: LCC JC323 .E45 2024 (print) | LCC JC323 (ebook) | DDC 912.09--dc23/eng/20240826
LC record available at https://lccn.loc.gov/2024034124
LC ebook record available at https://lccn.loc.gov/2024034125

ISBN 978-1-891011-57-3
Ebook ISBN 978-1-891011-58-0

Cover design by Jack Dunnington
Text design by EM&EN

Manufactured in the United States of America

First printing October 2024
10 9 8 7 6 5 4 3 2

For Agnes—God, I wish you were here to see this

Contents

PART TWO: LEGACIES

List of Maps

Introduction

An even briefer history

The main reason we know of the first recorded instance of a man-made international border is because of its abolition.

It won't have been the first to have existed, of course; people have been drawing lines on maps for as long as there have been maps to draw on, and even before that, our ancestors will have been keenly aware that this side of the stream is our tribe's land, while over there, in the distance, dwell the others. But the first example of an international border we can place with any degree of certainty is that which divided the lands of the Nile during the fourth millennium BCE. To the north of this limit was Lower Egypt, which lay in the low-lying river delta. To its south was Upper Egypt, which occupied the narrower band of higher ground towards Lake Nasser. The dividing line was somewhere around the thirtieth parallel, just south of modern-day Cairo.

But then, sometime around 3100 BCE, that border ceased to exist. Menes, who may actually have been called Narmer, became the first pharaoh by uniting the two kingdoms, in the process creating the world's first and most enduring national identity. For centuries to come, Egypt's rulers employed regalia combining symbols representing both halves of their kingdoms, and styled themselves as 'lord of the two lands'.

Several things are worth noting about this story. One is that borders and boundaries, the division between people like us and people like them, have been with us for the entirety of human history. Another is that, while both may sometimes have their roots in real physical geography, it's not always clear whether the border was shaped by political identities or whether the political identities were shaped by the border. A third is that boundaries can retain resonance long after they are effectively erased.

But probably the most important thing to take from this story is that, given a distant enough perspective by time or geography, almost any boundary can become baffling to the point of meaninglessness.

*

So, here's a game you can play at home. Stick the words 'map of the world' into a search engine's image search function and see what pops up. You will almost certainly get a couple of different map projections – and possibly an upsetting array of colour schemes too. But it's likely that all the maps on offer will otherwise be exactly the same, as the search engine assumes that, when you ask for a map of the world, what you really want is a *political* map of the world, which shows national boundaries and marks different countries in different colours.

This assumption is so embedded in the culture we've all grown up in that it might take a second to grasp it's an assumption at all – but it is. One could, in theory, be interested in natural geographical features, like rivers and mountains, rather than national boundaries. Even if we stayed in the realm of the human, one might be more interested in the question of where people actually live – maps of cities and population density – rather than the sometimes notional political control over places where they don't. Yet the search engine assumes that the thing we're most keen to learn about is the manufactured entities we call nation states. And it does so because, odds are, your brain does so too.

This is not necessarily how our ancestors would have conceived of the world. For much of history, had decent cartography or internet search engines been available, a 'map of the world' would have looked very different. So before we dive into talking about specific boundaries and what they mean, here's a map, as it were, of the territory ahead.

The earliest political entities recognisable to us as states – or at least, the earliest we have records of, which of course is not the same thing – emerged sometime in the fourth millennium BCE, in what is sometimes known as the 'Fertile Crescent', a region stretching from the Nile valley round to where the rivers Tigris and Euphrates meet the Persian Gulf. Later on, other civilisations emerged in other river valleys: the Harappan civilisation centred in Pakistan's Indus Valley; the earliest Chinese dynasties, beside the Yellow River.

The rulers of these places almost certainly had some sense of what land was definitely theirs and what was not, but the peripheries were more likely to be fuzzy areas where their influence was limited rather than hard lines marking out the point where it suddenly stopped. What's more, what lay beyond was less frequently a rival state than a sort of no man's land, free of political control and home to nomads, plus, probably, an exciting array of things that might kill you. There simply weren't enough humans in the world for all land to be claimed. It's probably not a coincidence that the first boundary we know of is the aforementioned one between Upper and Lower Egypt, as the Nile valley was one of the few areas fertile and prosperous enough to support rival states that could bang into each other.

This situation – islands of statehood in a great ocean of land – seems to have persisted for, well, almost all human history. The great empires of the classical era preferred to rely on natural features – mountains, rivers – for boundaries where possible. Where they did create their own, man-made boundaries, like Hadrian's Wall or the Great Wall of China, it was less about marking the boundary between states than between order and chaos, a way of giving them some form of control, even just highlighting their domination over man and nature alike. China's Han Empire, the American historian John Mears wrote in 2001, regarded its wall 'less as a clear, continuous line and more as a *cordon sanitaire*, a barrier restricting the movement of people and goods over what they regarded as the approximate boundary of their state'. Half a millennium later, on the other side of Eurasia, entire 'nations' could and did enter the Roman Empire, establishing themselves as *foederati* – client kingdoms – within its boundaries. For all the might of those empires, this is a much weaker conception of national boundaries than the one we're all used to.

The nation state – a way of organising the world so that political and ethnic/linguistic boundaries align – arrived later than we sometimes imagine, too. We live in a world still shaped by two western European countries, England and France, which coalesced early (both are over a thousand years old). This, along with misleadingly modern-looking maps with titles like 'Europe in 1000 CE', has sometimes led us to imagine a medieval Europe composed of a system of rival states not dissimilar to the one we have now. Until the early modern era, though, 'nation' was a distinctly fuzzy concept: people could move freely, provided they weren't enserfed or enslaved, but towns and territory were constantly traded between noble families by conquest, peace treaty or marriage alliance. Even in England and France, the edges remained fuzzier a lot longer than we sometimes assume – consider the fact that Lancashire, which later produced the major English cities of Manchester and Liverpool, doesn't feature in the Domesday Book (William the Conqueror's 11th-century Great Survey), or that Giuseppe Garibaldi, one of the most famous Italians of all time, was born in Nizza, better known today as Nice.

But then, in a few busy centuries around 1500, a couple of related things happened that fundamentally changed how people conceived of the world. One was that, thanks to improved tools and printing, maps got a lot better. That was useful as a way to, say, announce your control of that piece of land over there that you believed your family owned; it also gave political leaders a more spatial sense of their power.

Another change was in how Europeans, at least, thought of states. It may partly have been the shift to a form of government more based on centralised administration than feudal relationships that did it; a lot of it was also the Reformation. But at some point, the notion that much of their continent was under the sway of a vague and possibly non-existent thing called 'Christendom' was replaced by a sense of a world made up of independent sovereign states. This shift is sometimes credited to the Peace of Westphalia of 1648 (see page 78) but this turns out to be one of those things about history that everyone 'knows' which might be entirely untrue: the relevant treaties have almost nothing to say about sovereignty.

At any rate, by around the year 1700, maps were starting to show national borders in heavier lines than other forms of boundary: for the first time, the most important thing to know about a piece of land was which state it belonged to. At the same time, the bigger European powers were gobbling up unincorporated borderlands. Now, states mattered most, everywhere was part of one, and they were not just political units but sources of cultural identity, too.

This, via European expansion and imperialism, soon came – in relative terms, at least – to define the entire world. By the early nineteenth century, Thomas Jefferson's USA was setting state boundaries and parcelling out land to settlers based on little more than cartography. By the end of the century, the European powers were dividing up Africa – *an entire continent* – in much the same way. The words of British prime minister Lord Salisbury – which, in best British tradition, manage to be amusingly ironic about the terrible thing while also making clear he had no intention of stopping it – sum up the results best: 'We have been engaged in drawing lines upon maps where no white man's feet have ever trod; we have been giving away mountains and rivers and lakes to each other, only hindered by the small impediment that we never knew exactly where the mountains and rivers and lakes were.' Not that long before, this sentiment would have been meaningless – how can you divide the world using nothing but a map?

Eventually, of course, the empires fell (well, most of them; China, Russia and the United States are, I believe, still standing). But many of the lines they drew on the maps survived. And so today's maps divide the landmasses of planet Earth into roughly 193 discrete bits, most of which are fewer than two centuries old. What's more, they strongly suggest that the boundaries between them are not only clear but the only real way of dividing up the planet.

*

It's impossible to come up with an exact and unarguable measure for the length of a coastline; you can always zoom in further, get a more accurate measurement, include details invisible in a more distant view. By the same token, even with an infinite word count, it'd be impossible to come up with a history of a boundary that included every quirk of its past and geography. Things need to be compressed and summarised. So what you have here is not a definitive account, merely my interpretation of which parts are the most interesting, on the assumption that if I find them so, then you might, too. In the same way, I've had to be picky about which stories to include. This is not, despite its title, a definitive history of the world: there are entire centuries, entire civilisations I've been forced to leave out.

These gaps partly reflect the limitations on both time and space inherent in producing any book, and partly an urge to avoid repetition – but also, if I'm honest, my own limitations as a human being, and the fact I am, variously, English, British, European, a Westerner and white. I've tried to push outside my comfort zone, to acknowledge how many of the world's problems are the work of people who look more or less like me – but this is nonetheless my history with my biases. If I've missed your favourite border, or your favourite civilisation, I can only apologise – and invite you to buy copies of this book for all your friends and family to increase the likelihood I can correct that error in a sequel.

I should also make clear up front that what follows isn't a simple, linear history, stretching from past to present. It couldn't be, without jumping from border to border in an infuriating and confusing fashion, because many of these stories play out over so long. Indeed, most of the essays in this book include both chunks of history and commentary about the world as it stands today.

All that said, part one of the book, **Histories**, is roughly chronological. There I run through some of the most interesting lines drawn in the past, from the ancient world to the twentieth century – some because they feel particularly key to telling the story of borders as a concept and some because of the role they played in creating the world we live in now.

In part two, **Legacies**, I move on to the story of those borders whose most interesting feature is how they are still affecting the world today – by providing potential military flashpoints or less frightening foreign policy dilemmas, or simply because they make for strange or confusing lines on the map.

Finally, in part three, **Externalities**, I look at other types of border, less concerned with carving up control of the ground beneath our feet – temporal borders, between dates and time zones; borders at sea or in the air; and, finally, borders in space. Just as the book begins in the distant past, it ends by looking to the future.

While I'm explaining what lies ahead, some quick notes about language. Firstly, there is, technically, a subtle difference between boundaries and borders. A boundary is, in the words of Philip Steinberg, director of the IBRU Centre for Borders Research at the University of Durham, a 'line of no thickness where the territories of two states meet', while a border is the line you pass through to cross from one state to another. The former is about division, the latter about connection. This is why you can find signs alerting you to the fact you are about to cross a border inside an airport, hundreds of miles away from any physical boundaries. This is a distinction it feels worth noting, even though in the pages to come, I'm going to largely ignore it and use the two words interchangeably.

Likewise, the phrase 'Middle East' is obviously a problematic one, presuming as it does a European perspective on the world, rooted in a particular time, place and attitude. It is, if you think about it for half a second, just as absurd as the fact a large chunk of the eastern half of the United States is still commonly referred to as the 'Midwest'. There's an added complication, too, in that much of what we now call the Middle East – the stretch of the eastern Mediterranean once occupied by the Ottomans – would once have been termed the '*Near* East'. I did consider using less loaded terms like 'Western Asia', 'Southwest Asia' or 'SWANA'. But despite the fact that 'Asia' was originally the term for what is now Turkey, referring to that region as such today is likely to baffle a mainstream readership, and clarity is all. So as with the border/boundary distinction, I'm going to ignore it in favour of colloquial usage. This note is my way of saying, look, I'm not happy about it, okay?

Lastly, I should admit up front that the very title of this book is misleading. It contains 47 *chapters* but some are concerned with multiple borders. The lines humanity has drawn upon maps are innumerable. Apt, then, that the number of borders covered in these pages should be the same.

*

We are all familiar with the map of the world, or of our own corner of it. We are all so aware of where our bit stops and something else begins that it can be easy to imagine that the lines which carve it up are as natural a feature of geography as mountains, rivers or coasts. But they aren't. These divisions are ideas, more than physical facts, and to an animal or an alien they'd be invisible. What's more, what was made can be unmade. There was a time before those lines existed; there will be a time when they exist no more.

No border is inevitable or eternal. They are arbitrary and contingent and, in many cases, could have looked very different if a war or a treaty or the decisions of a handful of tired Europeans had gone a different way. Sometimes they are fleeting; sometimes they persist for centuries. Some are funny; some absurd; some brought forth a death toll that ran into the millions.

By telling the stories of these borders, we can learn a lot about human vanity and human folly, and see how what seems obvious and permanent in one century will come to seem random or ridiculous in another. These histories show us how decisions taken for reasons of short-term power politics or ego can have long-term, real-world effects for decades or centuries to come. And where better to begin than just south of Cairo 5,000 years ago, to consider what the first border in human history really meant.

PART ONE

HISTORIES

Borders are invented – empires rise and fall – nation states come into being – Europe screws up the world

The Unification of Upper and Lower Egypt

The first boundary in the world – possibly

The transition from prehistory to history is not the point at which stuff started happening, it merely marks the point at which people started writing stuff down. As a result, it's impossible to say with any certainty where the first borders appeared, since the urge to divide 'us' from 'them' almost certainly predates the urge to chronicle it in a form that will survive to be read in the twenty-first century.

Actually, the earliest city states/tribes/other peoples with some kind of group identity (delete according to ideology and taste) may have got away without borders in the modern sense simply because the world was, by modern standards, empty. They no doubt had a notion of where the land under their control came to an end – but beyond it there was less likely to be a notional line marking the border with another tribe than a no man's land controlled by no one. If anyone had invented maps, which they hadn't, they would have looked less like today's patchwork of nation states than like space or the sea: islands of order in a sea of chaos.

One of the first places where that ceased to be true was in northeastern Africa. In prehistoric times, this region had been home to nomadic hunter-gatherers, who moved from place to place in search of food, possibly with herds of cattle in tow. Sometime around the eighth millennium BCE, though, natural climate change meant the land began to dry out and, over many generations, the nomads settled down to farm the reliably fertile lands beside the river. Those lands, though, were narrow compared to the great desert beyond; the settled lifestyle meant a lot of people in a relatively small space.

So it is that, working chronologically, the first example of something resembling a modern international border you'll come across, sometime in the fourth millennium BCE, is almost certainly the one you'll find on the Nile. To the border's north lay Lower Egypt, the land of the delta, a relatively wide, fertile area prone to flooding. To the south was the higher ground of Upper Egypt, the land of the valley, where the band of fertile land was narrower and all the settlements crowded hard by the river. The dividing line, if there was anything as coherent as a line, has traditionally been placed somewhere around the thirtieth parallel. These two kingdoms had different customs, dialects and probably geopolitical interests too, with the north looking to the Mediterranean and the Levant, and the south to Nubia and into Africa. There's no reason to imagine they saw themselves as two halves of one divided whole, either. The idea of Egypt came later.

So why, at a point in history about which we know almost nothing, do we know of this border? Because, sometime around 3000BCE, some bloke abolished it. An Upper Egyptian king named Menes conquered the north and founded a new capital at Memphis from which to rule his newly unified kingdom, thus becoming the first pharaoh and creating a nation that still endures the entire length of human history later. For centuries to come, Egypt's rulers depicted themselves with symbols representing both halves of their kingdoms, using the title 'of the sedge and the bee' (emblems of Upper and Lower Egypt respectively) and styling themselves as 'uniter of the two lands' (exact translations vary). They even wore a double crown, the pschent, combining the white crown of Upper Egypt and the red crown of Lower Egypt. Key to the most ancient of Egyptians' sense of their nation was that they had once been two kingdoms but now, thanks to their beneficent rulers, they were one.

Of course, it's pretty difficult to work out what was going on in a world more distant from Socrates than he is from us; we also know much less about Lower Egypt than Upper because the slightly damper soil means that stuff was simply more likely to rot. And Egyptian history goes on for *ages*, so long that its conquests by the Persians and Alexander the Great – events we'd confidently categorise as 'ancient history' – take place in what's commonly referred to as its 'late period'. So you'll be unsurprised to learn there are a few question marks over this story.

In his book *The Rise and Fall of Ancient Egypt*, Toby Wilkinson highlights recent discoveries suggesting that the last two kingdoms standing before the unification around 3100BCE were based at Tjeni and Nekhen, both well inside Upper Egypt. When Egypt was divided again during later periods of instability, he notes, that division was generally at Asyut, a sudden constriction in the Nile valley north of both those sites but a good 200 miles south of the theoretical boundary. The political geography isn't nearly as clear cut as the traditional telling makes it sound.

It's also – this is awkward – possible that Menes never actually existed. His name barely appears in the archaeological record and so a consensus has emerged identifying him as a Tjeni-based king named Narmer, who has the advantage of being someone who definitely did exist. (Just to make life harder, pharaohs often had more than one name.) One side of the Narmer Palette, described by one Egyptologist as the 'first historical document in the world', seems to show him wearing the tall white crown of Upper Egypt and doing some smiting; the other has him cheerily ruling in the level red crown of Lower Egypt. That certainly suggests that what we're looking at is a record of conquest and unification. But even so, there's debate over whether the palette was intended to show an actual historical event or something more akin to a mythological origin story, of the 'raised by wolves, killed his brother then founded Rome' variety. The archaeological evidence does suggest a kingdom in the south of Egypt gradually extended its control – first over its immediate neighbours and then into the north – but there may not have been a moment when two clearly defined kingdoms merged to become one, or a particular king who made it happen.

Why does this border even feature in the historical record at all? Because, while we may not know much about what the earliest pharaohs did, the nature of the evidence we have (tombs, monuments, king lists, etc.) means that we know a lot about how they wished to be *seen*. And all that insignia – the double crown, both halves of which may have actually originated in Upper Egypt; the titles like 'lord of the two lands' – suggest that it was important that the pharaohs position themselves as the personification of the united Egypt. At least one, Djer, is known to have conducted a sort of tour referred to as the 'circumambulation of the two lands', knitting his vast kingdom together using his very presence.

Five thousand years later, after Egypt has survived occupation by everyone from Persians to Brits and still come out the other side as a single entity, the idea of it breaking into pieces again may seem fanciful. In ancient times, though, it was a very real worry: during the 'intermediate periods', between old, middle and new kingdoms, the land did fragment again and at times more than one dynasty ruled simultaneously from different capitals. Titles like 'uniter of the two lands' reflected the fact that pharaoh's prestige came, in part, from being strong enough to bind the country together.

Whether the boundary between the two Egypts had ever literally existed mattered less than the fact its ruler was strong enough to have erased it.

One last thing before we leave Ancient Egypt behind for the relatively recent events of the first millennium BCE. By the time of Djoser, the founder of the third dynasty in the twenty-seventh century BCE, Egypt was divided into provinces known as 'nomes'. Each of these was ruled by a 'nomarch', who seem to have been hereditary rulers with their own pseudo-feudal power bases. At the kingdom's height, there were forty-two of them and they persisted right down to the Muslim conquests of 640CE.

In other words, the nomes (it's a fun word to say, try it) were local government units which persisted in some form or another for upwards of 3,200 years. Puts English counties or American states into perspective, doesn't it?

The Great Wall of China and the Border as Unifier

Marking the limits of the Middle Kingdom since 221 BCE

You can't say 'the one thing everyone knows about the Great Wall of China is wrong' any more. That's because the one thing everyone knows about it *now* is 'it's not actually true that you can see it from space' and that, it turns out, is correct. The wall may be very long but it's only a few metres wide, and is, in any case, the same colour as the earth around it, which means you can't see it even from low orbit. If you want to see the Great Wall of China, you're still best off going to, well, China.

What is true, though, is that it is almost unimaginably vast: around 50,000km (about 30,000mi) of walls, which at that latitude is enough to circle the world and go halfway round again. That it clearly does no such thing is partly because it doesn't run in a straight line but mostly because it's not a single wall at all: it's a network of parallels and branches, stretching like a 2,500km (1,550mi) web across northern China, from the Jade Gate in the far west to the borders of Korea. Not all those walls still exist: the network that remains is estimated to be closer to 21,000km (13,000mi) in length. That is still, to be fair, a lot of wall.

To explain why the walls were necessary – and how they became a symbol of China's unification – it helps to step back a bit and ask a big question. Why did we start having borders in the first place?

For most of the Stone Age – which, at somewhere around 2.5 million years or so, accounts for roughly 99.8 per cent of all of human history – our species was overwhelmingly composed of hunter-gatherers: small tribal bands who moved about a lot, rarely ran into outsiders and got their calories from, well, hunting animals and gathering veg. But at some point, probably around 12,000 years ago, that started to change. In an event known variously as the Neolithic or Agricultural Revolution, someone – probably many someones – invented farming.

Exactly why anybody bothered is, strangely enough, a bit of a mystery: you might assume, in a whiggish, inexorable-march-of-progress sort of a way, that this made things better, but there's actually a fair bit of evidence that farming involved more work for fewer calories. Anthropologists have theorised all sorts of reasons why our ancestors did this ostensibly self-defeating thing, which is still, by any sensible definition, the most important thing to ever happen to our species: climate change; short-term benefits disguising long-term problems; benefits for the elite overriding problems for the masses. One possibility is simple demographics: you can support more people from a given area of land through farming than through hunter-gathering, which meant that those who farmed inevitably came to dominate. In all sorts of ways – more work, more inequality, the shift to settled existence allowing for more frequent pregnancies and thus the invention of patriarchy – life became harder. But with a rising population there was, at least, more life to go round.

At any rate, farming meant settling down, which had all sorts of implications for the relationship between humans and the physical world. For one thing, it meant more possessions: you could 'own' something without having to be able to carry it on your back. It also meant that control of good growing land became one of the most important factors in determining which groups of people would prosper and which did not. Where once, small groups of people moved about over vast areas, now much bigger ones were concentrated in relatively small ones.

But for one group to control a piece of land, that inevitably meant others could not. That gave the first an incentive to defend; the second, an incentive to attack.

You can probably see how this is the starter gun for, essentially, all human history.

The earliest civilisations – in Egypt, Mesopotamia, the Indus Valley of Pakistan and northwest India – all began in river valleys, where land was fertile and the seasons predictable. For obvious reasons, we know relatively little about life and politics in such places: as with the story of Menes/Narmer, we are dependent on disciplines like archaeology and anthropology because nobody had been kind enough to invent written history. But so far as we can tell, at some times, some of these places resembled unified empires, whose most important boundary was the fuzzy line between civilisation and barbarism; at others, they might consist of multiple states, competing for territory and hegemony, with power frequently shifting between dynasties and cities. A period of stability and success might cause the zone of civilisation and settlement to expand, but, at some point, the good times would inevitably end and the resulting array of different cities/states/*things* would inevitably come into conflict.

Such seems to have been the story of ancient China. At their height, the earliest dynasties controlled territories that, while a mere fraction of the size of modern China, were still vast by the standards of their era. As in Egypt, though, those empires had a periodic tendency to splinter into smaller pieces. So it was that, with a few centuries left to run in the first millennium BCE, the Zhou, China's third and longest-lived dynasty, still theoretically sat at the head of a polity they'd reigned over since sometime in the mid-eleventh century.* In practice, though, as early as the eighth century, real power had already begun to drain from the centre to an assortment of smaller local powers. By the fifth century, the king was forced to recognise the

* They may not actually have been the third. The dynasty that traditionally appears first in the list, the Xia, left no records and so is generally considered only a little more plausible than the legendary 'Three sovereigns and five emperors' period that preceded them. The next in line, the Shang, who seem to have reigned in the second half of the second millennium BCE, *did* leave some documentary and archaeological evidence. That means that, while there is still some debate about the Shang dynasty's starting date, finishing date and almost everything else, the consensus is that it did at least exist. In some way.

independence of some of these smaller states; by the third, he was little more than a figurehead and his recognition no longer even mattered. To give you some flavour of what this might have meant, the fifth to third centuries BCE are known as the 'Warring States Period'.

This is the world in which the Chinese first started building their walls. As far back as the seventh century BCE, the Chu – a Zhou vassal state centred on what is now Hubei province – began constructing a permanent defensive barrier, known as the 'Square Wall', to protect their capital. The Qi, to their north, used a combination of river dykes, impassable mountains and brand new structures of earth and stone to protect *their* perimeter. The Zhongshan built walls to protect them against Zhao and Qin; the Wei built two, one to protect their capital, another to defend their realms against nomadic tribes to their west and also against the Qin, again. The Qin, presumably a bit miffed by this, built their own walls to protect themselves from yet more nomads.

And so it went on. (There are more kingdoms, and many more walls, but that seems enough to provide a flavour.) These walls were defensive, yes, but they were also a way of marking territory. The impression you get is of local dynasties wanting to literally make their mark on the land – to show that they were as powerful as the next kingdom over.

All this reached some kind of conclusion in 221BCE, when Shihuangdi, leader of the by then extremely powerful Qin dynasty, completed the annexation of Qi, unified China and announced to the world that his dynasty would last '10,000' generations.*
This turned out to be a bit optimistic: in 207BCE, just four years after his death, his empire collapsed and, one quick civil war later, his dynasty was replaced by the rather more durable Han. Nonetheless, Shihuangdi has gone down in history as the first true emperor of China because of his many exciting schemes to turn the previously warring states into a single people with a single identity. His regime unified the various Chinese writing systems

* I did tell you they were miffed.

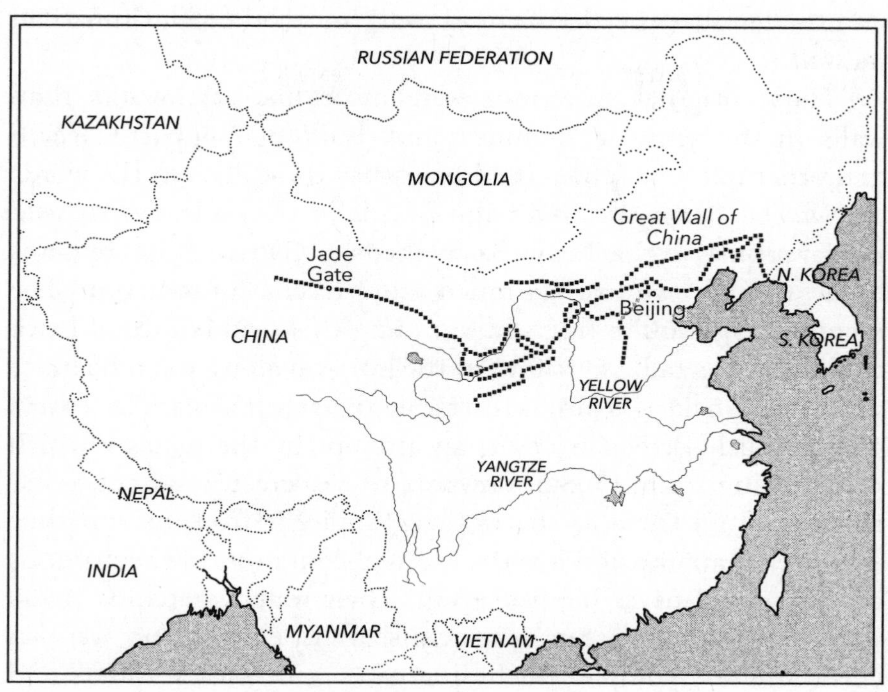

The Great Wall of China, superimposed onto today's map. Not every branch is shown.

into a single script; standardised weights and measures; even made rules about the width of cart axles to improve communications. There is a reason the Qin – pronounced, roughly, 'chin' – gave its name to the state.

And yet, the first emperor is also remembered as something of a villain because among these various schemes was a back-breaking programme of public works. Using a vast army of unpaid labourers, forced to work as a sort of tax, the state built new roads, canals and fortresses. It also began to link the various historic walls into a single system intended to defend against barbarian invasions from the north, but also as a symbol of the newly unified state. The literature of the period rails against the ruinous effect this would have on young men forced to work and the families they left behind. But, for good or ill, China had its wall.

Those original structures were more like earthworks than walls in the sense we'd understand, built of compacted earth and other materials that could be gathered locally – in the words of *National Geographic*, 'red palm fronds in the Gobi desert, wild poplar trunks in the Tarim Basin, reeds in Gansu'. What remains today, though, is mostly a much more recent construction. The mental image you've had while reading this – an edifice of brick as wide as it is tall, stretching to the horizon along the hills like a great, grey snake – is almost certainly the Ming Walls. These were a consciously defensive affair, an attempt by the dynasty which ruled China from 1368CE onwards to resurrect a system as far removed from them as the Roman Empire is from us and thus ensure that an invasion like the Mongol conquests of the previous century could never happen again. Their walls, stretching 4,500 miles from desert to sea, weren't just walls, either. They were an entire military complex, including gates and stables, towers and fortresses, with bombastic names like The Tower for Suppressing the North or (my personal favourite) The Tower for Suppressing the Goat-Like Foreigners.

This worked but, in the grand sweep of Chinese history, not for long. As the Ming began to falter, the state could no longer properly garrison its defences or properly supply those who remained to guard them: a wall, it turned out, was only as strong as the state it protected. When the Manchu mounted an invasion in the seventeenth century, the wall wasn't enough to stop them. That's not to say it didn't have its uses, however: the dynasty the Manchu established, the Qing, the last to rule imperial China, found the wall a useful bulwark against too much Chinese cultural influence finding its way back to their original non-Chinese territories in the northeast.

All of which brings us to one of the most important facts about the walls. Their purpose and meaning have changed radically over the centuries – which, given the likelihood of anything remaining the same over 2,000 years, should perhaps be no surprise. Their antecedents were a function of China's division, the Qin walls of its unification. In some centuries, the empire withdrew behind the walls, which came to symbolise the border between Chinese civilisation and the chaotic world outside. In others, the empire stretched far beyond, rendering them less a defensive structure and more a communications artery, a way of enabling and monitoring travel and trade from heartlands to provinces. In others still they've been forgotten and neglected and left to crumble away.

Then there's the inescapable role of tourism. At times when China has been more closed to the world, the walls have been the thing it hunkered down behind; when it's been more open, though, the beauty of its historic walls has been one of the main sights it offers to visitors, a major stop on the tourist trail among Westerners as far back as the fall of the Ming. Today, busloads of domestic tourists visit the stretch nearest Beijing – where once rich young Europeans would travel Europe on a Grand Tour, today, rich young Chinese students visit their walls.

So even if the walls do still serve a purpose as a symbol of the one, unified China they were built to protect, they couldn't hide the country from the world forever. And it wasn't just the Mongols and Manchu that managed to breach them: when Europeans arrived in the nineteenth century, they did so by sea, bringing gunships into Chinese ports. As the Chu, Qi and the others found all those millennia ago, and as the Ming discovered in the seventeenth century: no border can keep outsiders out forever.

Why Is Europe Not a Peninsula in Asia?

How the Greeks and the Church invented a continent

Different city transport systems have different levels of ambition. The New York subway stops dead at the city's northern limits, forcing residents of suburbs in neighbouring Westchester County to find another way. The Paris metro extends a few tentacles beyond the Boulevard Périphérique, which roughly traces the path of the city's last set of walls; the London Underground is all but inescapable in the city's northern and western suburbs but remains strangely in denial of the existence of its southeast.

The Istanbul metro can beat all of them. Six of its eight lines are in Europe; two – still within the city limits – are in Asia. The two areas are linked by the 76.6km-long (47.6mi) Marmaray commuter rail line, its name formed by combining that of the Sea of Marmara (which lies a little to its south) and 'ray', the Turkish word for 'rail' (which is what it is). Go to Istanbul and you can literally take a commuter train between continents.

This, though, is not as impressive as it at first sounds. In fact, you can switch continents by travelling just 3km (1.9mi) and one stop (from Sirkeci to Üsküdar, if you have the urge), and although the Marmaray runs in tunnel for 13.5km (8.4mi), only around 1.8km (1.1mi) of that is because of the Bosporus, the narrow strait dividing Europe from Asia. For most of its length, it's underground for the same reason that the New York subway or Paris metro are: because it'd be bloody inconvenient to start demolishing bits of Istanbul so as to run trains through them. The more you look at the Bosporus, the sillier it seems to consider the land on one side to be fundamentally different to the land on the other.

There are several points on Earth where continents meet, of course, and you could make an argument that, say, the Sinai Peninsula or the Isthmus of Panama are also pretty arbitrary points to tag as crossings from one to another. Those, though, are clearly narrow patches of land dividing two massive landmasses. What makes the Europe–Asia boundary different is that it doesn't get any less ridiculous if you zoom out. South of Istanbul the boundary runs through the Sea of Marmara and the Dardanelles, another strait which at its narrowest is just 1.2km wide. To the north, it continues via the Black Sea, the crest of the Caucasus Mountains, the Caspian Sea and the Urals – all impressive geographic features, I'm sure, but:

a) we don't generally divide continents by mountain ranges – North America divides at neither Rockies nor Appalachians;
b) there is, in any case, a gap between the Caspian Sea and Ural Mountains where no one seems quite sure where the boundary actually runs – the Ural and Emba rivers both come up but it's ultimately a judgement call because
c) look at a map of the world and it is extremely obvious that Europe and Asia, unlike North and South America, say, are one landmass with an arbitrary line drawn between them.

As arbitrary as this division is, though, it's also extremely old. The notion that there is some fundamental difference between the lands on either side of the Aegean Sea dates to the Ancient Greeks. One of the earliest known works of geography, Hecataeus of Miletus's *Journey Round the World*, which dates from the early fifth century BCE, took the form of a travelogue which worked clockwise around the Mediterranean, covering 'Europe' (from the Strait of Gibraltar to modern Greece) in book one and 'Asia' (modern Turkey to Morocco) in book two. This two-continent system later became a three-continent one with the boundary with 'Libya' – Africa – at the Nile.

The heartlands of the Ancient Greek world, you might notice – Attica and the Peloponnese on one side of the Aegean, and the western coast of Anatolia on the other – lay at the centre of this scheme. After all, if you were an Ancient Greek, where a place stood

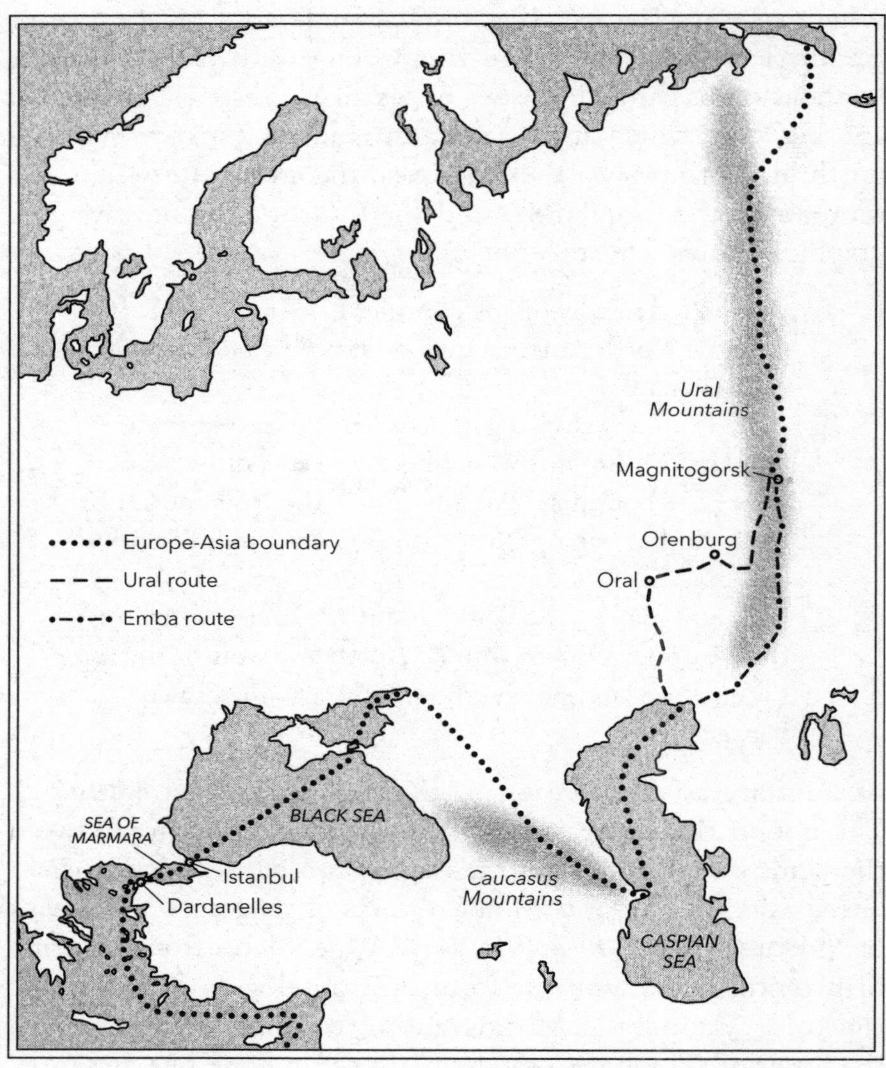

The strange, meandering route of the Europe–Asia boundary. Immediately north of the Caspian Sea, its route is contested, with some sources claiming it follows the Ural River, and others the Emba.

in relation to Greece was probably the most useful thing you could know about it. The fifth century BCE was also a time of conflict between Persia, whose empire dominated the lands to the east of the Aegean, and the Greek city states, which mostly lay to the west and whose national myth told of another epochal conflict with an eastern power named Troy. It's at least possible that this, too, contributed to the sudden enthusiasm for dividing east from west.

Even at the time, though, there were those who thought this ridiculous: before the fifth century BCE was out, the historian and geographer Herodotus was complaining in writing that he had no idea who had been responsible for dividing the world into three bits, or giving them names, but that everyone seemed very unclear about where the boundaries were. It may not have been a coincidence that he hailed from Halicarnassus – today's Bodrum in Turkey – a Greek city on the 'Asian' side of the Aegean, whose leaders had fought on the Persian side of the war.

The next thousand years or so were dominated by empires – Macedonian, Roman – that conquered parts of Europe, Asia and Africa alike. By the second century CE, a single state stretched from Carlisle to Kuwait, and while it had provinces called Africa and Asia, these covered tiny fractions of the continents to which we attach those names (a stretch of Mediterranean coast and western Anatolia respectively). There was no particular reason to expect an arbitrary system of geography, based on the Greek conception of the world sometime around 500BCE, to endure.

Quite obviously it did. Maybe this was down to Greek influence on the Roman imagination, not to mention Greek dominance of the eastern empire that survived nearly a thousand years after the western bit fell off. Or maybe it was the result of religion. In 200CE, there was no more to distinguish Greece from Syria than there was Greece from France. A few centuries later, though, the Islamic conquests happened, and the world to the east and south of Greece were very different places to the Christian lands to the northwest. Few in those lands may have thought of themselves as Europeans but they were very, very conscious of being a part of Christendom.

In the ninth century, a poet described the Emperor Charlemagne, a Frankish leader whom we'll meet in a few chapters' time, as *pater Europae*, the father of Europe, in an attempt to find a label flattering enough for a man who ruled over such a huge block of territory. As the centuries wore on, with classical knowledge all the rage, Christian forces trying to retake Spain and the Ottoman Empire edging ever closer to the heart of Europe, a view of the world that suggested a natural division between decent, European, *Christian* types and sinister Asiatics with their strange gods must have seemed rather appealing.

This was quite a different approach from that of the ancients. The Classical Greeks may have had political, as well as geographical, reasons for their tripartite division of the known world but they also had little enough information as to what lay in the far north that it was possible to genuinely believe there to be some fundamental physical divide between Europe and Asia. The Europeans of the Renaissance, though, *knew* that Europe and Asia made up a single landmass. This politically constructed and slightly false division is far from the only reason that Russia, which straddled the boundary, would spend the following centuries agonising over whether its people were proper Europeans or not, but it surely can't have helped.

It's not become any less absurd in the centuries since. The imperial age saw consensus over the route of the boundary through Russia shift several times – surely a sign that there was no fundamental reality to discover. By the mid-twentieth century, the theory of plate tectonics – the notion that the surface of the Earth was divided into plates, which over millions of years moved about the place banging into each other – was gaining acceptance and scientists discovered that most continents (Africa, Antarctica, Australia and both North and South America) had their own plate. Europe, however, was a mere western outpost of the Eurasian plates; if any parts of Asia deserved to be considered separate landmasses, according to this model it was the Arabian Peninsula and Indian subcontinent.

These places, though, have never been granted continent status: in a world largely built by those of European descent, the idea of Europe as a continent has survived, despite it being very obviously made up. And the Greek-speaking nation of Cyprus is still considered a European country, despite its breakaway Turkish-speaking north and the fact that it's closer to the Asian landmass.

I said earlier that Ancient Greece straddled the boundary. What I didn't mention was that modern Greece did, too. As late as the twentieth century, there were around 1.2 million Greek Orthodox Christians in Asia Minor, Eastern Thrace and other predominantly Islamic regions, as well as 400,000 Muslims in modern Greece. In 1923, both communities were forced to move: an act of legalised ethnic cleansing that created more than a million refugees. There had never really been a simple divide between a Christian Europe and an Islamic Asiatic world to its east – but the turmoil after the First World War provided an excuse to attempt to create one.

Istanbul, incidentally, is far from the only city to straddle the Europe–Asia border. Should you wish to take a tour, your stops will include Orenburg and Magnitogorsk in Russia, and Oral in Kazakhstan, all of which straddle the Ural River. In each of these – unlike in Istanbul – you can simply walk from Europe to Asia and back. Even when it's not being used as an excuse for ethnic cleansing this whole thing is just silly.

The Roman *Limes* and the Power of the Periphery

The centrifugal empire

Severus Alexander must have felt he had a lot to live up to. Of his two names, one was drawn from his great-aunt's husband, Septimius Severus, who had founded the dynasty which, at the turn of the third century, was in charge in Rome; the other was that of the greatest conqueror the world had ever known, the man who, half a millennium earlier, had brought lands from Greece to India under the control of tiny Macedon. Worse, he came to the imperial throne aged just thirteen – a difficult enough age for any boy, even without a fractious and tottering empire to manage – and in the full knowledge that his cousin had been murdered to clear his path.

It didn't go brilliantly. Young Alexander was widely seen as a figurehead for the real powers in Rome, his mother and grandmother, and the Romans, not known for their feminism, thought this sort of thing unseemly.* The city reportedly became so lawless that the Praetorian Guard, the emperor's personal bodyguard, murdered their own leader right in front of him, while one of the consuls for 229 CE, the historian Cassius Dio, spent chunks of his year in office outside the city to avoid a similar fate.

Alexander's biggest problem, though, was foreign policy. Despite some grumbling about their boyish and unworthy emperor, the Roman army defeated a Persian invasion of Mesopotamia, sort of. (The Roman counter-offensive was a disaster,

* Coins of the emperor show him with a rather wispy neck beard, suggestive of a boy who wants to look like he's a man but unfortunately isn't. The impression you get is of an emperor who uses a fake ID to buy beers for his mates.

especially the bit Alexander commanded personally; still, the Persians decided it wasn't worth the hassle and went home.) But then, almost before anyone could catch their breath, barbarian tribes began crossing the Rhine and Danube frontier. The army was depleted and the survivors exhausted, so in an effort to buy himself some time, Alexander attempted to bribe the Germans to go away again. This, for the troops, was just too much. What kind of 'emperor' was this, who, instead of defending the boundaries of the empire through blood and iron, attempted to buy his enemies off? And on the advice of a *woman*?

And so, they killed him. And then, for good measure, they killed his mother, too. In his place, they installed their own commander: Maximinus Thrax ('The Thracian'), a former shepherd and decorated military officer, who became the first Roman emperor to come from outside the empire's ruling class. Here, surely, was a man who could truly understand the needs of the soldiers tasked with defending Rome from its enemies. After all, he had been one of them!

Three disappointing years later, the troops killed him, too. This, it turned out, was to happen rather a lot. Over the next half-century, between the co-emperors, breakaway emperors and usurpers, the Roman Empire was to have at least twenty-six emperors* – roughly as many as it had got through in its first 220 years, even though those centuries had included unpromising periods by the name of the Year of Four Emperors (69 CE) and the Year of *Five* Emperors (193 CE).

There are a number of reasons the empire broke down and fractured during the period we know as the Crisis of the Third Century: the resurgence of Persia; the pressure of migration, sparked by some unseen crisis in central Asia; the economic crisis

* These exact counts are contested because it's not clear from this distance – and may not have been at the time – exactly who counts as a proper emperor. Honestly, the chaos of the Roman Empire is probably the single best argument for the hereditary principle. Okay, you sometimes end up with a dribbling idiot who, thanks to extensive inbreeding, only had five great grandparents, but at least it limits the number of claimants.

and inflation that followed Septimius Severus's debasement of the currency. A big part of it, though, was the collapse in military discipline that followed the murder of Severus Alexander, as commanders on the Rhine and Danube frontier realised that it was they who held all the cards. It was a crisis that stemmed, in part, from the empire's need to defend its own borders.

The gradual but inexorable expansion of Roman territory had been one of the main themes of the state's history. In its earliest centuries, the city had controlled little more than its immediate hinterland, and it was for a time dominated by the Etruscan state to its north.* In the mid-fourth century BCE, though – roughly the time when Severus Alexander's more impressive namesake was doing his thing in the east – the Romans had fought a series of wars, gradually defeating and absorbing much of the Italian peninsula. After that, they defeated the Carthaginians to become the dominant power in the western Mediterranean; swallowed Greece and Spain; and then expanded beyond, to Gaul, Africa, Egypt, and even to a distant, cold and generally unattractive island named Britain. For half a millennium, Rome had grown, until it encompassed much of the known world.

And then, around a century before Severus Alexander found himself in charge, it stopped. The emperor Hadrian, who came to power in 117CE, began to worry that the empire was becoming over-extended and withdrew from a few far-flung and recently conquered territories in favour of consolidating control over the land already in Roman hands. He also began moves to turn the previously shifting frontiers of the empire into something more understandable as a fixed border.†

You can probably guess at least one example of those borders because it still has the emperor's name on it. Hadrian's Wall

---

* Today's Tuscany.

† Both Hadrian and his immediate predecessor Trajan were born in today's Spain, although the former was certainly and the latter probably of Roman ancestry. It wasn't merely the boundaries of the state that expanded but the idea of who counted as Roman, right up to the Edict of Caracalla, in 212CE, which made basically all freeborn males citizens of the empire.

stretched for seventy-three miles across northern England and divided the firmly if restlessly Roman province of Britannia in the south from the wild lands of Caledonia to the north. Like those walls which had been built at the other end of Eurasia in China a few centuries earlier, it was probably never expected to be entirely impassable to outsiders; rather, it was a sort of tripwire, something which could slow down the enemy and provide, via its network of fortresses, an early warning system. More than that, it was a declaration of Roman power in a rebellious region and may even have performed an economic function, controlling the flow of goods in and out of the empire and levying taxes on them.

The wall was one of the more dramatic markers of the limits of Roman power but it wasn't completely unique. The empire's longest and most heavily fortified border was the *Limes Germanicus*, the German frontier: a line of over 350 miles, defended by at least 60 forts and 900 watchtowers. This, too, was probably as much a way of controlling trade and monitoring the periphery as it was a clear line between us and them, or a way of blocking the German tribes from entering the empire entirely. But to bridge the gap between the two great rivers which made up the *Limes*, Danube in the east and Rhine in the west, there nonetheless lay 190 miles of heavily defended earthworks.

Elsewhere, the limits of Roman power faced onto other natural barriers to movement, whether rivers, seas or deserts – notably the Sahara. Beyond, lay client kingdoms, or more barbarian tribes requiring careful management, or land hostile to human existence. It was only in the far eastern province of Mesopotamia, where Roman interests directly faced onto those of Persia, that the empire butted up against anything like a comparable state.

So while the build-up of legions along these borders, especially the German one, was partly about protecting the empire against external threats, it also served another purpose: defending the people who ran it from internal ones. Centuries earlier, responsibility for ensuring troops were paid had rested with individual generals. This was all very well, in a 'keeping costs down' kind of way, but in the last century of the Republic it had caused chaos when a succession of politically ambitious generals (Marius, Sulla, Pompey) had realised that this effectively gave them a loyal private army. The result had been half a century of chaos, as well as one of the most famous border crossings in history when, in January 49 BCE, Julius Caesar and his army crossed the Rubicon – the river that marked the northern frontier of Italy – thus precipitating yet another civil war.

When Caesar's adopted heir Octavian – Augustus, as he became – had eventually won enough civil wars to be the last man standing and become Rome's first emperor, he therefore set about reforming the military, ensuring troops were paid from the imperial treasury and not by their commanding officers. He also drew a distinction between the senatorial provinces of the empire's Italian and Greek core, whose governors were appointed by the Senate and which barely needed to be guarded, and the more militarised imperial provinces of the periphery, whose governors were appointed by Augustus himself. In this way, potentially troublesome troops were kept loyal to the emperor and a very long way from Rome.

All this worked pretty well – two and a half centuries is a decent run for any political order – but it also contained the seeds of its own destruction. For one thing, it was expensive, and the cost was funded largely through conquest and plunder: Hadrian's decision that the empire was quite big enough may have, paradoxically, made an empire that size harder to preserve. The decision to shift the army from a machine for conquest and glory to a border force made it less glamorous, too, so that service became less attractive to Romans and the army came more and more to depend on barbarians. That probably didn't make it any less effective or less loyal, no matter what some of the snobbier Romans would later argue. But it probably *did* create space for the idea that the Roman Empire did not, necessarily, need to be focused on Rome.

Last but very much not least, it meant that when the empire tottered, many of the forces in a position to contest it were not at its core but on its edge, especially along the Rhine and Danube frontiers, and, since military service had fallen out of fashion in

Rome, very few of them were actually Roman. The result was (this is where we came in) the decades-long Crisis of the Third Century, in which emperors were declared by their own troops after promising them the earth, and discarded and murdered as soon as they failed. Some of these 'barracks emperors' attempted to clear things up by setting out a formal line of succession, naming their sons as their heirs. What this generally meant was that, when the time came to murder them, their sons were slaughtered, too.

Among the shortest reigns of all belonged to co-emperors Balbinus and Pupienus, who, in the chaos of 238CE, the Year of *Six* Emperors, ruled for just ninety-nine days. This was an eternity compared to their predecessors, the ill-fated father/son team of Gordian I and Gordian II, who managed just twenty-two, but during those fourteen weeks, they fell to bickering, each believing the other was plotting their downfall, and were in the middle of yet another argument when the Praetorian Guard burst into the room, grabbed them and hacked them to death.

Later on, the empire began to fall apart. In around 260CE, with the crisis decades old and still no end in sight, a general named Postumus took advantage of his troops' irritation at being ordered to give up some booty to the imperial treasury and had himself declared ruler of a new *Gallic* empire, consisting of Gaul, Germania and, later on, Britannia and Hispania. A decade later, at the other end of the empire, a Palmyran queen named Zenobia took control of the Syrian, Arabian and Egyptian provinces. Both of these breakaway states maintained some of the structures of the empire they were overthrowing – indeed, their revolt may have resulted as much from the desire for order that Rome could no longer provide as for independence.

There's some debate about when, exactly, Rome fell but nobody has ever put the date as early as the third century. Returning the empire to stability, though, was a job too big for one man and it took almost as long as the breakdown had. In 274, the emperor Aurelian managed to restore a measure of order by ruling his troops with an iron fist and defeating both breakaway empires. The same reputation for ruthlessness that had earned him the title *Restitutor Orbis* ('Restorer of the World') may also have caused his death, however, as a secretary who had told him a lie decided that his best chance of survival lay in forging a document outlining the emperor's plans to execute assorted officials. True to form, the officials got Aurelian before he could get them.*

A decade after that, the emperor Diocletian instituted yet another set of military reforms, weakening the border forces and instead backing them up with mobile forces who could be moved about as they were needed. That, and a decision to move non-Roman troops to distant provinces, was enough to weaken the frontier generals and make their troops less likely to declare them emperors. That wasn't quite the end of the story – Diocletian's abdication in 305 was followed by yet more civil wars, which ended only with the victory of Constantine in 324. But the fact he *could* retire, to die of natural causes, says something in itself about his impact.

Other boundaries, drawn up by Diocletian himself, would turn out to have a much longer legacy. One of his biggest reforms was the 'Tetrarchy', under which the empire was split into halves, east and west, and then the resulting halves split again. Two of these four sections would be run by senior emperors named *augusti*, the other two by their junior colleagues and designated successors, the *caesares*. These were always zones of influence with only rough boundaries rather than states in themselves, but the intention was that this would deal with the succession problem, as well as recognise the fact that the empire was clearly now too big for one man.

You can tell how well this attempt to prevent conflict between rival power bases went from the fact that the wars that inevitably followed Diocletian's abdication were known as the Civil Wars of the Tetrarchy. But the fourfold division survived the reunification as new regional power bases, known as prefectures. More

* Bonus fact about Aurelian: some coins suggest his wife Ulpia Severina may have ruled briefly in her own right after his death. If so, she was the only woman ever to rule the western empire.

importantly, the idea of a western, Latin half of the empire and an eastern, Greek one never quite went away again; in 395, after the death of the last unifying emperor Theodosius I, the empire was permanently split.

The forces that had caused the crisis had not entirely abated. Barbarian tribes still kept trying to cross the *Limes Germanicus*, asking for sanctuary from the chaos outside the empire, then generally being hired to guard the border from the next lot. Until, in 476, the last western emperor, a small boy named Romulus Augustulus, after both the founder of Rome and the founder of the empire, was finally deposed by a passing German warlord in favour of the other, *better* emperor in the east.* For nearly a thousand years, an empire calling itself 'Rome' would persist in Constantinople, the new capital Constantine had founded to be equidistant between the troublesome German and eastern frontiers, and then modestly named after himself; but it would hardly ever include the city of Rome.

Even later than that, in 1054, the church that was one of Rome's more enduring legacies would also split in two, in the event known as the Great Schism; the resulting halves would again be a Latin-speaking Catholic west and a Greek-speaking Orthodox east, a division which persists, sort of,† to this day. Even now, the legacy of Rome is still defined, to some extent, by its borders.

---

* As is so often the way of these things, this is contested: some historians prefer to count Romulus's predecessor Julius Nepos as the true final western emperor, as he was more widely recognised, never renounced his claim and lived until 480. But the slightly sad boy emperor with the thematically resonant name is generally recognised as the last, possibly because it makes for a better story, so that's what I've gone with.

† By this I mean that the division *is* still there; it's just that there are also quite a lot of other divisions there, too.

The Legacies of Charlemagne

The Treaty of Verdun, 843, and its eleven centuries of consequences

On Christmas Day in the year 800CE, Pope Leo III crowned Charlemagne, king of the Franks, emperor in Rome. Since the fall of the west over three centuries earlier, chaos had reigned in the ever-shifting patchwork of states that occupied what had once been Italy and Gaul. Now, at long last, the western empire was back.

Slightly less than half a century later, Charlemagne's descendants carved his legacy into three and then, as if this wasn't messy enough, almost immediately started chewing one of the fragments into smaller pieces still. A thing calling itself the Roman Empire would persist in the west for nearly another 1,000 years – far longer, indeed, than the original had held sway there – but it never approached its namesake in territory or power, and it would often not involve Rome. Even so, the legacy of Charlemagne's empire, and the way his territories were divided, would still be doing unpleasant things to Europe over a thousand years after his death. Indeed, by some reckonings, it's still affecting the map to this day.

There are several things worth knowing about 'the father of Europe'. Firstly, his name wasn't actually Charlemagne – that's a contraction of Charles-le-magne, Charles the Great, an honorific reflecting his achievements, rather than the thing Mrs Charlemagne would shout when she wanted his attention. On the lists of rulers drawn up on either side of the Rhine (we'll be coming back to that), he also counts as Charles I. More surprising, perhaps, he had a pet elephant: Abul-Abbas, apparently a gift from the recently established Abbasid Caliphate in Baghdad.

Fierce academic debate has long raged regarding whether he was an *Indian* or *African* elephant.

The key thing to know about Charlemagne for our purposes, though, is that his legitimacy wasn't all it could have been. For one thing, he may have been a bastard. For another, he actually only inherited half of Francia, a post-Roman barbarian kingdom centred on the Rhine: the core territories of most of France and southern Germany had been left to his brother, Carloman. But Carloman, rather conveniently, it must be said, died in 771, sometime before he reached the age of twenty-one.*

The biggest issue, though, was that Charlemagne was from a line of usurpers. His grandfather, Charles Martel, for whom he had been named, had been mayor of the palace, a sort of chief of staff to the Merovingian kings of Francia. Those kings, though, had been increasingly symbolic for some time and by the time Charles was winning battles against all and sundry, it was fairly clear that he was now the true power in the kingdom. When, in 751, Charles's son – Charlemagne's father – Pepin got himself made king, he also got himself anointed by some passing bishops, to make up for the lack of magical royal blood.

So in 768, when Charlemagne ascended to the throne, his dynasty was less than a generation old, and much of what he did seems to have been an attempt to shore it up. For one thing, there was the investment in learning and culture that's gone down in history as the Carolingian Renaissance, which was an attempt to build something less like a tribal kingdom and more like a Christian state. (To be specific: Rome.) Then there were the endless military campaigns against the neighbours, to expand the kingdom to include Saxony, Bavaria, Lombardy, the Pyrenees. This not only spread the light of the church to new peoples, as any good Christian king surely should; it also, as a helpful side effect, provided a sense of national mission and spoils for the military, who tended to grow restive when there was no foreign treasure to plunder. 'As long as the snowball keeps rolling, it gets larger,' the

* Apparently this was natural causes. Sure.

historian Mary Garrison has said. 'When it stops rolling it starts to melt.' The parallels with Rome, half a millennium earlier, all but scream at you.

And then, three decades into his reign, after taking the time to protect the pope from a rampaging mob of disgruntled Romans, came the ultimate mark of Charlemagne's legitimacy. Nearly a thousand miles away in Constantinople, there still ruled an empress: Irene, the latest in an unbroken line stretching all the way back to Augustus, before even the birth of Christ. In the west, though, there had not been an emperor since Romulus Augustulus had been kicked out back in 476. But in Charlemagne, with his domains stretching from Pyrenees to Elbe and North Sea to Adriatic, much of the west had one ruler again. It only took some muttered questions about whether you could really have an emperor who was a girl, and for Leo III to do a spot of crowning to fill the vacant western imperial throne and, hey presto, there was an emperor of Rome again. The empire was back.*

These old and new versions of empire, however, were not entirely comparable. The original Roman Empire, too, had been built on military conquests and complicated rituals involving Latin-speaking priests, yes, but it was also the work of a city, polity and culture that had grown up over centuries. Charlemagne's version, by contrast, was really just the work of Charlemagne, and even he seems not to have expected it to survive him in one piece. The Franks, after all, didn't practise primogeniture, the system of inheritance in which the oldest son gets the lot; instead, they divided territory between all male heirs, which is why Charlemagne had briefly ruled only half of his empire.

So, in 806, Charlemagne published a decree, the *Divisio Regnorum*, which outlined how his realms would be divided on his death – on the grounds, one assumes, that this would make it marginally less likely that the sad event would be followed by

* Charlemagne's biographer claims the king was surprised by this turn of events. I'm sure it was just as big a surprise as the unexpected death of his brother.

immediate civil war between his sons. As it happened, the *Divisio* was never enacted because two of the three sons who stood to benefit made the rookie error of dying before their father, thus leaving the entire empire to go to the youngest, Louis the Pious. But he too began fretting about the succession almost immediately – as early as 817, just three years after his father's death, he published his own decree, the *Ordinatio imperii*, outlining a complicated plan involving appointing his eldest son co-emperor and making his younger sons kings, but making it clear that the empire was absolutely not ever, under any circumstances, ever, *ever* to be divided. In theory, this seemed like a pretty nifty way of matching Frankish custom with the need for imperial unity. In practice, it almost immediately led to civil war.* Back to the drawing board.

That pretty much set the pattern. Eventually, Louis abandoned the *Ordinatio*, instead publishing his own *Divisio Regnorum*, but that wasn't enough to put an end to years of intermittent war between father and sons. We don't have space to go through all of it – though the highlight is surely the 'field of lies', the event in 833 at which Louis believed he was just meeting his eldest son, Lothair, to settle their differences, only to find himself faced by all three sons, their supporters, the pope and, most hurtfully of all, his childhood best friend, every one of them demanding he abdicate, which he did, briefly – but the key point is that, if no one would accept a plan for holding the empire together while Louis was alive, preventing it from falling to bits after his death was surely impossible.

And so it proved. In 840, Louis died, Lothair's brothers declined to accept his inheritance and the result was civil war. Again.

Eventually, after three years of that, the three brothers agreed on how the empire would be divided. By the Treaty of Verdun of 843, *Francia Orientalis* – East Francia, the lands east of the Rhine

* The problem seems to have been the failure to take account of Louis' nephew Bernard, king of Italy, who responded by plotting to remove his kingdom from the empire. Louis marched in with troops, had Bernard blinded (deliberately) and killed (accidentally), and then became the first king to perform public penance for his actions.

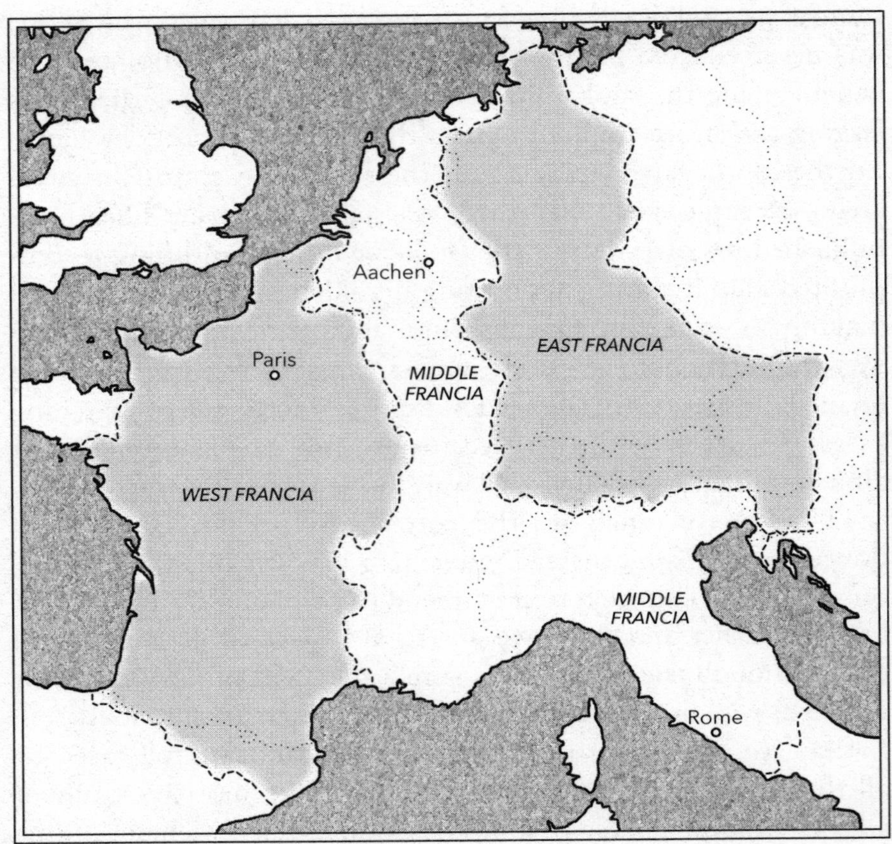

The division of Charlemagne's empire between his grandsons at the Treaty of Verdun, 843. Middle Francia would be contested for centuries.

and north of Italy – would go to the middle son, Louis, the ruler of Bavaria. *Francia Occidentalis* – West Francia, the lands west of the Rhône – would go to the much younger son, Charles, who already ruled Aquitaine. That left the heart of the empire, *Francia Media* – Italy, Burgundy, the Rhineland – for the eldest son, Lothair.

This latter creation looks rather weird to modern eyes. While East Francia and West Francia feel coherent and familiar today, Middle Francia is a faintly bizarre set of territories stretching from some damp Dutch seaside villages all the way to Rome. It was, however, considered the best, richest and most prestigious bit, containing as it did both the old imperial capital in Rome and the new one in Aachen. It should have been the heart of the Frankish lands, which is why it went to the eldest son, along with the imperial title.

Unfortunately, the weird, spread-out nature of Middle Francia left it simultaneously vulnerable to attacks from two of the age's most enthusiastic groups of marauders: the Vikings in the north and 'Saracens' – the various Muslim caliphates – in the south. That made it a bugger to defend and Lothair, pushing fifty, was already looking down the barrel of his own succession crisis. So barely a year after Verdun, he made his eldest son, Louis, king of Italy and co-emperor; eleven years later, feeling increasingly unwell, he partitioned his territory into three parts again at the Treaty of Prüm, handed the imperial title to Louis, retired to a monastery and immediately died.

That, if you're keeping count, left what had been Charlemagne's rebooted Roman Empire split into five parts. This was more than the original had ever managed in even its most exciting bouts of civil war.

The two largest of these fragments would have long enough histories to remain recognisable in successor states today. One was West Francia, a territory centred on Paris, whose significance doesn't need spelling out. The other was East Francia, which was more disparate, with a mobile court and with no clear capital. A little more than a century later, in 962, the East Frankish king Otto the Great, scion of another upstart dynasty, would cosplay as Charlemagne in roughly the same way Charlemagne had cosplayed as Augustus: visiting Rome, getting himself crowned emperor and beginning the process through which East Francia would develop into the Holy Roman Empire. Their kings – let alone their citizens – would not have recognised them as any such thing, of course, but here, in embryo, were France and Germany.

Middle Francia's history would be very different. After that second tripartite division in 855, part of it became the Kingdom of Italy; another, a nebulous area that would go through multiple identities – Burgundy, Provence, Arles – would spend some centuries as independent but would eventually be absorbed by France.

The most interesting chunk, though, is the northern bit, stretching from Geneva to the North Sea. This went to Lothair's second son, helpfully known as Lothair II, who entirely failed to produce a legitimate heir of his own. He had, as it happened, an *illegitimate* one and so came up with a complicated scheme by which he would denounce his poor, infertile wife for infidelity, divorce her and marry his lover instead. This resulted in some poor sod named as the queen's champion being forced to undergo trial by hot water, plunging his hand into a boiling kettle so as to grab a red-hot stone. When his skin failed, miraculously, to blister, the queen was universally declared as innocent and Lothair received not a shred of sympathy.

I'm getting distracted. The point is that, when Lothair II died, his kingdom was split *again* by yet another treaty, this time between Charlemagne's great-grandson in East Francia and his great-great-grandson in West Francia, both of whom, delightfully, were called Louis III. These territories – Lotharingia, as they are sometimes known – were to become a sort of no man's land, sometimes attached to France, sometimes to the Holy Roman Empire, sometimes to neither. In the ninth century, long before most states we're used to today had emerged, when debatable lands were everywhere, this was not unusual: as Simon Winder writes in *Germania*, if Lotharingia 'was to become ultimately a crucial European fault line then it is fair to say that until the fourteenth century it was one among many'.

In that latter century, though, King John II of France handed some of those lands – by then known as Burgundy, not to be confused with the other Burgundy, some distance to the south* – to a younger son, in another sort of Charlemagne tribute act. Several generations and a convenient marriage later, they ended up in the

* As many as a dozen different states have gloried in the name, from the Baltic to the Mediterranean. If this entry has induced the first twinges of migraine then all I can say is be thankful I am not writing about them.

hands of the Habsburg family. Who were also, as it happens, Holy Roman emperors. This had not been John's plan.

At any rate, as the European state system began to consolidate, the existence of a block of land that could plausibly be either French or German began to have consequences. Some of these – the eventual emergence of the Netherlands, Belgium and Switzerland, buffer states that were proudly neither French *nor* German – we could mark as broadly positive. Others – for example, Alsace-Lorraine, a territory where people and place names alike could be either French or German, resulting in a whole lot of conflict – were not. It's probably not fair to blame, say, the Franco-Prussian War of 1870–1 on the way Charlemagne didn't sort out his succession. But it's not entirely *unfair*, either.

That's the final point to make here. It's easy to look baffled at the way Charlemagne built a state which could quite plausibly justify him being called 'emperor of Rome' and then entirely failed to make sure it survived his death. But his concern was not with an abstract notion like a 'state' that could endure down the centuries. In fact, he would no doubt be baffled to hear himself described as the founder of concepts like 'France' or 'Germany'. He was simply looking to provide for his kids.

After a couple of generations of fratricidal conflict, though, it was becoming pretty obvious that this was no way to run a family business. So gradually, most of western Europe abandoned the partible inheritance system they'd inherited from the Franks, which meant splitting stuff between heirs, in favour of exciting new concepts like 'primogeniture', in which everything went to the eldest. This allowed them to keep their lands together and meant they no longer needed to hold a civil war every time anyone died. Charlemagne's final legacy is that people stopped doing things like Charlemagne had – even if it was sometimes useful to pretend otherwise.

The Borders of Great Britain

England, Scotland, Wales and the contingency of nationhood

There are, by common agreement, three nations on Europe's largest island. The bulk of Great Britain, some three-fifths of its land containing five-sixths of its population, we call England. The island's northern third, the bit that if you start anthropomorphising too much could pass as the head, is the once and very possibly future independent kingdom of Scotland. Then, extruding west from the middle of England, like our person-shaped island is clutching something to its chest, there's a mountainous country named Wales.* All three of these places have political or cultural identities that date back a thousand years or more; both they and the borders that divide them feel natural, inviolable, even inevitable.

I'm not so sure. All three British nations were, in their earlier history, divided into many smaller kingdoms. Roll the tape back to the early medieval centuries when these coalesced into the countries we're familiar with, and other nations, with other boundaries, come to seem like a possible outcome.

When the Romans began their conquest of Britannia in 43CE, they found an island populated by disparate tribes, whose names

* Actually, I can already hear a very small number of pedants somewhere to my southwest furiously googling my email address so as to remind me there are four. Cornwall does have a flag, a fading language and an independence movement, and is classed at times as one of the Celtic nations. But perhaps because of size, obscurity or how early it got absorbed by its much bigger neighbour, its nationhood is less widely accepted than that of, say, Wales, and it is for the most part treated as the westernmost county of England. This actually feeds nicely into the point I'm making here about historical contingency but space, alas, is limited.

now seem, for the most part, meaningless. (Two exceptions: the Dumnoni, in the southwest, and the Cantiaci in the southeast, which gave their names to the English counties of Devon and Kent respectively.) There was nothing resembling a *state* on the island, which from the Roman perspective was quite helpful – as Tacitus wrote towards the end of the first century, 'We have no better weapon against the stronger tribes than this lack of common purpose' – but it does mean that trying to map these tribes onto later nations is a waste of time.

This period contributed to those future boundaries, even so. For starters, the Romans didn't actually conquer the entire island: after eighty years of trying, they seem to have decided that the wild, cold northern bit they called Caledonia wasn't worth the hassle and built Hadrian's Wall to divide it from the empire. They did think again – another structure, the line of stone, wood and turf known as the Antonine Wall, briefly placed the northern limit of civilisation eighty miles further north in what today is the central belt of Scotland, but this was abandoned pretty quickly. So for much of the occupation, the boundary between empire and barbarians lay in the far north of England. The impression you get is that, having come this far, the world's most terrifying military machine decided it just didn't fancy the last bit. The people of what would one day be Scotland were simply too tough for them.

Wales, by contrast, *was* in the empire – it had roads and forts and everything – but it differed from much of England nonetheless. The relatively prosperous lands closest to mainland Europe seem to have ultimately become as Romanised as anywhere in, say, Gaul, so could be trusted to civilian rule. The wilder, more mountainous lands to the north and west, by contrast – not only Wales, but the extremities of England, too – always remained slightly more troublesome and required more militarised occupation. As far back as ancient times, you can already see a division emerging between the southeastern lowlands and the other parts of the island. Score one for those who argue geography is destiny.

When the Romans pulled out in the early fifth century, though, everything seems to have fragmented. It's difficult to be certain – for the next 200 years we have remarkably few sources; it's basically a load of archaeological evidence plus one furious rant by a monk named Gildas, who gives the impression of everything going to hell but also has the same vibe as the average *Daily Mail* columnist, so who knows if he can be trusted – but what we *do* know points to a warring tribes and/or kingdoms sort of situation.

At some point, peoples named Angles, Saxons and Jutes arrived from the German lands, though we can't be sure how many of them there were, whether they were just men, families or entire tribes, whether they were invited or invaded, or quite possibly were invited *and then* invaded, or really anything much. In the traditional telling of events, these guys conquered the southeast of the island and pushed the remaining Romano-British peoples into the far west, with one of the British kings who fought back possibly being a chap named Arthur but actually probably not being called anything of the sort. It's quite possible that much of that never happened at all, though, and that the Germans instead won a sort of culture war, in which the people of the east found it profitable and/or cool to start playing up their Anglo-Saxon habits and connections and downplaying their Roman heritage. Meanwhile, those in the west who had previously been Roman holdouts started to talk, in a bloody-minded sort of fashion, about how the Romans had in fact been really great, actually, and how they were their last representatives in Britain.

The next bit of the standard narrative has the Anglo-Saxon invaders, who drove the Britons out of England, gradually coalescing into seven kingdoms: four big ones (Wessex, Mercia, East Anglia and Northumbria), plus three smaller ones (Sussex, Essex and Kent), a period of English history known as the 'heptarchy'. But, you'll be shocked to hear, that's probably an oversimplification too. The northernmost kingdom of Northumbria may for a long time have been divided into Bernicia, Lindsay and Deira, while a Mercian land survey from this period, known as the 'Tribal Hidage', lists the kingdoms familiar from school history lessons but then goes on to baffling additions like the Hwicca,

Noxgaga, Hendrica and Unecungaga. Trying to map these places is a wasted exercise, Max Adams argues in *The First Kingdom*. For one thing, we simply don't have the evidence; for another, the key fact of each kingdom was not its borders and its limits but the places at its heart, 'a core group of . . . centres of itinerant power, allowing for much fluidity or uncertainty at the edges'. It's probably less accurate to imagine a map of petty kingdoms than an ever-shifting kaleidoscope.

Gradually, these places vanished until, by the early 800s, even the smallest of the seven famous kingdoms seem to have been dominated or absorbed by their larger neighbours, leaving just four. So, even though the heptarchy has long taken up perhaps 300 years of the standard telling of English history, it's not clear how long it lasted or whether there was a time when there were precisely seven kingdoms at all.

Oh, and then in the ninth century, the Vikings invaded and everything changed *again*. They conquered East Anglia and Northumbria; they fought the once-dominant Mercia to the point of collapse. Under the leadership of Alfred, the only native English king to be blessed with the suffix 'the Great', Wessex defeated the Vikings at the Battle of Edington (878) but failed to drive them from the country. With neither side strong enough to knock out the other, the two came to an agreement, dividing the country in two along a diagonal line running from the Thames in the southeast to the Mersey in the northwest. To its south was a bigger, stronger Wessex; to its north an array of Viking kingdoms now known as the Danelaw.

That new division left a substantial legacy in terms of place names and dialect words – any name ending in -by, -holme, -thwaite or -thorpe suggests Vikings were knocking about these parts at some point – but this is odd, in some ways, because the Danelaw didn't last very long. After only a few decades, the kings of Wessex began to push the Vikings out. As they did so, they started to call themselves first the kings of the Anglo-Saxons (a way, perhaps, of retroactively justifying the Wessex takeover of its neighbours), then the kings of the English. After centuries of division, they'd unified the bit of the island that had been most Romanised, and then most heavily settled by the Anglo-Saxons, into a new nation: England.

The obvious question is – why stop there? Alfred's grandson Athelstan, the king who in 927 conquered the last Viking kingdom, Jorvik (York),* was the first to call himself king of the English and thus has as good a claim as anyone to be the first king of England. He was also recognised at times as sort of overlord by those running the rest of the island. Extending his territory was very much Athelstan's bag. So why didn't he finish the job?

The short answer is, probably, he tried, for a while demanding homage from those smaller, weaker kingdoms. But conquering people who don't want to be conquered is a tiring and difficult business, and even as England was unifying, as long ago as that was, there were already alternative identities developing in Great Britain.

The lands to the north seem to have consisted of multiple kingdoms, just as in England, but those don't map anything like so neatly onto Scotland as you might think. The northwest was dominated by a Gaelic kingdom, known as Dál Riata, focused on the islands and parts of Northern Ireland; in the northeast was a variety of sub-kingdoms of people known as Picts. The southeast of these lands, though, all the way up to Scotland's modern capital Edinburgh, was for a long time part of what we now think of as an English kingdom, Northumbria (which insisted, when marking out its boundaries, on ignoring Hadrian's Wall entirely). Most confusingly of all from a modern perspective there was Strathclyde, which stretched from Glasgow far down into northwest England. That was the last remnant of a region known as the *Hen Ogledd* – the old north – whose inhabitants spoke a Brittonic

---

* Fun fact! If you've ever looked at a map of England's traditional counties – and if you're reading the footnotes in a book like this, you probably have – you may have wondered why it is that Yorkshire, in Northern England, is so much bigger than the rest of the counties – big enough to contain four or five smaller ones. The reason is that this is Jorvik, swallowed whole: the entire kingdom looked to the regional capital at York and so it didn't break neatly into smaller, county-sized chunks.

language and were thus considered another branch of the people who'd held the island before the Anglo-Saxons came. To put it another way: the people of ancient Glasgow spoke, essentially, Welsh.

At any rate, identity and nation emerged in Scotland through conquest, unification and shared political interest, just as they had done in England – both the historic fact of having been outside Roman control and the rather more live one of not wanting to be ruled from England no doubt fed into that. But it was not obvious where, exactly, in the dozens of miles of relatively unpopulated land between Hadrian's Wall and the Antonine effort, the boundary should be. So unclear was it that for centuries this region was known as 'the Debatable Land'. At no point, incidentally, has the boundary been where the Romans put it.*

As to the other boundary on the island, there is a more obvious geographic line between the relatively flat lands of England and the mountainous ones of Wales. There's a man-made barrier there, too – the earthwork known as Offa's Dyke, after the eighth-century Mercian king believed to have constructed it as a defensive measure. This isn't the official boundary, either.

But while there was a clear Welsh identity that may be even older than the English one – that existed in part *in opposition to* the English one – the existence of the Hen Ogledd, a shared sense of nationhood with the people of northern England and western Scotland, is a reminder that this may not be a historical inevitability, either.† What's more, Wales was never really a single

* It has also moved. The largest town on the border, Berwick-upon-Tweed, changed hands so often that it was often mentioned specifically in statutes and royal proclamations to make sure it wasn't accidentally left out. This led to the sadly apocryphal tale that it was forgotten by the peace treaty that followed the Crimean War, meaning the town was still technically at war with Russia until well into the twentieth century. Today, incidentally, Berwick is in England but Berwickshire is in Scotland. Why not?

† Another fun fact! The word 'Cumbria', a modern county name drawn from an ancient word describing the inhabitants of the far northwest of England, has the same root as 'Cymru', the Welsh name for Wales. Both names mean, basically, 'fellow countrymen'.

unified state like England and Scotland: it almost always consisted of several petty kingdoms (Powys, Gwynedd, Deheubarth, Gwent), culturally united but politically divergent, which was pretty helpful to the English forces when the thirteenth century rolled round and they finally got around to invading. Two centuries later, a member of a Welsh dynasty, the Tudors, won the English crown, Augustus-style, by being the last man standing in a civil war and went on to rule as Henry VII. Perhaps thinking of his roots, perhaps simply cognisant of the dangers of an enemy within, his son Henry VIII began moves to fully reclassify the Welsh counties as merely another part of England.

*

One of the recurring themes of the pages ahead will be how nations happen. The point of this whistlestop tour of my primary school history lessons and why they were wrong is to show quite how big a role is played by chance. Geography is obviously a big factor in creating a nation, but it's equally obviously not enough. Shared institutions matter, so do shared stories, and so, too, do shared enemies. (Shared enemies can mean both shared institutions *and* shared stories, of course.)

So, even if it's possible to explain why the lines on the maps ended up where they did, it's often much harder to explain why they didn't end up elsewhere. There's a sense of inevitability that comes from reading history as just the series of events that could only have brought us to now. But if we could roll the tape back and play it again with just a few minor details going differently, the result could have been very different. Scotland could have included Cumbria, or England the Lothians. Wales could have been absorbed entirely.

In some ways, of course, this entire passage has been a cheat. Even if Great Britain does contain three nations, it only includes one *state*: the United Kingdom of Great Britain and Northern Ireland, better known as Britain or the UK. (A nation and a state, the political unit that contains it, don't always map neatly onto one another either, even if the existence of a state can help to create national identity, too.) Depending on how you define the word, England, Scotland and Wales may no longer count as countries at all.

So why was Welsh national identity allowed to persist, as something even other Britons still recognise as a *nation*, while Breton or Bavarian, say, are more contested? A separate language is clearly helpful but equally clearly not sufficient: only around a fifth of Welsh people actually speak Welsh; the language was discouraged, if not outright suppressed, by British institutions for centuries. There are also plenty of minority language communities around the world who don't get to have their own devolved national institutions.

I'd put the continuing existence of Wales down to three things. Firstly, in 1603, before Wales *could* become merely another part of England, a Scottish dynasty, the Stewarts, inherited the crown from their Tudor cousins. Full political unity followed a century later, when the Act of Union 1707 explicitly carved out space for multiple identities beneath the British one. Perhaps the existence of a British Scotland preserved the space for a non-English Wales.

Secondly, the new unified nation was soon busy building the largest empire the world had ever seen. That, among other, less flattering achievements, also created plenty of room for multiple, overlapping identities.

Thirdly, and perhaps most importantly, the nations of the UK still have separate national football teams.

That too is a function of empire, of course: this island not only spread its sports of choice around the world, it got to set the rules, too. Spoiler alert: the legacy of the British and other European empires is going to come up rather a lot over the next few chapters.

Of Feudalism, Marquises, Margraves and Marcher Lords

Life on the edge

One of the aspects of the noble hierarchies that dominated Europe for so long that feels strangest to modern eyes is the inclusion of a whole extra rank for people who lived near a border. It's one thing to grasp that kings and queens are at the top, that dukes rank higher than counts or earls, that counts or earls are actually just different words for the same thing,* or that if you stick the word 'arch' on the beginning of a title that probably makes it bigger and scarier. But what the hell's a margrave? Or a marquis? Why would you need a whole different category just for people who live way out in the sticks?

Before we get on to that, there's something else I should probably tell you – partly because it's useful to understand what follows but also, frankly, because it's worth knowing in its own right. It's this: very likely, your entire mental model of medieval Europe is wrong.

Thanks to books and school history lessons and so forth, you likely have some idea that the continent spent several centuries dominated by a thing called 'feudalism'. This, you no doubt remember, was a hierarchical social system in which kings would grant titles and land ('fiefs') to lesser lords ('vassals') in exchange for loyalty and service; these lords would then make further

* 'Earl', like 'shire', comes from the Germanic languages that gave us Old English. 'Count' and 'county' come via the French: the fact England ended up with counties called -shire is an artefact of the Norman invasion of 1066 and the centuries of domination by a Francophone ruling class that followed.

grants to those below them in much the same way, and through this method, everyone in medieval society, from the smuggest monarch to the humblest serf, was connected. This, we were told, is how a society functioned in the absence of things like universal rights and strong central government.

The thing about feudalism, though – the thing that medievalists have spent at least half a century *saying* about feudalism but which has yet to filter down to the rest of us – is that, in several quite important senses, it probably never existed. Part of the problem is that the word is used to apply to several different things – a legal framework, an economic system, a set of social relationships – interchangeably, as if they're the same thing when they're often not. There is also a problem of language. There clearly were reciprocal relationships between king and lord, lord and peasants, and so on, with the bigger men nominally granting land and protection in exchange for military service and labour. But the word 'feudal' was an early modern creation which, like many of the other words attached to all this, was never actually used in the Middle Ages. If you could ask an eleventh-century lord about the system of feudal relationships they enjoyed, they'd have no idea what you were on about, and then would almost certainly have you killed.

Probably the biggest issue with the notion of the feudal system, though, is the idea it was a *system*: not merely a rough description of a society based on hierarchy and reciprocal relationships, but an actually existing, universal framework that could play the role later played by a state. This is just nonsense. As with, say, the heptarchy, it's an attempt to force a messy world in which things varied wildly in both time and space into a single, easily comprehensible pattern; at some point, we've all just mistaken the model for the reality.* But, since it's a model that remains useful when

* The idea that feudalism was a sort of post-Roman, Europe-wide legal system seems to date to the *Libri Feudorum*, a legal text about 'fiefs' in twelfth-century Lombardy. This, assorted historians assumed four centuries or more later, was not only a description of how things actually worked in twelfth-century Lombardy, rather than a simple academic exercise, but a reliable guide to how

explaining economic and social relationships in the era before strong states, and since it's simpler than constantly reminding everyone that things may have varied wildly between times and regions, and since no one has come up with anything better, so the schoolchildren of the Western world are still taught about feudalism as if it's a thing that actually happened, rather than merely a rough and ill-informed description of what happened, and thus we're all probably stuck with it.

Anyway. What is true is that emperors or kings often granted lands or titles to their supporters to thank them for their assistance in some campaign or another, and that many of these titles ended up becoming hereditary. It's also true that, in theory, lower-ranked lords often owed fealty to higher-ranked ones, even if there were times when it didn't work quite so well in practice.

The result of all this – to edge us back to our theme – is that, as the powers of medieval monarchies ebbed and flowed, their borders shifted, too, as territories that owed them fealty became more or less independent. This is why early maps don't necessarily privilege national borders: the identity of the local lord sometimes mattered more than which monarch they nominally answered to. It's also how there could be a period in the twelfth and thirteenth centuries when places like Normandy and Aquitaine formed part of the 'Angevin Empire', ruled by the kings of England, even though they were still officially part of France: they may have technically owed fealty to Paris but, given the French crown's relative weakness, the fact their duke was also king of England came, for a time, to matter more.

Border territories seem, by virtue of their distance from their centres of power, to have been particularly prone to this collision between neat feudal hierarchies and messy *realpolitik*. So, just as the Roman emperors had distinguished between secure, senatorial provinces and wobblier imperial ones, from the earliest days

---

things worked across a much wider area of Europe over a period of several centuries. In a book packed full of stupid footnotes, this is surely, on scale of error alone, the stupidest.

of medieval Europe, its monarchs began distinguishing between heartland and periphery. After all, if you wanted security at the centre of your state, you needed territorial integrity, too. That meant securing, if not expanding, your borders, which required those who defended them to have both a measure of independence and substantial military strength.

It was to that end that Charlemagne issued special forms of land grant, with greater independence from the empire, to encourage good, Christian folk to settle in what became known as the Spanish March; in this way, he hoped to create a military buffer zone between his empire and Islamic Spain. A couple of centuries later, the Ottonian dynasty that inherited the eastern half of his empire created a new system of 'marks' (marches) on its eastern frontier. These were mandated not merely to defend the empire's borders but to push north and east into territory still held by the pagan Slavs.

These territories were often ranked as counties, rather than more powerful dukedoms, but because their holders had greater power than most counts, a new title began to emerge. In German, they became margraves, from *markgraf* ('mark count'), a word translated into French as 'marquis'. In England, where such noblemen ran the contested lands of the far north and the border with Wales, they were often known simply as 'marcher lords'.*

The advantage of this model of border management was that it gave border princes the independence required to do their job. When the realm was threatened, they didn't have to wait for troops or permission from the court before defending it: they could just raise an army or build a few castles and get stuck in. The downside of this model of border management was that, if you give people the power to raise their own armies and build their own castles, it's a bit optimistic to assume they're always

* In the later Middle Ages, some of the more pretentious English kings began to hand out peerages which used the French word 'marquis', which, in some cases (there seems to be no rhyme or reason to this), they spelt 'marquess'. Because the latter looks a bit girly to English eyes, the *female* form of marquis/marquess is 'marchioness'. Of course it is.

going to use those powers to defend *your* realm from outsiders and otherwise do as you say.

So some of those strong border territories transformed, gradually, into powers in their own right. The County of Barcelona was originally a position to which the Carolingian kings appointed someone to defend their empire's southern flank; gradually, though, it absorbed neighbouring counties and became first a hereditary title, then independent, and ultimately entered a union with neighbouring Aragon. This is why the region ended up not in France but in Spain.*

Two of the German marks followed a similar path of becoming hereditary and then expanding their power. The Saxon Nordmark ('northern march') turned eventually into the powerful Margraviate of Brandenburg, whose rulers were important enough that, by the mid-fourteenth century, they got a vote for the elective Holy Roman Emperor. Meanwhile, the Bavarian Ostmark ('eastern mark') would become known as Austria, about which we're going to be hearing quite a bit more.

Not all the marches followed this pattern, of course. Gradually, medieval Europe's borders ceased to be about the line between Christendom and paganism, civilisation and barbarism, and became merely lines between, or even within, states. In England and Wales, the marcher lordships eventually became counties like any other: this is why Shropshire, say, doesn't get a seat at the UN.

So by the end of the Middle Ages, nobles whose lands lay on the borders no longer needed exceptional powers, and 'margrave' and its various equivalents had ceased to have any special meaning – it was just another title, more prestigious than earl or count, but less prestigious than duke. As a hereditary title in France, 'marquis' was all but lost altogether, the lands of its holders absorbed into bigger estates. Instead, it became a title adopted by minor lords who held several titles, to distinguish themselves from mere counts, who held only one.

---

* This is also at least part of the reason some of the locals aren't happy about it.

But the self-granted nature of this title had the unintended side effect of raising questions about the lineage of anyone who held it – everyone knew who a count's ancestors had been, but a *marquis*? That meant that, by the seventeenth and eighteenth centuries – even before the Marquis de Sade embarked upon his long career of sexual adventurism – it was a sign of ill-repute. Where once the title had been a sign of special power and influence, today it lives on in the French verb '*se marquiser*': to mark oneself.

The Open Borders Policies of Genghis Khan

The man who created the modern world

The Mongol Empire was the largest contiguous empire the world has ever seen. It brought peoples stretching from Ukraine to Korea, the wastes of Siberia to the deserts of the Middle East, under the sway of a single polity - and, come to that, a single family. The decades of Mongol domination that followed the conquests of the thirteenth century are a major interlude in the histories of both Russia and China, and the very thought of its mounted warriors and the pyramids of skulls they were said to leave behind was enough to strike terror into hearts right across Eurasia, including in places that never so much as saw a scimitar.

All this you probably already knew. You probably know some basic facts about that empire's founder, Genghis Khan, too. That the invasions which he led killed as many as 40 million people, as many as one in ten of everybody alive at the time, which makes him by some distance the individual with the highest body count in history.* That, despite - or perhaps because of - this record, he's seen as a national hero in Mongolia and, more confusingly, in China, too. That there was a lot of excitement around 2003 when a paper in the *American Journal of Human Genetics* claimed to have identified a gene that suggested he had around 16 million living descendants, even though it offered no sense of whether, after a couple of dozen generations, this was actually a lot. (A bunch

* You could, I suppose, make a case for Christopher Columbus, since his voyages led to the conquest of the Americas, the resulting genocides and the Atlantic slave trade. But a) those things were indirect effects, not direct actions, and b) his discoveries would have happened anyway soon enough; his is merely a convenient name to put on a major historical process. So we won't.

of other geneticists later dismissed the whole thing as 'merely speculative'. Spoilsports.)

Something it's less likely you'll know, because it's a whole lot weirder to get your head around, is that Genghis and his empire pretty much created the conditions for the world we live in now. He set processes running that can still be seen in the relative positions and attitudes of Russia, China, Europe and the Middle East today. And it was Khan's post-marauding commitment to both open borders and free trade that lay behind it all.

At the time the boy then known as Temüjin was born into a Mongol tribe, possibly in 1162, possibly somewhere in the vicinity of Lake Baikal – the Mongols, it turns out, were not great record keepers – Eurasia was then pretty divided. The classical empires – Roman, Parthian, Han – had fallen to bits centuries ago, of course, but even their successors, like the great Muslim caliphate that had risen in the seventh century, were now shadows of their former selves. The Byzantine Empire, who still thought of themselves as Romans, were restricted largely to the Balkans and Anatolia, while the Holy Roman Empire, which thought itself a successor in the west, commanded not that much more territory than mere kingdoms like England or France. What had been and would again be China, meanwhile, was split between the Jin state in the north and the Song one in the south.

The region where Temüjin lived was more divided still – a world of warring confederations made up of warring tribes, made up of often warring clans – and the sort of place which makes medieval Europe look like a holiday destination. You can get some sense of quite what a vicious world it was from *The Secret History of the Mongols*, an anonymous and likely fallacious account of Temüjin's life and works, published several decades after his death. After some of the standard genealogy – wolf meets doe, nature takes its course; you know the sort of thing – it tells of how a widow named Alan has a torrid affair with a supernatural entity who enters her tent via the smoke hole in its roof, then leaves again disguised as a dog. The resulting sons realise that they can get what they want by robbing people and kidnapping women. Sometime later, one of their descendants, our hero's father Yesügei, kidnaps his mother, Hoelun, only to be murdered by some Tatars when his son is just nine years old.

All this, by the way, happens in chapter one.

Somehow, Temüjin overcame the death of his father and – after taking revenge on the Tatars by killing all those taller than a cart axle – came to rule his tribe, then his confederation, and then all the other confederations, too. In 1206, a great meeting of the people of the steppe gave him the name by which the world would come to know and fear him: Genghis. It probably – again with the poor record-keeping – meant 'great ruler'.* After that, there was no stopping him. By 1209, the Mongols had squeezed submission from the Uyghurs and the Tanguts. In 1215, they overthrew the Jin. By 1220, they held much of central Asia and three years after that, they were in Russia, with predictable results.

The reason the Mongols were so good at conquering was (there's no gentle way of putting this) that they were so good at violence – so good, indeed, that they often didn't even need to employ it. Those who were sensible enough to surrender would be spared and welcomed into an empire which, some scholars now suggest, they might find surprisingly tolerant, even meritocratic. But those who resisted, which was quite a lot of them, would be enslaved or slaughtered in quite astonishing numbers. You probably haven't heard of the Tanguts, the Buddhist people in the middle of what is now China who I mentioned in the previous paragraph. There's a reason for that: the Mongols systematically wiped them and their culture out, an event the historian

---

* Consensus these days seems to be that 'Jinggis' or 'Chinggis' are more accurate transliterations of the original Mongolian, but I'm sticking with the name by which the conqueror is best known in the English-speaking world because that's the language I am writing in. While you're down here, though: there are, annoyingly, two different words translated into English as 'Khan'. The one with the shorter 'a' sound means 'king'; the one with the longer one means 'emperor' or 'king of kings'. Genghis was probably never Khaaaan (my own transliteration) in his own lifetime but was given the title posthumously by a successor, so as to clarify who was the boss in a family where everyone was going around calling themselves Khan.

John Man has said could be the 'first ever recorded example of attempted genocide'. At the other end of Eurasia, one English monk described the Mongols as a 'detestable nation of Satan that poured out like devils from Tartarus'. The interesting thing about this is that the Mongols never got within 1,500 miles of his monastery. That is quite the reputation.

Genghis died in 1227, during the campaign against the Tanguts, which was probably a great comfort to those watching their relatives murdered and cities destroyed. The empire he founded, though, kept growing, swallowing Persia, Tibet, Korea, Crimea . . . As for China, from which the Mongols took large chunks of their culture, it had long held a quaint belief that there would ideally be one, single ruler for the world. For all its grandeur, though, China itself was far too settled to attempt to impose its will much beyond East Asia. It took an outsider to actually have the ambition to put this grand ideal into practice.

Perhaps unsurprisingly, China took the Mongols quite some time to digest. It wasn't until 1271 that Genghis's grandson, the man known to history and students of romantic poetry alike as Kublai Khan, managed to establish the Yuan dynasty that'd rule China for another century. By then, though, his status as Great Khan was already largely notional. When Kublai's brother Möngke died without naming a successor in 1259, the result had been (stop me if you've heard this one before) civil war, followed by the empire fragmenting into four vast chunks: an eastern European bit (the Golden Horde), a vaguely Middle Eastern bit (the Ilkhanate), a central Asian bit (the Chagatai Khanate) and the Yuan, who ruled China and East Asia. In theory, the others all owed fealty to the Yuan emperor; in practice, not so much.

Even though the Mongol Empire's time as a single polity had been short-lived, it remained as a cultural space for decades to come. It also, more to the point, became a sort of free trade zone. The network of trade routes we know as the 'Silk Road' had been operating since the second century BCE: 4,000 miles of caravan routes carrying Chinese luxuries like silk and spice west to the

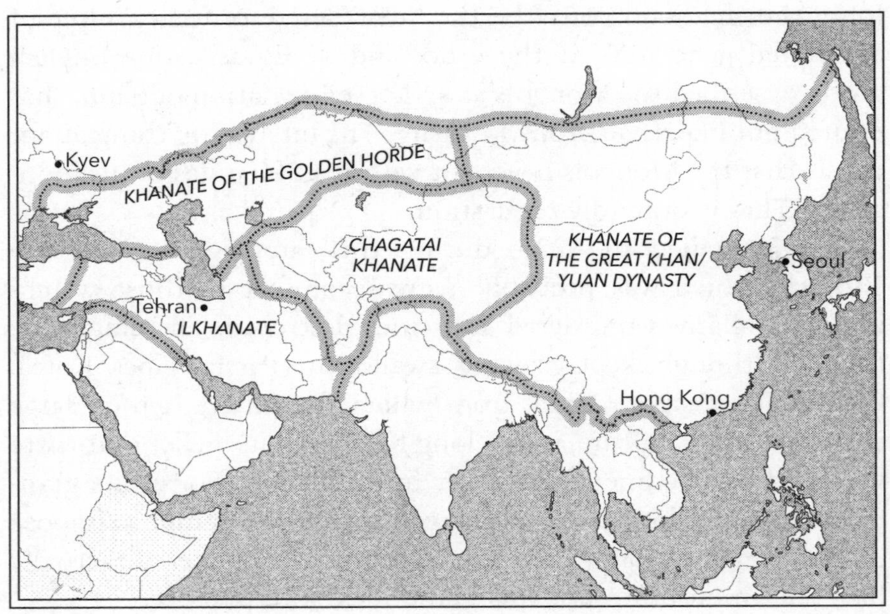

The division of the largest contiguous empire the world has ever seen in the late thirteenth century. Many regions bordering the empire, such as Kievan Rus', were still forced to pay tribute.

Mediterranean, and gold, silver and other useful commodities back to China as payment. But with the fragmentation that followed the fall of the classical empires, these routes had become more perilous: more petty local rulers keen to exact tribute, more warring kingdoms making travel unsafe, fewer authorities capable of dealing with bandits.

The Mongols, though, were quite keen on a spot of free trade. Their nomadic, pastoral lifestyle had always meant an economy based more on herding cattle than on making anything, so many of the products they needed had to be acquired from more settled peoples, who had the sort of workshops that could make pots, clothes or weapons. In China, merchants were looked down upon as a low-status class who didn't create anything; the Mongols valued them as a group of people who brought them *stuff*.

So although it probably wasn't their main priority, one of the benefits they drew from their empire was simply that it boosted communication and commerce; so much easier did travel become after the Mongols had finished their conquering and marauding that it's sometimes referred to by the mildly ironic label of the '*Pax Mongolica*'. More than that, the Mongols actively introduced policies intended to help trade flow: a network of relay stations to provide food and lodging, and 'ortoghs', trade associations with official backing through which merchants could pool their resources and their risk as a sort of insurance scheme, even lending them money at low interest rates.

We tend to think of the Mongol period as a great time to be a guy with several horses and a sword, and a bad time to be almost anyone else. We don't tend to think of it as a golden era of free trade. But it was. The reason that this is the era that produced *The Travels of Marco Polo* is because it was the first time an Italian merchant could plausibly nip back and forth between Venice and China along safe routes and well-maintained roads.* Advanced Islamic mathematics, science and astronomy spread right across the continent. So did other useful innovations like banking and insurance.

And the region that benefited most was Europe. The part of the Mongol forces that would become the Golden Horde had invaded regions like Poland and Hungary but in 1242, after Genghis's son and successor, Ögedei Khan, had died unexpectedly, the conquerors had decided to turn back. What mattered most to the various members of the imperial family was staking their claim in the empire's internal power struggle; the conquest of Europe could wait.

---

* As an aside, Polo's memoir fails to mention a number of fairly major features of Chinese culture, like tea and chopsticks and the practice of foot-binding, which would, you'd think, be of interest to a medieval Italian. This has led some scholars to suggest it's possible he never visited China himself, but merely heard stories from his father and uncle, or perhaps even just read about it in books he found in relatively nearby destinations like Persia. If this is true it would fit with the fact that, even at its height, few merchants travelled the entire Silk Road, instead ferrying things back and forth along their own, relatively short stretches of it.

It would wait forever, in fact. The blow never came and, while parts of eastern Europe would be paying tribute to the Golden Horde for generations, much of the continent was spared the horror of Mongol conquest. That did not, however, stop it from benefiting from the massive trade boom unleashed by the *Pax Mongolica* and the access to world-shaking Chinese technologies like papermaking and gunpowder that it brought. It wasn't all great news. When the 1340s rolled round, the Black Death spread just as easily as all those nifty technologies (although once it had passed, the 40–60 per cent of Europeans it didn't kill probably ended up with a better life by virtue of a hefty increase in labour bargaining power and wages). Nonetheless, it's not an exaggeration to say that the *Pax Mongolica* helped kick off the Renaissance.

Even in its divided form, the Mongol Empire didn't last long. The Persia-focused Ilkhanate disintegrated after 1335 and the central Asian Chagatai Khanate after 1347, thanks largely to the conquests of Timur, another man well-known to students of English literature as Christopher Marlowe's Tamburlaine the Great. (It may actually have been him with all the pyramids of skulls: Genghis should sue.) In China, the Yuan held on until 1368 when, weakened by famine and growing resentment over their discrimination against the majority Han Chinese, they were overthrown by the homegrown Ming dynasty. In the west, some fragments of Mongol power lasted longer – Crimea did not escape the 'Tatar Yoke' until 1502 – but even there it had long been fragmenting and weakening (and yes, that man Tamburlaine was partly to blame). Genghis's atrocities and achievements were incredible; they were also short-lived.

His effects on the world, though, proved rather more durable. The Islamic world would never recover either the political or intellectual leadership it had held since late antiquity. Ming China reinforced its Great Wall, building some of its most famous stretches, and hid behind it, in the hope of keeping the nomads out – a large, rich and technologically advanced power effectively disengaged from the world. Elsewhere, the Mongols had destroyed Kievan Rus', an east European principality from which Russia,

Ukraine and Belarus all claim descent. Leadership of the Russian lands now passed to an up-and-coming duchy named Moscow – less interested than its predecessor in tentative experiments in democracy, more interested in making sure its borders were a very long way from the capital.

But surely the biggest impact the Mongol Empire had was on a region it never conquered. In 1200, western Europe was a political, economic and technological backwater struggling to feed itself. By 1400, it had acquired a bunch of useful technologies, which helped it close the gap, and a taste for eastern luxuries, which, following the collapse of the *Pax Mongolica*, were suddenly no longer forthcoming. In a move which would resonate for the next six centuries, some Europeans decided it was time to go looking for them, and started building boats.

Spain and Portugal Carve Up the World

The Treaty of Tordesillas, 1494

Imagine, best beloved, that you and I and our needy friend Jules are sat together on a beach one evening. On the horizon, beyond a stretch of sparkling sea, we can see a scattering of lush green islands.

And so, being in a whimsical mood, and several cocktails drunk from coconut shells into our evening, you and I make a pact. Everything to the left of that jagged rock, we agree, is henceforth and from now until eternity to be your domain, for you to reign over with whatever title you like the most. Everything to the right of the rock, by contrast, is mine. Jules doesn't get anything but so keen is he for our approval that, after some thought, he agrees to witness and approve our agreement, and the three of us shake hands. And so it is decreed.

Were this to happen, I suspect we would wake the next morning, rather the worse for wear from the coconut shells, and feel a little embarrassed, on the grounds that we know nothing about those islands, who lives there or what they might have to say about any of this. The rulers of early modern Iberia, however, felt no such compunction: on 7 June 1494, the Spanish and Portuguese crowns, which at that point between them occupied somewhere comfortably under 1 per cent of all the land on Earth, agreed the terms on which they would divide the planet between them. If you could pinpoint a single moment when someone fired the starting gun on nearly half a millennium of European imperialism, the Treaty of Tordesillas would be it.

The 1490s was an exciting time to be Spanish.* In 1492, the Reconquista, the 700-year-long process by which assorted Christian kingdoms 'reconquered' the parts of the peninsula that had been under Muslim rule since the eighth century, finally reached its conclusion with the destruction of the Emirate of Granada. What's more, most of the peninsula's various kingdoms were now, if not a single state, then at least a union of the crowns, under the rule of a single family: Ferdinand of Aragon and his wife, Isabella of Castile, known collectively as the 'Catholic Monarchs'. After centuries of division, there was a thing one might term 'Spain'.

Even more exciting was the other big thing that happened in 1492. Christopher Columbus's voyage of discovery may have failed in its ostensible mission of finding a new, western route to India (he had screwed up the maths and was under the impression the globe was about a quarter smaller than it actually is) but he did have the sizable consolation of 'discovering' the Americas. Because his voyage had been funded by the Castilian crown, he'd claimed his newfound lands for Castile. Spain was ready to become an empire.

There was just one small fly in the ointment. Of the two kingdoms on the Iberian Peninsula that remained outside Ferdinand and Isabella's grasp, one was Navarre, which was small and rocky and would anyway be conquered soon enough.† The other, though, was more of a challenge. The Kingdom of Portugal had been busily building its own empire for most of the fifteenth century: by 1492, it had a sizable navy, with which it had discovered and claimed various Atlantic islands, planted assorted

---

* I should really say it was an exciting time to be *Christian* and Spanish because 1492 was also the year the region's Jewish population was given an unappetising choice between conversion, exile and death. Its Muslims would face a similar choice in the decades that followed. Basically, 1490s Spain: great for the Catholics, not so great for everyone else.

† Well, one bit of it, anyway. The area that was once Navarre is the bit that today we generally know as the Basque Country. Part of it ended up in Spain; the bit on the far side of the Pyrenees would become part of France.

trading posts along the West African coast and navigated as far as the Cape of Good Hope. In the 1470s, under King Alfonso V, it had fought a war against the Spanish kingdoms, in an attempt to put Joanna, who was upsettingly both Alfonso's consort *and* his niece, on the throne of Castile. It had lost but the resulting Treaty of Alcáçovas of 1479 had recognised its exclusive rights of navigating, conquering and trading in any new land discovered in the Atlantic south of the Canary Islands.

And so, when Christopher Columbus rocked up in Lisbon in early 1493, claiming to have discovered new land for the crown of Castile, the new Portuguese king, John II, who was both Joanna's cousin and her stepson – I did say it was upsetting – was not too happy about it. He dashed off a furious letter to his neighbours, reminding them of their treaty obligations and also, in not so many words, which of them it was who had the big navy.

Luckily for the Spaniards, though, Sixtus IV, the pope who'd ratified the Treaty of Alcáçovas in the papal bull* *Aeterni regis* ('Of the eternal king') had since found that he himself wasn't that eternal after all, and died. The new pope, Alexander VI, had, as of Columbus's return, only been in the job a few months. He was a Spaniard, born in the Kingdom of Aragon, and was currently, in his other role as sovereign of the Papal States, in the early stages of a war with pretty much every other significant Italian power. His name was Roderic Llançol i de Borja.

The fact that the Italianised version of his name – 'Borgia' – has gone down in history as a byword for corruption, nepotism, fathering bastards and generally shagging around might be a clue that he was not above earthly things. Such as, for example, revoking previous papal bulls to suck up to the rulers of Spain, in the hope they'd keep out of the Italian wars.

So, in May 1493, Alexander issued a new papal bull. (In fact, he issued three in two days – a succession of warring drafts which suggest a certain amount of fevered negotiation.) *Inter caetera* –

* Basically, just a public decree. There are going to be a few of these so I'd get comfortable with both the term and the Latin, if I were you.

'Among other works' – reaffirmed Portugal's existing colonies. But it also recognised Spain's exclusive claim to any new non-Christian lands it happened to come across to the west of a meridian 'one hundred leagues towards the west and south from any of the islands commonly known as the Azores and Cape Verde'.

A few months later, another bull, *Dudum siquidem* ('A short while ago'; whimsical names, these papal bulls) extended the Spanish right to lands reachable from the west, even if they were also – the globe being what it is – east of India. The pope – who was, let's remember, a Spaniard and also massively corrupt – was essentially saying to his fellow countrymen: 'There's gold in them thar seas. Go get it.'

John II wasn't wild about any of this; he might have accepted Spanish rights to a few distant islands in the Atlantic but the reference to India, a place the Portuguese had ambitions to reach by sailing round the Cape, was just too much. But he had no more enthusiasm for a costly and exhausting war than the Spanish did. And so, he decided to go around the pope, in roughly the manner his ships were going round Africa, and opened direct negotiations.

After some back and forth, the two sides agreed, in the Castilian town of Tordesillas, a new meridian dividing the Spanish and Portuguese spheres of influence, 270 leagues (810 miles) to the west of that set out by the pope. That guaranteed Portuguese access to its shipping routes down the African coast and, as a bonus, the easternmost tip of South America. It also guaranteed to the Spanish that they didn't have to have a war with a country with a much bigger navy. Both sides were happy, and if Alexander was at all annoyed to find his decree ignored, he had bigger problems, as the whole of Italy exploded into war.

A dozen years and two popes later, yet another pope, Julius II – nephew of Sixtus IV – ratified the treaty the Iberians had agreed among themselves, ostensibly in the hope of keeping on the good side of the powers that were busily conquering the world. A couple of decades after that, when the two sides found themselves banging into each other in today's Indonesia, they agreed yet

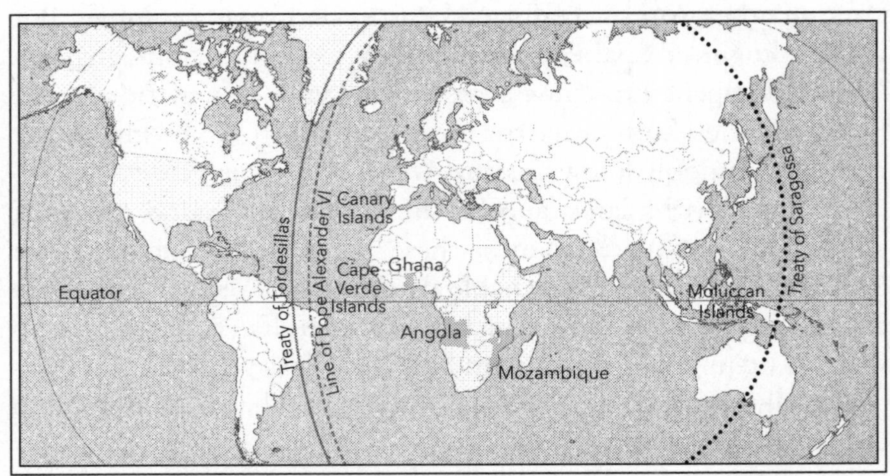

The various lines Spain, Portugal and the pope agreed in their attempts to divide the planet among the Catholic powers in the 1490s and 1500s.

another treaty, which created an *anti*-meridian, splitting the Pacific region between them, too. Less than forty years after Columbus had set out, the two rival powers on the Iberian Peninsula had divided the entire Earth between them.

The odd thing about all this is that very little of the land the powers of Europe were claiming for themselves had ever even been seen by a European (a habit, as we'll discover, those powers would acquire something of a taste for over the following centuries). More than that, they didn't even know where the land *was*. There's been some debate among modern scholars over whether the Portuguese demand to move the line westwards was a clever attempt to make sure the coast of Brazil was on their side of the line, thus giving them a helpful toehold in South America, or whether all this was a lucky coincidence, but the latter seems more likely: in the words of maritime historian J. H. Parry, 'Both sides must have known that so vague a boundary could not be accurately fixed, and each thought that the other was deceived.' The Europeans didn't really know what they were dividing.

Another problem was that it was not exactly clear where these world-shaping new lines were. The Treaty of Tordesillas specified a line a number of leagues west of the Cape Verde Islands but since it did not specify either which island or the length of the league, it was followed by decades of debate about where to put it.

Not that it mattered, particularly, since soon enough there were other naval powers – the English, the Dutch, even the French, who unlike the first two were still, by the seventeenth century, Catholic – zooming about the New World ignoring it. The treaty settled relations between Portugal and Spain, at least for a time; when it came to the rest of the world, though, it was unenforceable.

Oh – and let's not forget that nobody involved in the Treaty of Tordesillas ever thought to ask the people who actually lived in the Americas, Africa or Asia what they thought. That was, from some perspectives, a problem too.

The multiple absurdities, though, didn't stop the treaty from having effects that would persist for centuries. It explains why, when the entire rest of Latin America speaks Spanish, Brazil speaks Portuguese (because, having got their toehold, the Portuguese merrily expanded into the interior, to harvest wood, plant sugar plantations and dig mines). It's been used by Chile to justify its claim on the Antarctic and by Argentina to justify its claim on the Falkland Islands, on the grounds that both were, by the terms agreed at Tordesillas, parts of the Spanish Empire. This is odd because, as early as 1750, the colonial era still in full swing, John V of Portugal and Ferdinand VI of Spain had signed the Treaty of Madrid, which settled the borders between Spanish America and Brazil, thus superseding the Treaty of Tordesillas – essentially rendering it void.

One thing the Treaty of Tordesillas did not succeed in entrenching was the precedent that non-Christian lands could be handed out by the pope like sweeties: within a few years, the Reformation would kick in and large chunks of Europe would decide they need not listen to the papacy about anything ever again. The idea that the powers of Europe could divide the world up between them based on little more than their own military might, though – that idea would prove rather more durable.

Holy, Roman and an Empire

The sandals of Jesus and the many Heinrichs of Reuss

In the summer of 1789, the philosopher Wilhelm von Humboldt and friends travelled from Brunswick, capital of the small, fragmented but prominent Duchy of Brunswick-Wolfenbüttel, to Paris to have a look at the French Revolution. In the twelve days it took the party to reach the border between the Holy Roman Empire and France, it passed through four bishoprics, ruled directly by the church; six duchies, in the hands of secular princes; seven knightly estates, tiny patches of territory in the hands of relatively low-ranked nobles whose right to independence came directly from the emperor; and the free city of Aachen. That's eighteen different states, and seventeen different border crossings, in a distance of perhaps 350 miles.

They'd barely scratched the surface. At this point, the increasingly optional Holy Roman Empire of the German Nation contained untold hundreds of sovereign entities. That's as specific as I'm going to be because, thanks to constant splits, mergers, semi-independent exclaves and the like, no one actually seems to have a more definite figure: estimates range from as low as 250 (not, you will note, terribly low) to as high as 1,800. It's not merely that there wasn't a single Germany – a fact which anyone with even the slightest familiarity with European history will recall. It's that nobody knows how many Germanys there were.

Some of these states were big enough to be almost plausible: Prussia, Hanover, Saxony, Bavaria. The several dozen free imperial cities were smaller, of course, but not inherently sillier than, say, Singapore. The vast majority, though, were not just tiny but almost gleefully absurd. There was, for example, the House of Reuss, which ruled over a selection of constantly merging or dividing states in Thuringia and insisted on naming every male born into the family 'Heinrich' to commemorate the patronage of Emperor Henry VI back in the late twelfth century. The dozens of resulting Heinrichs were then numbered like kings, regardless of whether they got to be ruling princes or not. Then, once the regnal numbers began to get *really* silly – just in case you're worried some sanity might come into play here at some point – they'd reset the numbering, either once a century or once a hundred Heinrichs, depending on which branch of the family you're in. (At the time of Humboldt's journey, the house's various counties were in the hands of Heinrichs XXX, LI, XXXVIII, XXXV, XLIII, XLII and XLVII respectively.)

Then there were the imperial abbeys, which acted as independent states and had a seat in the Imperial Diet (parliament) despite being big stone buildings full of either monks or nuns. The Benedictine abbot of Prüm, for example, ruled over several dozen towns, villages and hamlets in the Trier area and made a living flogging the chance to see the abbey's most prestigious relic, the sandals of Jesus Christ. Two hundred miles to the northeast lay the Imperial Free Secular Foundation of Gandersheim, a Lower Saxon state whose population consisted entirely of unmarried daughters of the nobility, and whose abbess was on occasion an actual child.

You won't find a decent map of this patchwork – or possibly, as with the numbering, you'll find many clearly contradictory maps, because the borders were hazy, if not entirely undefined, and both they and the states they delineated were constantly changing. And this fragmentation, remember, was not a merely theoretical problem: the empire also contained numerous currencies (some states used several), and each state had the right to impose its own taxes and tariffs on those travelling through. If there is such a thing as the opposite of the European Union's single European market, the Holy Roman Empire of the eighteenth century was it.

In early modern Europe, of course, internal tariffs were pretty much the norm. The thing that made the empire stand out was that all these problems were *getting worse*. Across much of the continent, rulers were building stronger governments with armies to match, and to the German lands' west lay an increasingly volatile superpower named France. The Holy Roman Empire, though, was going in the opposite direction – the emperor becoming weaker, power moving from centre to periphery rather than the other way around. It isn't merely in retrospect that all this looks weird: German intellectuals were fretting about how mad and backwards their bit of Europe was at the time, too. They even had a pejorative term for it: '*kleinstaaterei*'. Small state-ry.

The most famous comment on the Holy Roman Empire is Voltaire's quip that it was 'neither holy, nor Roman, nor an empire'. In the eighteenth century, he was right on all counts, but it's terribly unfair that this is the only thing many people should remember about the place, because he was writing during the empire's sunset years. Once upon a time, things had been very different.

When last we left this part of the world, it was the mid-tenth century and Otto the Great, as he would be known, had taken a leaf out of the Charlemagne playbook and got himself crowned emperor by the pope. He and his successors would rule over a vast central European territory, including East Francia (western Germany), large chunks of what had in the ninth century been Middle Francia (stretching from the Netherlands down to northern Italy) and the newly civilised lands on the eastern frontier, too. So, although that name wouldn't come into vogue for several centuries, Otto's state really was holy, in that it had the papal imprimatur; it included Rome; and it was, by any reasonable contemporary standard, an empire.

You'll notice I said 'successors' rather than 'descendants'. That's because the thing that made the empire different from most medieval European states was the way it determined who got to be in charge. Firstly, although the king of Germany* was gener-

* This title varied a lot. It was (these translated from the Latin) 'King of the Franks', then 'King of the East Franks' for a few centuries; then 'King of the

ally (but not always) also the emperor of Rome, this elevation did not happen automatically: the pope still needed to give the nod and get the imperial regalia out. Secondly, no one automatically became king of Germany either: when the Carolingian line had died out with the death of Louis the Child in 911, the German nobles had reverted to the ancient Frankish custom of electing their next king. Who got to do the electing wobbled a bit but by the late twelfth century the rules had been formalised to create seven electors: three archbishops (Mainz, Trier and Cologne), plus four secular lords (the King of Bohemia, Duke of Saxony, Margrave of Brandenburg and Count Palatine of the Rhine).

The stage was set for a three-way battle of strength that would ebb and flow for centuries. Kings would generally want to pass the crown to their son, and all else being equal they would. If the crown got too strong, though, the nobles began murmuring darkly about how the throne was really elective and the king should watch his step or they'd pick someone else when he snuffed it. If it got too weak, and the realm was threatened, they might turf out a dynasty in favour of somebody stronger. On occasion, just as there might be a pope and a rival anti-pope, there were kings and anti-kings, too.

Meanwhile, the king still wanted the prestige and the titles that only a papal coronation could give, which gave the popes a lever, too. But that only worked so long as the emperor didn't show up with an army to threaten Rome, or fail to show up to protect it, or find some other way to undermine the papacy. In one particularly messy period of the mid-eleventh century, the emperor Henry IV persuaded a bunch of bishops to declare the election of Pope Gregory VII invalid, leading Gregory to retaliate with excommunication. The Investiture Crisis, as it's known, involved both anti-popes and anti-kings, and ended with Henry

---

Romans' in order to retaliate against the sneery way certain popes dismissed them as mere kings of Germany; then later they added 'King in Germany' because that's literally what they were. I'm going with 'king of Germany' as, although it's ahistorical, it's also a-confusing.

making a penitential walk to the castle of Canossa, then kneeling, praying, in the snow for three days. No one could ever be confident they'd come out on top.

The histories of most medieval European states include a certain amount of tussling over the strength of the monarch, the power of the barons and whether the pope gets a veto, of course. And for a while, just as in England and France, it looked like the German crown was on course to win this one. In the mid-fifteenth century, with wars raging in the east, the electors moved into one of their occasional 'oh crap, we need a stronger Reich' phases and began habitually handing the crown to whoever was next in line in the House of Habsburg. Over the next few decades, thanks to a combination of clever marriages and luck, the Vienna-based family moved itself into pole position to inherit the latest in a series of disparate territories calling themselves Burgundy – that meant control over the Netherlands, the richest area of northern Europe. Later, it also got its hands on the newly unified Spain, which helpfully came with a chunk of southern Italy and a promising overseas empire, too.

The mastermind behind much of this good fortune was Maximilian I. From 1495 onwards, he moved to modernise the Holy Roman Empire – as it had been calling itself for a couple of centuries by then – through all sorts of newfangled ideas like stronger courts and centralised taxes. Then he named himself emperor without all the hassle of travelling to Rome and getting crowned; and the papacy, keen to stay on the right side of what looked increasingly like a superpower, acquiesced. Viewed from, say, 1519, when Maximilian's grandson came into his terrifyingly vast territorial inheritance as Charles V, you'd probably have expected the empire to emerge as Europe's strongest state.

But no. Two years before Charles inherited his titles, a chap by the name of Martin Luther had nailed a piece of paper to a door to complain about the corruption of the Catholic church, and thus kicked off the Reformation. Converting to this new 'Protestantism', assorted German princes soon realised, would be a great way of throwing off an increasingly troublesome imperial authority, while also getting their hands on all the wealth of the local church. The result was intermittent but exhausting civil wars, which only ended once nobles on both sides made it clear that they would rather call in backup from France than let Charles indulge his fantasies of absolute rule. In the Peace of Augsburg of 1555, the emperor made the massive concession that the empire's individual princes could pick whatever religion they wanted for their people – and there was nothing he could do about it.

Meanwhile, it was becoming clear that the empire was just far, far too big to manage. The Italian territories, battered by decades of use as a battlefield by the Habsburgs and the French, had been pulling away for some time; almost everyone resented the fact that their nominal rulers were seemingly always somewhere else. The year after Augsburg, Charles abdicated, exhausted, and his empire was split in two, the Spanish and Dutch bits going to his son Philip, the German and Austrian ones to his brother Ferdinand. That wasn't enough to stop the Netherlands launching a revolt, in 1568, that would go on for another eighty years.

If the tug of war between its various factions had kept the empire weak during the medieval centuries, other forces were doing so now. The Habsburgs were more interested in sustaining and expanding their dynasty than they were in building a nation. Other states – the Netherlands, Prussia, eventually the Habsburgs' own Austria – would emerge with one foot inside the empire but one outside it, and thus had no particular interest in the consolidation of anything one might term 'Germany'. Meanwhile, groups of cities or other communities – the Swabian League, the Hanseatic League, the Swiss Confederacy – were banding together to guard their powers, privileges and ability to make money just as jealously as the nobles ever had. There were a lot of people with an interest in keeping the empire weak and apparently no one with an interest in making it strong.

Except, perhaps, the people who lived in it. In 1618, with the imperial heir who'd soon become Ferdinand II rubbing his hands with glee about the prospect of Counter-Reformation and to hell with Augsburg, some Catholics got themselves chucked out of a window in an event known, amusingly but inaccurately, as the Defenestration of Prague.* They survived, but the incident nonetheless proved the trigger for the long, draining hemoclysm known as the Thirty Years' War, during which virtually every power in Europe – France, Spain, Sweden, Denmark – took it in turns to march their armies across the German lands, killing a third of the population in the process. In some cities, like Magdeburg, the death rate was over 90 per cent.

The Peace of Westphalia, which finally ended the war in 1648, has gone down as a key event in the history of international relations: the moment Europe invented the modern state system and everyone agreed that, from here on in, no state should be able to interfere in another's domestic affairs. This is slightly baffling given that the treaties† actually say very little about such things.

They *did* recognise the independence of both the Dutch Republic and the Swiss Confederacy. They also introduced a measure of equality for all feudal vassals within the empire, no matter how big or small; those states were also now entitled to make treaties, both with each other and with others outside the empire. But other key aspects of what would become known as 'the Westphalian system' – mutual recognition, territorial integrity, non-interference and so on – are conspicuous by their absence from the actual Peace of Westphalia. The name seems to have been adopted merely as a convenient label for a shift from the thing we call feudalism to modernity, a process that had begun long before 1648 and that

---

* To be clear, it is not inaccurate that they were defenestrated (that is, thrown out of a window) or that the window in question is in Prague (it's in the castle; you can still visit it today). It's inaccurate merely because it should in fact be known as the *Second*, or possibly *Third*, Defenestration of Prague. The first, in 1419, led to the Hussite Wars. There was a second in 1483, too, though this is often discounted because it didn't lead to a big war. People getting thrown out of windows in Prague Castle, thus precipitating major wars, is a surprisingly common theme of European history. Just don't hold any EU summits there, that's all I'm saying.

† Two of them: Osnabrück and Münster.

still had another couple of centuries to run – centuries, what's more, in which plenty of Europeans would be running around the world depriving other peoples of *their* territorial integrity and generally interfering.

Within the empire, though, 1648 did mark a big shift: suddenly its states had a degree of sovereignty and autonomy that their forebears could have only dreamed of a little over a century earlier. And the Holy Roman emperors, who only a few generations before had been the most powerful monarchs in Europe, now found themselves severely diminished and in line to be mocked by any French philosophers who happened to be passing.

The newly semi-autonomous states, though, were not 'nations' in the sense we'd understand them today: they were places like Prüm Abbey or the ever-splintering counties ruled over by the dozens of men named Heinrich von Reuss. What had a little over a century before been the most important power in Europe was now an absurd patchwork of silly little statelets, which everyone knew had been little more than a buffet for predatory foreign armies. The era of *kleinstaaterei* had arrived.

Later German thinkers would look back on this era and see a country too weak to defend itself and too divided to punch its true weight. It was a situation that both the Prussian militarists who would unify Germany in the nineteenth century, and the people who'd take their legacy into the twentieth, were absolutely determined to address. What could possibly go wrong?

Britain, Ireland and the Invention of Cartographic Colonialism

The most dangerous map in imperial history

The 1570 Mercator map of Ireland is clearly a product of a different age. It isn't merely that it's facing the wrong way, so that north is on the right, or that the title or elegantly scripted labelling of the seas are all in Latin: it's that the country is very clearly the wrong shape. The rivers and lakes are far too wide; the curving east coast is a near straight line and the jagged west one is missing most of its jags. Meanwhile, the island's northwest corner has what looks suspiciously like a right angle.

Gerardus Mercator was no slouch when it came to cartography – the projection he invented for his 1569 world map is still in use, giving people a misleading sense of the relative sizes of Greenland and Africa to this day. But still, this was a map made by people who fundamentally didn't know what shape the thing they were mapping was. Those elegantly scripted labels might as well read 'Here Be Dragons'.

The Down Survey maps, drawn up just eighty years later, are a different sort of thing entirely. It's not just that the coasts and islands are the right shape, and the inland waterways on a sensible scale, it's also the level of detail they contain. There are county maps, showing towns and roads, castles and inns, and more local ones, of baronial estates or parishes, too. You no longer feel you're looking at a map of a strange and unfamiliar land that would not seem out of place in the opening pages of a high fantasy novel, but one of the real European country which you can still find in an atlas today. The Down Survey maps, based on the first full, national survey, are proper, modern maps. But more than that, they are beautiful.

It was of course the latter sort of map that would end up doing all the damage – not just to the Irish but to other colonised peoples all over the globe.

The start of England's interference in Irish politics – the eight-hundredth anniversary of which was marked by the beginning of the 'Troubles', a faintly euphemistic name for three decades of intercommunal violence – is generally dated to 1169, when a deposed king of Leinster, Diarmait Mac Murchada (Dermot MacMurrough) requested English help in regaining his throne. In exchange, he offered land and loyalty to King Henry II, accidentally giving the English crown a permanent foothold in Ireland in the process.*

For the next few centuries, bits of Ireland were ruled by earldoms of English descent but fairly questionable loyalty. And while the English kings claimed to be Lords of Ireland, in practice, control was restricted to 'the Pale', a narrow strip around Dublin. Beyond the pale – the *Oxford English Dictionary* is cynical about whether this specific historic phenomenon is the origin of the phrase† – lay a world where the king's writ did not run and civilised behaviour, in English eyes, could not be guaranteed. This was clearly a form of colonialism but it also wasn't substantially different from the sort of messy feudal politics going on all over Europe.

What changed that was the Reformation, when the kings of England, and Scotland, abandoned Catholicism but the people

* Whether it's fair to describe either Le Mans-born Henry II, whose empire included half of France, or the Normans more generally as 'English' – as opposed to what was, initially at least, the force occupying them – is an interesting and controversial question which I am shamelessly avoiding answering by means of this footnote.

† Other notable pales in history: the Pale of Calais, the stretch of northern France in English hands between the fourteenth and sixteenth centuries, and the Pale of Settlement, the western chunk of the Russian Empire (modern Belarus, Lithuania, eastern Ukraine, and so on) in which Jews were allowed to live.

of Ireland did not. England in the sixteenth century was not the imperial behemoth it would later become but a relative minnow, terrified about the possibility of aggression or invasion by bigger, Catholic powers like France or Spain. Ireland, a Catholic island lying at its own backdoor, was thought – not entirely unreasonably – to be a security risk. Its people, what's more, were not merely potential agents of hostile foreign powers, they were heretics, too. And heretics were legitimate targets.

So far as the English crown was concerned, there was only one solution: conquest. In 1541, Henry VIII unilaterally upgraded himself from lord to king of Ireland and demanded allegiance from the Irish barons. The next decade, his successors began the policy of 'plantation': essentially, ethnic cleansing, clearing Irish lands of their existing occupants to make room for new, more loyal English settlers. After 1603, when James VI of Scotland also became James I of England, the Scots got into the game, too, and the plantation of Ulster became a British joint venture.

But the original occupants of Ireland were, of course, still there. The result was a predictable and apparently endless cycle of oppression, followed by uprising, followed by yet more violent oppression.

It was one of the most violent – certainly the most infamous – periods of English violence that produced the Down Survey. In 1641, much of Ireland rose in revolt against foreign rule and all the anti-Catholic discrimination, plantation and land confiscation that came with it. The resulting war was a complicated affair: the row in London over how to fund a military response was a key factor in the road to the English Civil War, which led ultimately to the temporary abolition of the monarchy and the execution of Charles I; the whole archipelago-wide conflagration is sometimes described today as the War of the Three Kingdoms. But for our purposes, a few key facts should suffice.

One is that the 1641 uprising saw the rebels slaughter perhaps 4,000 English and Scottish settlers in events like the Portadown massacre, when they forced around 100 Protestants off a bridge into the River Bann, then shot the survivors. Another is that, as horrific as atrocities like this were, their scale and frequency were both exaggerated by lurid pamphlets published back in London, which claimed that as many as 200,000 Protestants had been slaughtered by the savage Catholics, thus creating pressure for the British response to be equally savage. In 1642, the English parliament passed the Adventurers' Act, which raised money to fund the military reconquest of Ireland through public subscription. Repayment would be funded through extensive confiscation of Irish land.

Civil war meant the invasion didn't come for some time, but in 1649, with King Charles separated from his head and parliament now running the show, a fleet of ships carrying Oliver Cromwell and his New Model Army landed in Dublin. Over the next few years, they crushed both rebel Catholic and remaining royalist forces in Ireland, and engaged in mass slaughter – of surrendering troops, priests, civilians – in towns whose names would become bywords for atrocities: Drogheda, Wexford, Clomnel. What proportion of Ireland's population died during the conflict, either directly from the violence or through starvation or disease, is difficult to say, but few estimates seem to get below 10 per cent. Some put it at over 40 per cent. This, if you've ever wondered, is why Cromwell, far from the only Briton to oversee horrifically violent acts in Ireland, is still synonymous with English oppression today.

As the war approached its conclusion, the English government began to think about how to repay its war debts, both those generated by the Adventurers' Act and its massive unpaid military wage bill. So in 1652, it passed another bill, the Act of Settlement, which laid out plans to dispossess the rebels of their land: that way, it could then be redistributed to soldiers to cover unpaid wage bills, or possibly flogged off for cash. As to the surviving native population, well, they could be transported to the Caribbean or to the poorer land west of the River Shannon, comfortingly far from Great Britain. The plan is summed up in Irish popular memory by the suggestion they would be sent 'to hell or to Connaught'.

All this, though, required the English to find out what they actually had to redistribute – that meant a land survey. The first man given the job was the surveyor-general, Benjamin Worsley, who hired professionals and began a careful and fastidious job that he confidently expected to complete in as little as thirteen years. But a younger, more impatient man, on leave of absence from academia to serve as the army's physician general, thought he could do the job rather quicker.

William Petty was the son of a Hampshire clothier who had run away to become a ship's cabin boy at the age of thirteen, broken his leg and been unceremoniously dumped on the shores of Normandy. (This was apparently the sort of thing that ships at that time did rather a lot.) There he was found by some Jesuits who recognised his potential, took him in and gave him an education. After a stint in the Royal Navy and another as private secretary to the philosopher Thomas Hobbes, he'd ended up in Oxford, teaching anatomy at Brasenose College, and then joined up with Cromwell.

Petty's great insight was that using a small team of trained specialists for every little job was a waste of time. New technology like Gunter's chain – a standardised measuring chain of 100 links, invented by the clergyman and mathematician Edmund Gunter a generation before – was simple enough that even ordinary soldiers, who were not in short supply, could use it. The difficult bit, of collating the results and turning them into a map, could be left to a much smaller group of specialised cartographers in the warm and dry back in Dublin. By essentially handing the grunt work over to non-specialists, Petty's team managed to survey half of Ireland in thirteen months instead of thirteen years.*

Both the improved quality and sheer quantity of data collected were key in facilitating the shift from Mercator's vague, faintly fantastical map to Petty's detailed, modern one. The Down Survey was the first full-scale land survey of a nation conducted anywhere

* One possible explanation for why it's called the Down Survey, incidentally, is because using Gunter's chain involves laying it down on the ground. Another is that the results were put down in a map.

in the world. It was not, however, a merely academic exercise: it would have a number of enduring effects.

The least of these was that Petty made good. He came out of the survey wealthy and with powerful friends, and would soon enough win a knighthood and seat in parliament, too. He also served on the commission which distributed the land to creditors, many of whom preferred to sell up rather than wait for some theoretical future in which they could safely take possession, and thus managed to end up with vast estates in County Kerry: a result that brought forth furious allegations of corruption over the years to come. He married well, too: his descendants would be earls and marquesses; one would be prime minister (William Petty, the second Earl of Shelburne, a Whig who managed not quite nine months in Downing Street in 1782–3). Petty himself is remembered today mainly as an economist, which makes sense given that the survey's main insight essentially amounted to the theory of specialisation and division of labour. Samuel Pepys would later describe him as 'the most rational man in England'; Karl Marx preferred 'a frivolous, grasping, unprincipled adventurer'.

But the Down Survey had another, more philosophical consequence. Not so long before, titles of lands had relied upon archaic systems like 'metes and bounds' (metes were directions and distances of straight sections; bounds referred to other features like rivers, rocks and trees often used to define boundaries). Such things inherently involved an intimacy with the land: possessing a place required you to *know* it. The rise of the professional surveyor, though, made it possible to assert land ownership on a previously unimaginable scale. You didn't even need to visit; you just needed a map. And if force was sometimes required to enforce ownership, the thing that fired the starting gun could be little more than a piece of paper.*

* This was not merely a colonial issue. Hannah Rose Woods's brilliant 2022 book *Rule, Nostalgia* quotes one early modern observer's complaint that professional surveys were used to boost domestic rents, too. 'The world was merrier before measurings were used,' he complains. 'A tenant in these days must pay for every foot, which is an extreme matter.'

This was a shift whose consequences would be creeping across the globe for centuries to come. To give just one example, in the years after the American Revolution, Thomas Jefferson – a man feted for his authorship of the Declaration of Independence, but whose personal politics frequently failed to live up to those values – came up with the nifty idea of the Public Land Survey: an official US government programme to divide the uncolonised lands beyond the Eastern Seaboard into a grid of one-mile squares. These could then be distributed to veterans of the Revolutionary War in lieu of unpaid wages or sold off to the highest bidder to raise some cash. (All this might sound familiar.) So successful was this scheme, and so vast were the lands it swallowed as the US expanded farther and farther west, that features created by the 'Jefferson grid' can still be viewed from plane windows over the US today.

As in Ireland, however, 'uncolonised' did not mean 'unoccupied': the Jefferson grid was, among other things, a machine for the systematic dispossession of the Native American populations. And this division of territory – so vast that its grid lines occasionally needed to dog-leg, to take account of the curvature of the Earth* – was done not using natural features or landscape as seen by its occupants; it involved one-mile squares divided by the stroke of a pen, hundreds of miles away in Washington.

The advance in the political use of cartography represented by the Down Survey would soon, in other words, be dividing up whole continents. This is a theme we'll be coming back to.

* Because you can't divide the surface of a sphere into a grid: lines of longitude are not quite parallel but converge at the poles. The sheer size of the US is also a problem addressed through its national coordinate system, a reflection of the fact it's big enough to need something taking the curve of the Earth into account but not quite big enough for longitude or latitude to be the most useful way of doing this.

The Much Misunderstood Mason–Dixon Line

A metaphor waiting to happen

The Mason–Dixon line – thanks to its imagined status as the boundary between the northern free states and the southern slave ones, its role in the American Civil War in the nineteenth century, not to mention US hegemony since the twentieth – is one of the most famous boundaries in the world.

The funny thing is, though, that the line originally had absolutely nothing to do with slavery. It wasn't about dividing the US into north and south. It certainly had nothing to do with a civil war that was still nearly a century off, in a nation that didn't yet exist. The men who drew the line, astronomer Charles Mason and surveyor Jeremiah Dixon, may well have been surprised to learn their names would forever be associated with this one job: both were born and based in England and neither lived to see the newly formed United States adopt the constitution that'd play such a big part in the trouble.

The original Mason–Dixon line, in fact, had its origins in the turmoil surrounding a different civil war entirely. In 1632, Britain's Charles I granted the second Baron Baltimore – a man who gloried in the magnificent given name of Cecilius Calvert – a charter to start an American colony as a haven for the Catholics fleeing persecution from England's Protestant majority. It would lie north of the existing colony of Virginia (by now recovered from the rather unpleasant false start of Jamestown, a period known as the 'Starving Time', in which its population fell by nearly 90 per cent and the survivors engaged in some light cannibalism). It would stretch northward to the point 'which lieth under the Fortieth degree of north latitude' and west to the source of the Potomac River. The colony's main settlement would be named

'Baltimore' for its absentee governor, who spent the rest of his life safely at home in England, but the colony as a whole would be named for the queen, or possibly for Christ's mother: Maryland.

Nearly fifty years, one civil war, a republic and a restoration later, Charles I no longer had a head, and his eldest son, Charles II, was on the throne. He, like his dad, was widely believed to have Catholic tendencies and ruled a country riven by religious division. He also had rather a lot of debts.

So in 1681, when one of his creditors, the Quaker William Penn, came calling for his money, Charles had a bright idea: why not give him a grant of land in the New World instead? At an estimated 45,000 square miles, the proposed colony was almost as large as England itself – surely enough to cancel a trifling £16,000 debt. And like Maryland before it, it could act as a haven for some of England's religious minorities, far away from where they could do any political damage. Charles even named it 'Pennsylvania' to sweeten the deal. Penn, quite touched by the idea of a colony for Quakers, and rather fancying himself as the largest non-royal landowner in the world, agreed.

Here's the problem, though: maps of the New World were still pretty shoddy (the clue was in the name). Pennsylvania was clearly supposed to be the area immediately north of Maryland, stretching from the forty-third parallel to the existing border at the fortieth. But the terms of the grant also described its southern boundary as extending westward from 'a Circle drawne [sic] at twelve miles distance from New Castle . . .' The king had assumed, from the map, that such a circle would meet the previously defined boundary but it didn't – even its northernmost point lay a good ten miles south of the fortieth parallel. That meant that, if that previously defined boundary became official, it would leave Penn's chosen capital of Philadelphia sited, inconveniently, in Maryland.

The solution favoured by the Penn family and their supporters was to note that Maryland's charter had said merely that the colony 'lieth under the Fortieth degree of north latitude': 'under' didn't necessarily have to mean 'immediately under', did it? Not

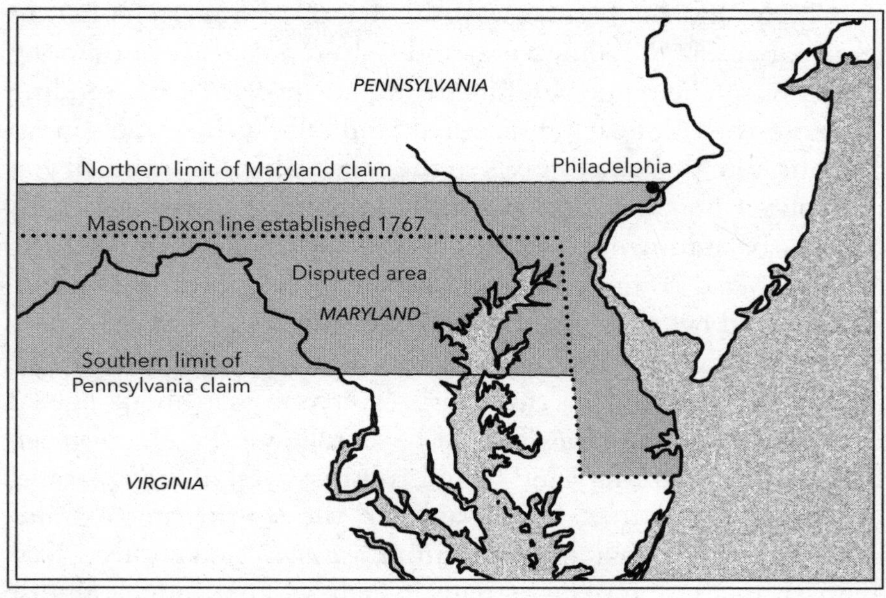

The overlapping territorial claims of Pennsylvania and Maryland, eventually settled by the Mason–Dixon line in 1767.

unnaturally, though, the Calvert family and their supporters preferred the original interpretation. The two descriptions, one favouring each colony, simply couldn't be reconciled.

As if that weren't enough, there was the slight issue of what would later become Delaware. The reason that circle around New Castle had been excluded from Penn's grant is because the king had granted it to his brother, James, the Duke of York – the settlement, along with a vast stretch of land between the Delaware and Connecticut rivers, had been a reward for his role in kicking the Dutch out of North America. Penn, though, wanted his colony to have access to the sea. And so he persuaded the duke – who would later briefly reign as James II before being chased out of England by, ironically, the Dutch – to lease him that circle, plus the three 'lower counties' on the peninsula to its south. This came as some surprise to the Calverts, who had confidently believed they were part of Maryland.

Charles did his best to wash his hands of a mess he had in large part created, telling Penn and Calvert to sort it out among themselves. Their first attempt to do so involved each sending letters to the colonists on disputed land telling them that on no account were they to pay taxes to the other, which tells you all you need about how well that was likely to go. The scene was set for decades of arguments, official commissions, failure to heed the results of said commissions and expensive litigation in London, all peppered by occasional bouts of violence.

After approximately eighty years of this, and with a fair amount of nudging by the courts, everyone just about agreed that the local boundaries should be as follows: the line between Pennsylvania and Maryland would run east–west along a parallel fifteen miles south of what was then the southernmost point in Philadelphia. That put it at around 39°43', guaranteed that Pennsylvania's capital was actually in Pennsylvania and felt almost anticlimactically straightforward as a resolution to a row that had lasted as long as the Dutch War of Independence.

The line between Delaware and Maryland was more complicated. That required finding the midpoint of the Transpeninsular Line, which divided the aforementioned peninsula between Virginia in the south and Maryland/Delaware in the north,* drawing a line from there to the western side of the twelve-mile circle around New Castle, Delaware (the 'tangent line'), then following another line north until you hit the Maryland–Pennsylvania border (the 'north line').

Got that? Good, because there's another bit. The agreement also stated that any land within the twelve-mile circle but west of the north line would remain a part of Delaware – a fact now visible in an almost imperceptible kink in the state boundaries in the western suburbs of the town of Newark, Delaware.†

* You can probably guess at this point how the Delmarva Peninsula got its name, though the label wasn't in use until at least a century later.

† Actually, there is yet another bit. Something the agreement did not state, because until the survey was over no one had considered it as a possibility,

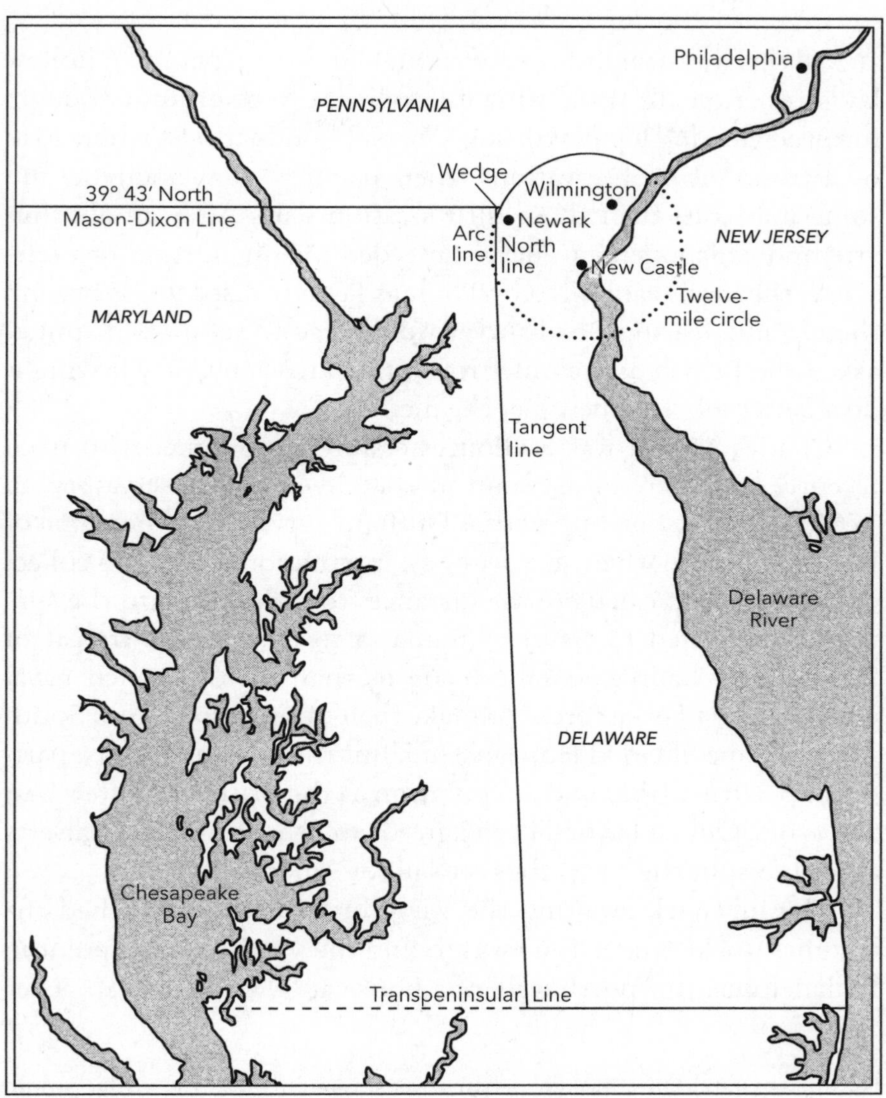

The assorted geographical features used in determining state borders on and around the Delmarva Peninsula.

---

is what would happen if there turned out to be any land that was east of the north line (so clearly not part of Maryland) but outside the New Castle circle (so not part of Delaware) *and* south of the Maryland–Pennsylvania Parallel (so not obviously part of Pennsylvania either). Initially, this didn't matter, as both Pennsylvania and Delaware were in the hands of the Penn family. Once the two

All this was straightforward enough in theory (pause for hollow laughter). Actually translating it into lines on the ground, though, involved clearing a path through forests, conducting a whole load of astronomical observations, then using a star catalogue and some maths to turn those into location data. After an abortive attempt, which seems to have succeeded mainly in ruining a telescope, the local team hired by Thomas Penn realised it was beyond them. Penn, fearing a bad survey would lead to yet more disputes, asked the British astronomer royal if he knew anyone who might do a better job. He knew just the men.

Charles Mason was a Gloucestershire astronomer who until recently had been an assistant at the Greenwich observatory. In 1761, he had teamed up with a Durham surveyor by the name of Jeremiah Dixon, when, as part of an international effort to collect data that'd help calculate the distance from the Earth to the sun, they'd attempted to travel to Sumatra to observe the transit of Venus. They hadn't actually made it, thanks to a French naval attack, and had been forced to make their observations from South Africa's Cape of Good Hope instead. But they'd established a partnership, a friendship and a reputation as the British Empire's best surveyors. Once a fee had been agreed, and the Penns and Calverts agreed to split the costs, they set sail for America.

The first task awaiting the surveyors when they reached the colonies in November 1763 was to find the southernmost point in Philadelphia: the 'north wall' of a house at 30 Cedar Street.* They

---

became separate states, though, debates over sovereignty over the 'wedge' would keep the locals busy for another century and a half. It was only finally resolved in Delaware's favour in 1921.

* How the north wall of a house in a city could be the southernmost point of that city is not exactly clear – according to Thomas Pynchon's 1997 novel *Mason & Dixon*, it's because the southern wall was private property, though since a) that's a novel, and b) it has a bunch of stuff about alien abduction in it, I'm not sure we can trust it as a source. Anyway, it's too late to check: the house was demolished in 1960 to build the I-95 highway. The street it stood on is called South Street today.

spent the next four summers surveying the various lines involved in the boundary; the winters, when the weather made both astronomy and movement impossible, they spent sightseeing. As the survey proceeded, they left milestones, labelled 'M' and 'P' on either side, to mark the boundaries; every five miles, they placed a 'crownstone', which included the two families' coats of arms.

Then, in October 1767, some 233 miles west, the Iroquois who'd been helping to clear the ground and acting as guides declared that they were done. Any further, they said, and the party risked running into Shawnee war parties; they would go no further. And so, after returning east and making a map of what they had found, Mason and Dixon were done, too. Their four years of work had gone on rather longer than anyone had predicted and had cost the Calverts and the Penns over £3,500 – nearly £500,000 in today's money. But, finally, the matter was settled: at long last, everyone agreed where Pennsylvania ended and Maryland began.

So that's the Mason–Dixon line: an 83-mile north–south line dividing Maryland from Delaware, and another 233-mile east–west one dividing it from Pennsylvania, a boundary which makes it barely a third of the way to the Mississippi. Put like that, it doesn't seem very important and it's possible that the men it's named after, who seem to have been far more excited by the research into the size of the Earth they did along the way, would be surprised to find their names still attached to it. Both returned to England, where Dixon died in 1779. Mason researched and published a catalogue of 387 stars, and started a family, but seems to have struggled to make ends meet. In 1786, he moved to Pennsylvania, apparently in the hope his friend Benjamin Franklin might help him find work, but died there soon after arriving. Neither could have had the slightest inkling of what their line would come to symbolise.

The reason we've all heard of the Mason–Dixon line, of course, has very little to do with Mason and Dixon, or the Penns or the Calverts, or even, particularly, Pennsylvania or Maryland. In 1787, the year after Mason died, the great and the good of the now independent United States met in his adopted city to work out how to transform thirteen colonies who had spent over a century squabbling over matters just like this one into a single, cohesive nation. One of the difficulties they were struggling with was the fact that the new country was composed of two increasingly divergent halves: a south, with an agricultural economy based on slavery, and a north, more interested in industry and reform. Managing the conflicting values and interests of these two regions was to dominate US politics for decades; the inability to reconcile them would lead to civil war.

It was in 1820, during one of the periodic crises that all this threw up, that the first references to the 'Mason–Dixon line' appear. The topic at hand was what to do with Missouri, a territory which allowed slavery and which was hoping to become a new state. Participants in congressional debates on the subject referenced the boundary between Maryland, one of the northernmost slave states, and Pennsylvania, a free one. It's not quite true to say even the original line was the boundary between the slave and free states: slavery in some forms persisted in Delaware and even New Jersey for several more decades. Nonetheless, the name became attached to the entire concept of a line between a free north and slave south.

What eventually emerged from these debates was the 'Missouri Compromise', which maintained the fragile equilibrium by simultaneously admitting Maine as a free state and Missouri as a slave one. It also ruled that a new line, along the latitude of 36 degrees 30 minutes north, would mark the northern limit of slavery in the west. Perhaps, even though this was some way south and a long way west of anywhere Mason and Dixon ever went, people simply mixed up the lines. Or perhaps there was another source of confusion: the name 'Dixie' for the south, popularised by an 1859 song, may have referred to the name French-speaking residents of New Orleans gave to $10 notes ('Dix'). But it sounds a bit like 'Dixon', so perhaps someone, somewhere, assumed it came from the line and thus that the line marked the boundary with the north.

Either way, in a pattern we'll meet again, the Mason–Dixon line became a sort of synecdoche: a label attached to a boundary or a concept very distant from the line the name had originally referred to. The need for Mason and Dixon's survey had resulted, in a roundabout way, from the fallout from one civil war. Perhaps our misunderstanding of their work and their line resulted from another.

The Local Government Reforms of Emperor Napoleon I

A young man from Corsica redraws the map

There are many great tales one could tell of the French Revolution and the Napoleonic Wars which followed. There's the story of how a popular uprising in favour of *liberté, égalité, fraternité* gave way to the slaughter of the Terror; of how Maximilien Robespierre betrayed and executed his friends, and was betrayed and executed himself for his trouble. I could write about how it sparked decades of war and instability, not only in France but across Europe, and from there across the world; or tell of how a soldier from an island backwater used this chaos as a ladder and climbed to rule over the largest empire Europe had seen in centuries. I could explore how the revolution's effect on political thought was so great that when the Chinese premier Zhou Enlai was asked, nearly two centuries later, what its impact had been, he said: 'It's too early to say.'*

What I'm really interested in, though, is the revolution's impact on the map of Europe and, more specifically, on French local government structures. So let's talk about that instead.

So radical was the idea of overthrowing the *ancien régime* – the basket term for the political and social order which had held sway in France for centuries, and the monarchy which had ruled

---

* Actually, probably not. An interpreter who was present at that event, in 1972, later clarified that Zhou had understood the question to refer to the then recent student protest movement of 1968, rather than the years that followed 1789; this was less a comment about China's long-term view of history than about France's addiction to revolution. But that wouldn't make for so useful a pithy quote to end the paragraph, now, would it?

it for considerably longer than that – that the revolution opened the door to rethinking absolutely everything. Some of the new ideas which originated in that period stuck (the metric system, a new, more rational set of weights and measures that many of us use every day, was first proposed in the French National Assembly in 1790); others, alas, did not (proposals for a new, more rational calendar, in which the months were named after natural phenomena like the weather and 1792–3 was rechristened 'Year I', were abandoned on 1 January 1806).

One reform which fell somewhere in the middle was the one concerning France's boundaries, internal and external alike. Before the revolution kicked off, the Kingdom of France was made up of thirty-four, ish, provinces. But because they had been acquired at different times and in different ways, not all provinces were created equal. Some of them, like Aunis, a small patch of Atlantic coast around La Rochelle, were small enough that they'd look a bit titchy when placed beside an average English county. Others (Guyanne and Gascony, Languedoc, Brittany) were big enough their size can be given in multiples of Wales. They often had different systems of laws and taxes, too. None of it made for rational administration.

So in September 1789, with the revolution four months old, Emmanuel-Joseph Sieyès – a junior clergyman and political writer who coined the word 'sociology', and who is generally known to history as Abbé Sieyès – suggested to the national assembly that this might be a good moment to sort this mess out. The first and silliest proposal was to borrow a 1786 proposal from the cartographer Mathias Robert de Hesseln, which divided the country into a sort of chess board, of 81 squares measuring 18 leagues (approximately 70km, or about 45mi) on each side. This would have allowed everyone, anywhere in the country, to be within a day's ride of their provincial capital, assuming that there weren't any rivers or mountains in the way; the problem was, of course, quite often there were. So while Sieyès's proposal for new, straight boundaries looked perfectly rational on the map, boundaries cutting across natural landscapes and people's houses were entirely *irrational* on the ground. Unsurprisingly, the plan was never implemented.

After several months of deliberation, the committee charged with reorganising the map of France came up with an alternative. The rough size and number of new divisions remained: there would be eighty-three instead of eighty-one but the goal was still to put everyone within a day's ride of their local centre. Sieyès's plans to sweep away the class-inflected names of provinces and replace them with those of rivers, mountains or other natural features stuck, too. The only change was that the borders would follow the landscape – or, though no one much wanted to draw attention to the fact, old provincial boundaries.

The workings of these new departments would change a lot over the years: they'd be divided into communes and merged into regions; their original democratic councils would be replaced, under Napoleon, with prefects appointed by central government. But broadly speaking, the divisions of France created in the months after the revolution remain: around seventy-nine of the ninety-six departments which exist today have been there since 1790.

One reason for the increase in the number of departments is because some of them were subdivided: Seine, for example, a sort of Greater Paris, and Seine-et-Oise, the even *greater* Greater Paris which surrounded it, were split into eight departments between them in 1968. The other reason for the increase is that France got bigger.

Which is where the other part of our story comes in.

There were many reasons why the French Revolution led to war: some powers wanted to support the *ancien régime*, others to prevent pernicious ideas like 'liberty' and 'equality' from spreading, still others to take advantage of perceived French weakness. At any rate, from 1792 onwards, France fought a series of wars with, basically, everyone – not for nothing are the conflicts of this period known as the wars of the first, second, third, fourth, fifth, sixth *and* seventh coalition, after the shifting collections of European powers who opposed it. Despite 'basically everyone' seeming on the face of it to be a pretty formidable opponent, all this went surprisingly well for France, which was already the largest country in Europe, and which, over the next few years, started swallowing bits of neighbouring states – some Austrian Netherlands here, the left bank of the Rhine there.

Then, in 1799, our old friend Abbé Sieyès instigated a coup and installed a successful Corsican general as first consul of the French Republic. This, his thinking went, would outmanoeuvre his more radical opponents and allow him to call the shots. Napoleon Bonaparte, though, wasn't wild about this whole figurehead proposal and decided that instead he'd rather be the most powerful man in Europe. And that was when the map really started to change.

Once Napoleon had had himself crowned emperor in 1804, he swiftly got to work marching about the continent redrawing borders, kicking out incumbents and installing friendly regimes: turning the mess of the western German lands into the Confederation of the Rhine, appointing his brother king of Spain and so on. Much of this was done with the express intention of leaving the British, who stubbornly insisted on retaining naval supremacy, politically and economically isolated. But, along the way, as a bonus, France annexed a whole bunch more territory, too.

Until, by 1811, there weren't eighty-three departments. There were around 130.*

Some of the additions, especially in the southeast – Savoy, Nice – were places that make up part of today's France, and which it feels almost strange to discover were ever anything else. These, though, are the exceptions and most of these extra departments cover parts of Europe that are very definitely not, at time of writing, French. Napoleon's empire absorbed the entirety of the Low Countries, from Forêts (a department centred on Luxembourg) in the south

* I'm being a bit vague about the number because, so dynamic was the First French Empire – a nice way of saying that bits kept dropping out of it, even as other bits were added on – that certainty about which provinces were in the empire at the same time, and how many departments they functioned as, has proved surprisingly elusive.

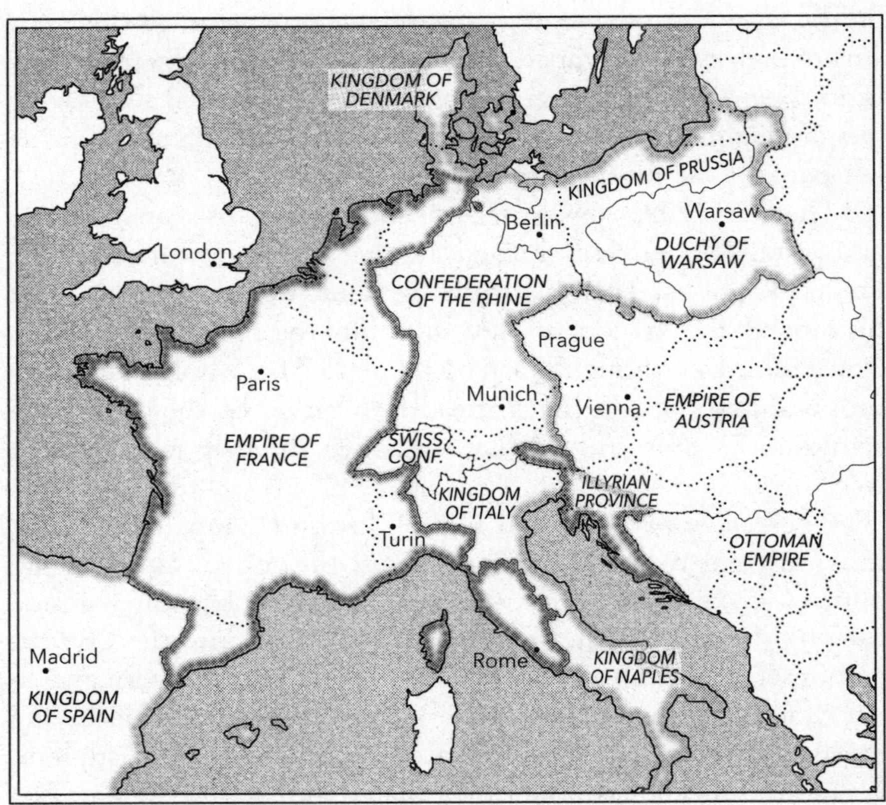

Napoleon's empire at its greatest extent, c. 1812, overlaid on modern boundaries. The darker line shows the borders of the expanded France; the lighter one, client states. The empire of Austria was sometimes allied, too.

right up to Bouches-de-l'Elbe (Hamburg) in the north. Another line of departments stretched down the west coast of Italy as far as Rome (in the imaginatively named department of Rome). Then there were the four departments briefly covering Catalonia (Barcelona was in that of Montserrat) and another seven in the 'Illyrian Provinces', conquered from Austria in 1809 and held until 1814, which included large chunks of today's Slovenia and Croatia. These were not mere client states like the Kingdom of Italy, which made up the rest of the northern end of that country, or the Duchy of Warsaw; they were intended to be as much a part of France as Brittany or Languedoc.

From two centuries on, this looks both unnerving and faintly absurd: of *course* the Netherlands and northern Italy aren't a part of France, and it's ridiculous to imagine they could have remained so.

I'm not so sure. This was a time before the age of the nation state, an era in which both the map of Europe and the national identities it contained were in flux. Eric Hobsbawm has noted that, on the eve of the revolution in 1789, only around half the population of France spoke French and perhaps a quarter of those spoke it well. When Corsica became a part of France in 1769, it was after nearly five centuries as part of the Republic of Genoa; Napoleon Bonaparte, born there the same year, likely spoke both Corsican and Italian before he spoke French. He learned the language of Paris for the same reason many others would: because that was how you got on in life.

Furthermore, the borders of France still had decades of change ahead. Alsace-Lorraine would be lost to, and regained from, Germany twice; the leading Italian state of Piedmont-Sardinia would happily hand over Savoy and Nice in exchange for French support for unification. There's no obvious reason why, say, the Belgian region of Wallonia, which once had its own language but was increasingly speaking French, could not have ended up a part of France, too: it had been so before. So had some of the Dutch-speaking lands to its north. And almost all of the extra territory swallowed by Napoleon's empire, with a couple of far-flung exceptions, had once been part of the Lotharingian third of Francia, which is one reason why the French thought it only right and proper to make them true parts of France in the first place. If they had remained French politically perhaps nationalism would have won out and they would have broken away again. Or perhaps their people would have learned the language and adopted French customs to further their careers, just as that Corsican schoolboy once had.

Or perhaps not. Perhaps other national identities were already too established in some of those conquered territories; perhaps a bigger France would have been unable to indulge in the nation building required to create the country we know today. Perhaps, even if those seven coalitions had all failed, the British industrial machine would have somehow found the money to fund an eighth, or a ninth, or a tenth, that would succeed.

At any rate, none of this was necessary. Napoleon was defeated and exiled to Elba by the sixth coalition in 1814. When he escaped and returned, the allies assembled a seventh coalition and defeated him again, at the Battle of Waterloo, this time for good. The map of Europe that emerged from the Congress of Vienna peace conference pushed France back inside its pre-revolutionary boundaries. To keep it there, the great powers – Russia, Prussia, Austria and Britain – created a bigger Netherlands, which would last all of fifteen years before the Belgians held their own revolution and broke away. They also gave a load of coal-rich territory on the Rhine to Prussia, setting off the chain of events that meant the military power which would be tearing up the map a century hence would not be France at all, but Germany.

Still – and please forgive my lack of British patriotism here – I can't help but wonder about that other universe, where Napoleon wasn't defeated after all; where his attempts to rationalise the European map and replace a jigsaw of microstates and duchies with sensible-sized modern states survived. How big is today's France in that world, I wonder? And does it still have a department named Rome?

The American Invasion of Mexico

The imperial pretensions of President James K. Polk

The first thing to say about the Trump Wall is that it is not, in fact, a wall. It would more accurately be described as 'some fence'.

Much of the discourse concerning plans for a physical barrier along the US–Mexican border, which Donald Trump began talking about at campaign rallies in early 2015 to enthusiastic cries of 'Build the wall!', has focused on his entirely fabricated claim that Mexico would pay for it; the question of whether it's a waste of money; and the issue of whether it's fundamentally tacky for the world's largest superpower to build a physical barrier between itself and its poorer southern neighbour, and then top it with aggressive spikes that point south. Relatively little of that discourse has focused on the fact that this wall mostly never appeared – or that it's surprisingly easy to breach where it did.

But this, as it happens, is the case. The US–Mexican border is around 2,000 miles long, of which around half consists of the natural barrier of the Rio Grande. Of the remainder, around 450 miles is marked by scary thirty-foot metal fences; fewer than fifty of those miles are in areas that were previously unbarred. That leaves a surprisingly large number of miles unfenced, even if many are not particularly passable.

What's more, while Trump may have described the boundary as 'virtually impenetrable', that phrase came with a silent 'providing you don't have the sort of power tools you can buy in any DIY store'. These, it turns out, are exactly the sort of thing people who help smuggle other people across borders tend to have. Even better, the people building the wall sometimes smuggled armed Mexican security teams across the border to guard their work, even building illegal dirt roads to help them do it, thus making life easier for other smugglers. It's all gone terribly well.

There's something else the wall debate has tended to skip, however: that those who did succeed in crossing the border would have remained on land that had once been Mexican. It only stopped being so after the US won it in a war that sounds suspiciously like – there's no easy way to say this – imperial expansion.

Much of the western United States was once part of 'New Spain', a vast territory that at its height included the whole of Mexico, Central America, large chunks of North America, some areas of northern South America and, most vexingly, the Philippines, which are 8,000 miles away across the Pacific.* But in the early nineteenth century, the newly independent US expanded westwards into what had been French territory, in a deal that happened largely because Napoleon needed cash (the so-called Louisiana Purchase). Suddenly, the Spaniards found themselves with an expansionist new eastern neighbour and a border that nobody had yet managed to pin down.

That border was finally agreed by the Adams–Onis Treaty of 1819: the Americans would get Florida and, in exchange, they'd give up their claims to Texas, even though that left the Spaniards unnervingly close to the vital Mississippi port of New Orleans. The treaty came into effect two years later but, in what was presumably at least a mild irritation to both Adams and Onis, it lasted all of 183 days. By 1821, the Mexicans had been attempting to follow in their northern neighbours' footsteps, by fighting a war to throw off their European imperial overlords, for eleven years. On 24 August, local Spanish military officials finally recognised the fact that Mexican independence was not one of those things they were going to be able to undo, and that was pretty

* Actually, if you go back far enough, the western United States was Native American territory, of course, but you will be amazed how little those guys are going to feature in our story.

much it for Spanish power in North America. And so, for the next few years, nobody knew where the border was again.

In 1828, the newly minted Mexican Republic signed the tediously named Treaty of Limits with the United States. That said that the border was, well, exactly where the last treaty had said it was. The entirety of what are today California, Nevada, Utah, Arizona, New Mexico and Texas, plus parts of Wyoming, Colorado and Oklahoma, were all established as Mexican territory in perpetuity.

You can see where we're going with this, can't you.

The problem was that the nineteenth century US had this quaint idea of 'manifest destiny' – a sense it had a God-given right to expand right across its continent. The northern half of Mexico was in its way.

The most pressing issue was Texas. By the time the Treaty of Limits came into force in 1832, Americans of northern European origin had been migrating to the area in significant numbers for around a decade, thanks to the depression that followed a financial crisis known as the Panic of 1819. Many of them were attracted by Mexico's land policies; many also brought with them a very enthusiastic attitude towards the institution of slavery. This was a problem for the younger of the two republics, which had its own quaint idea that bondage slavery was bad; in 1829 it abolished it, then attempted to ban further American settlement just to be on the safe side.

The newly arrived residents of Texas weren't keen on this, so came up with a system of long-term indentured service contracts, which looked suspiciously similar to actual slavery. Over the next few years, while the increasingly panicked Mexican authorities stepped up the scale of military force in the area, the Texans held a couple of conventions, then a revolution, then declared they were an independent republic and then established a congress. This, too, may all sound suspiciously familiar.

The Mexicans weren't wild about any of this. They were even less pleased when the US recognised the independence of the new republic, which they still maintained was an integral part of

Mexico. And they were absolutely fuming when, after the 1844 US presidential election, in which the key issue had been 'so are we annexing Texas then or what?', the new pro-annexation president James Polk annexed Texas. Both sides sent troops to the disputed border, the US in large part because its president quite fancied a spot of war but needed congressional permission to hold one. The following year, after an attack by Mexican troops, he got his wish.

In the twenty-first century, we would expect any conflict between the US and Mexico to be a fairly one-sided affair, but in the 1840s, it was not yet clear which of the two was on course to be a superpower. Both were former European colonies that had thrown off their imperial masters. The US was bigger and richer, but not outrageously so, and this was the first war it had fought where the other side wasn't the British, or Native American tribes, or some pirates. It was also, unlike Mexico, deeply divided on the Texas question: not everyone wanted to admit another slave state into the nation – an issue that would blow up in a pretty big way within fifteen years – and presidents including Andrew Jackson, not a man known for his tender-hearted nature what with the whole 'Trail of Tears' thing,* had resisted calls for annexation out of fear the US might lose the war that would inevitably result.

Once the fighting began, though, the US leadership largely held it together, while the Mexicans, agreed though they were on the issue of beating the Americans, were horribly divided on almost everything else. During the twenty-one months of the war, they went through somewhere between four and eleven presidencies, depending on how you count (always a sign of a stable, functioning country). By the time the war ended in February 1848, Mexican casualties were five times those of the US and the country was ready to cede vast chunks of territory in an act known to history by the mildly euphemistic title of the Mexican Cession.

* An act of official ethnic cleansing, in which 60,000 Native Americans from the southeastern United States were forced to relocate to reserves west of the Mississippi. Around a quarter died on the way.

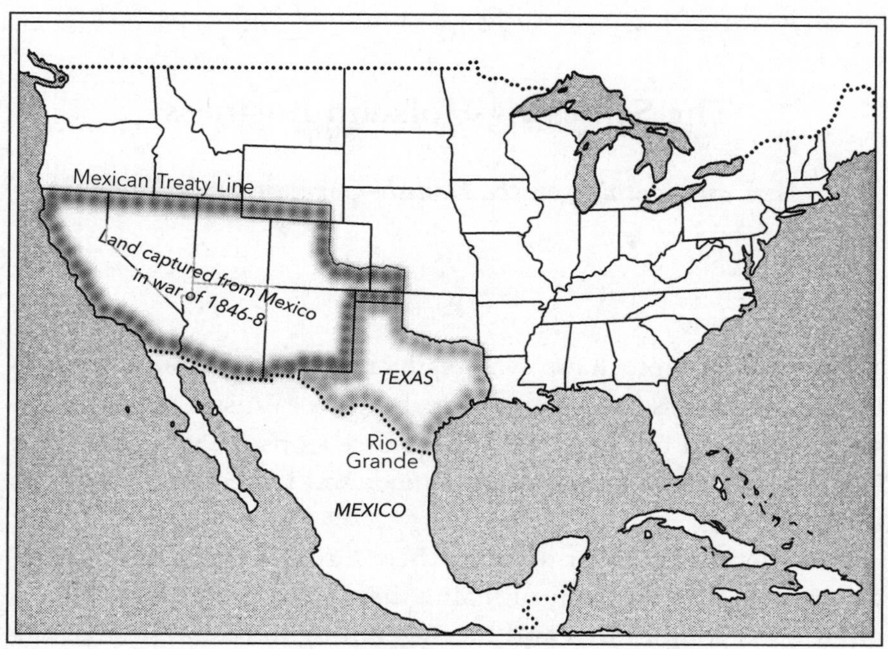

Territorial change in the US–Mexican War of 1846–8, superimposed on a map of the modern United States. The war saw the US capture territory that would form nearly six more states.

And so, today, something like 60 million Americans live on land conquered from Mexico by military force.* And where Americans once crossed the border in search of economic opportunities, now the US builds a wall in an attempt to stop Mexicans from doing the same. It hasn't worked. But still.

* A fun bonus fact! In the early 1930s, the government of President Herbert Hoover attempted to blame Mexicans for the Great Depression and deported somewhere between 335,000 and 2 million of them to Mexico. At least half of them were US citizens. This almost certainly meets the definition of ethnic cleansing, too!

The Schleswig-Holstein Business

Fear and loathing on the Danish–German borderlands

'Only three people have ever really understood the Schleswig-Holstein business,' occasional British prime minister Lord Palmerston is reputed to have said. 'The Prince Consort, who is dead; a German professor, who has gone mad; and I, who have forgotten all about it.'

I sometimes wonder whether there's a little bit of self-aggrandisement going on from ol' Palmy here. The Schleswig-Holstein question is complicated and messy – taking in feudalism, nationalism, liberalism, a divided population and the Salic Law – but it is hardly incomprehensibly so. By making it a byword for impenetrability, the man who dominated Britain's foreign policy at the height of its imperial age was making his specialism sound Very Difficult and himself sound Very Clever Indeed.

Schleswig and Holstein are a pair of territories which between them make up the southern part of the Jutland peninsula: if you think of it as a sort of thumb, Schleswig-Holstein make up the lower joint. The eponymous question, which hung over northern European politics for decades, was whether they should be Danish or German.

They had at various times been both. Schleswig had been a part of Denmark during the Viking era, but then so had a lot of places, and in the later medieval period it had become a duchy, attached to the state but annoyingly independent of it. The County of Holstein, by contrast, was a fief of the Holy Roman Empire and not part of Denmark at all.

The complicating factor was that, at some point, following a certain amount of feudal to-ing and fro-ing, both ended up in the

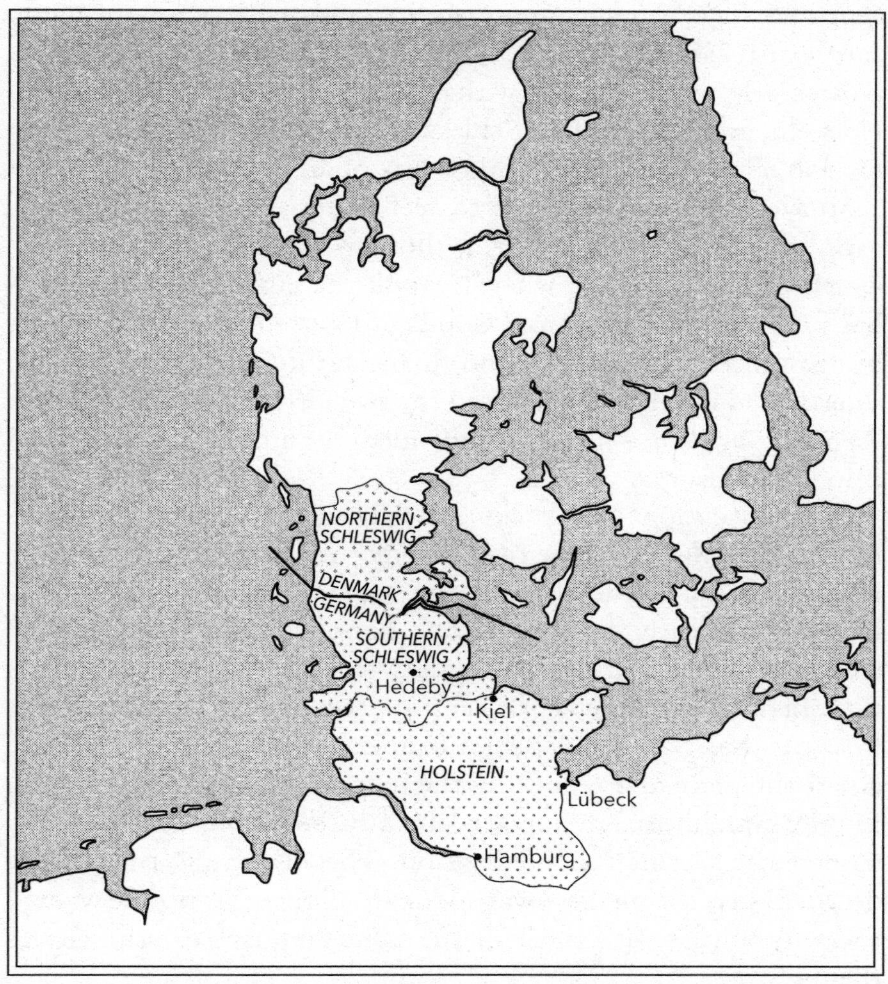

Schleswig-Holstein, on the Jutland peninsula.

hands of the same dynasty, who, a couple of generations later, died out. So in 1460, both territories came into the possession of King Christian I of Denmark. This, though, was a mere personal union, not a unification – a situation one might summarise as 'different territories, same king' – and there were a number of issues preventing Denmark from simply swallowing its southern neighbours.

One was that Holstein was still a fief of the Holy Roman Empire. And while that august body was to spend the next few centuries increasingly ruling over its lands with a sort of damp cardboard fist, it was still, in 1460, not the sort of body one particularly wanted a war with. Another was that everybody in Holstein, and a fair few in Schleswig, spoke German, rather than Danish, although this was much less of an issue in the fifteenth century than it would come to seem later. The biggest complicating factor in the long term, though, was the Treaty of Ribe, which Christian signed when he took the gig. He would rule as both Duke of Schleswig and Count of Holstein, the treaty stated, but to protect the political and financial interests of the regions' intertwined nobility, it promised the two territories would remain '*Up Ewig Ungedeelt*' – 'Forever Undivided'. Significantly, it promised it in German.

This situation – Holstein basically German, Schleswig half-heartedly Danish, and the two, despite this divergence, an indivisible possession of the Danish king* – persisted for a surprisingly long time. In early modern Europe, nobody particularly expected ruler, national identity and borders to meaningfully match up. But then, in the nineteenth century, two things happened. The first was that Napoleon spent a couple of busy decades storming about the place and redrawing the map, so that the Holy Roman Empire was ultimately replaced by a rather more rational body named the German Confederation. The other was that, a few decades later, nationalism was suddenly all the rage: people wanted to be in polities with those of the same language or ethnicity as themselves.

And so, the equilibrium was broken. The German majority in Schleswig-Holstein wanted the two to stay together as part of the German Confederation; the Danes, in both Schleswig and

* This whole thing, incidentally, brought to my deeply broken mind the mathematical impossibility of the UK's single market policy in c. 2018, in which there could be no borders between Great Britain and Northern Ireland, and no border between Northern Ireland and the Republic of Ireland, but there absolutely *had* to be a border between the UK and EU which meant a border between the UK and the Republic of Ireland. On that occasion, alas, Lord Palmerston was unavailable.

Denmark itself, wanted the two broken up, even though that meant custody of a substantial minority of grumpy Germans. By the 1840s, Denmark's National Liberal Party had begun to campaign under a new slogan, a reference to the river that marked the traditional boundary between the two territories: 'Denmark to the Eider!'

Matters came to a head, as so many matters did, in 1848, when an uprising by the German majority led to a Prussian invasion, which led, in turn, to a three-year war.* Denmark won but, under pressure from the great powers, the resulting treaty, the 1852 London Protocol, stated that both of the contested territories would be Danish *but* that Denmark would never attempt to force Schleswig into a closer union with itself than it had with Holstein.

'Never' in this case turned out to mean 'not for the next eleven years'.

In 1863, Frederick VII, last of the male line of the House of Oldenburg – the dynasty that had been ruling Denmark since Christian I, four centuries earlier – died and a long-looming succession crisis finally hit. Denmark and Schleswig both followed a complicated set of rules set down in the seventeenth century, which stipulated that, in the event of the male line's extinction, the crown would pass to the most recent possible *female* heir and then her male descendants. This meant that the crown passed to the late king's second cousin, who became Christian IX, first king of the House of Glücksburg.

The only slight problem with this was that Holstein followed a much simpler interpretation of the Salic Law, which can be summed up as, essentially, 'No girls allowed'. Under these rules, Christian had no claim. A pretender, another Frederick, claimed Holstein for himself and then claimed Schleswig, too, on the grounds that treaties right back to Ribe had said the two territories were one. And so, in something of a panic, the government

* That conflict, incidentally, is known to history as the 'First Schleswig War'. Great sign!

in Copenhagen changed the constitution to make Schleswig an integral part of Denmark.

This, you might recall, was a breach of the London Protocols agreed just eleven years earlier, and helpfully provided Prussia with a pretext to invade. Again.

The Second Schleswig War didn't go quite so well for the Danes. With Austrian help, the Prussians – by now led by the Iron Chancellor, Otto von Bismarck – took just nine months to defeat them. Denmark was forced to surrender the duchies it had been clinging onto for centuries to an Austrian-Prussian condominium,* which, after another war two years later, became straightforward Prussian rule. Those who wished to remain Danes were given six years to move north.

In some ways, all this was a neat reflection of the radically different points these two countries had reached in their histories. Denmark had been at the peak of its power eight centuries earlier, when its king Cnut had ruled an empire stretching to England and Norway; in medieval times, Denmark-proper had included lands in what is today southern Sweden (Skåneland) and northern Germany (the Principality of Rügen), too. Slightly unusually for a modern European state,† though, it spent much of the millennium gradually getting smaller, losing the empire in the eleventh century, Rügen in the fourteenth and Skåneland in the seventeenth. The loss of Schleswig-Holstein, roughly a quarter of its remaining land, was the final step in the transformation of what had once been a significant power into the likeable but fundamentally diddly country that exists today.

Germany, by contrast, literally didn't exist when the Schleswig-Holstein mess kicked off: the German Confederation wasn't a state but a loose association of thirty-nine of the things. But having knocked out first Denmark, then Austria, in 1870 Bismarck's

---

* Not an American term for an apartment but exactly what it sounds like: shared rule.

† But not unique: Lithuania and Hungary were also once a heck of a lot bigger than they are today.

Prussia marched west and defeated the real enemy, France. The new German Reich was declared in the Palace of Versailles on 18 January 1871. War with Denmark was the first step in the creation of what would soon become Europe's most powerful country.

That wasn't quite the end of the Schleswig-Holstein question. The 1866 Treaty of Prague, which concluded the Seven Weeks' War between Austria and Prussia, stipulated that northern Schleswig had the right to rejoin Denmark if a majority of its inhabitants so wished. In 1878, both parties agreed to drop that provision; it took defeat in the First World War and the collapse of both empires before anyone bothered to ask the inhabitants what they wished. In the event, the northernmost third of Schleswig voted overwhelmingly to join Denmark and the middle part overwhelmingly to remain German. (The southernmost third was so Germanic that no vote was felt necessary.)

And so the Danish-German border was finally settled. In the decades that followed, ethnically Danish farmers marooned on the wrong side of the border would protest the fact they weren't allowed to hoist a Danish flag through the novel means of breeding 'protest pigs' – red with a suspiciously Danish flag-like white stripe across their middles. Generally though, after seventy years of intermittent fighting, all was quiet on the northern front.

As to Lord Palmerston, it's just possible he had another motive for talking up the complexity of the Schleswig-Holstein question. Back in 1864, he had promised that, were the Prussians to use force, 'it would not be Denmark alone with which they would have to contend'. As it turned out, though, it was: Britain's offer of support had encouraged Denmark to fight, rather than negotiate, while its decision to back down weakened the hand of the pro-British liberals that provided the main German opposition to Bismarck's Prussian militarism.

Perhaps it wasn't merely that Palmerston was trying to make himself look clever. Perhaps he also wanted to discourage anyone from looking too closely at a situation in which he had made rather a hefty mistake.

'. . . Where No White Man Ever Trod'

The Congo Free State and the Scramble for Africa, 1884–5

Leopold was finding family get-togethers to be increasingly embarrassing. His wife's cousin Franz Joseph was the emperor of the Austro-Hungarian Empire, which covered most of central and eastern Europe. His own cousin Victoria was queen of England, by virtue of which – this being the late nineteenth century – she sat atop the largest empire the world had ever known and had just been named 'empress of India' to boot. All Leopold had to his name was the tiny, damp kingdom of Belgium. What was worse, his own government was showing a disappointing lack of interest in even *trying* to build an empire. Didn't they see that they were embarrassing him in front of his family? Did they even care?

But then, one day, he noticed something: there was a large chunk of central Africa just sitting there which no one – this meant, of course, no white people – had ever tried to claim. What's more, the Congo basin was full of lovely, valuable stuff, like rubber and ivory. The latter was still largely attached to elephants, yes, but there were ways of fixing that.

And so, he created a holding company, calling it the International African Association, to disguise it as a scientific, philanthropic sort of a thing. And he hired the British adventurer Henry Morton Stanley – best known for having tracked down the Christian missionary David Livingstone on behalf of the *New York Herald* and greeting him by the shores of Lake Tanganyika with the words, 'Dr Livingstone, I presume'* – and persuaded him to

---

* Actually, he may have done nothing of the sort. Livingstone never mentioned these words; the relevant pages of Stanley's journal were mysteriously torn out.

explore the Congo basin on the company's behalf. If the Belgian state didn't want to build an empire, well, then Leopold II would do it himself.

Eight years later, in November 1884, men from every significant European power, plus the United States and Ottoman Empire, were sitting round a table in Berlin beneath an enormous map of Africa. Their task was to decide on the rules for dividing up a continent three times the size of Europe. Not a single African was in the room – one who had tried to get an invite, the Sultan of Zanzibar, had been laughed at – and only two delegates had ever even set foot on the continent. Yet within a few years, 80 per cent of Africa would be under European rule – and the state Leopold founded would be the site of some of the worst crimes that European imperialism, hardly a stranger to atrocities, had yet committed.

Neither Leopold, nor the conference his adventures summoned into existence, fired the starting gun on the Scramble for Africa – an oddly euphemistic term for the military conquest of the planet's second largest continent. Parts of Africa had had a European presence for centuries: the Portuguese had held Angola, in the southwest, and Mozambique, in the southeast, since the sixteenth century; the Dutch East India company had held the Cape but lost it to the British; the French were moving in on Algeria.

For most of the imperial age, though, attempts to explore the continent's vast interior had been stymied by the fact that white people who ventured there had an awkward habit of dying of malaria. The European presence in Africa had been restricted to coastal trading posts and had often been informal and commercial in nature. Full-scale political conquest had never really been the goal.

In the nineteenth century, three things changed that. Firstly, the discovery of quinine as a treatment for malaria made it easier

---

But it made the meeting between the only two white men for hundreds of miles sound gentlemanly, rather than sinister, which tells us something about the spirit of the age all the same.

for Europeans to get a foothold in the tropics. Secondly, there was the industrial revolution, which brought steamships, railways and guns: that meant it would now be easier to carry people into the interior, carry valuable resources out again and keep any locals who objected at bay.

The third thing to change was the arrival of a Belgian king who was so determined to get himself an empire that he went after that attractively empty middle bit of the map.

For nearly five years, Stanley explored the Congo basin, agreeing treaties which swapped miserly quantities of European luxuries for vast swathes of territory with people who couldn't read them. In one, the chiefs of the Ngombi and Mafela tribes pledged political control, military support and full rights over fishing, foresting, mining and game to the International African Association. In exchange, they received a promise that the Europeans would 'promote to its utmost the prosperity' of their territory, plus one piece of cloth per month. They did at least receive one each but, nonetheless, this was a pretty abhorrent way to behave, even by the standards of European colonialism.

This did not, of course, bother Leopold. What was more of a concern was the growing number of other European powers enthusiastically descending on the Congo basin, on what one might term the 'dog in a manger' principle. The French joined the rush in 1881, sending in an Italian explorer by the name of Pierre Savorgnan de Brazza, who charmed the locals, travelled deep into the interior and founded a city on the right bank of the river which he modestly named Brazzaville.*

That unnerved the other powers, so the Portuguese attempted to reassert their right over the Kingdom of the Kongo, some way

* The Republic of the Congo is sometimes known as Congo-Brazzaville, to distinguish it from the *Democratic* Republic of the Congo, which is sometimes known as Congo-Kinshasa (and once, a very long time ago, Congo-Léopoldville) and lies on the other side of the river. The resulting confusion seems to me to be a very good argument for the latter to revert to Zaire, the name it held between 1971 and 1997, but the locals disagree and given this entire entry is about white people buggering up Africa, perhaps I should keep my opinions to myself.

to the south, which they claimed by a combination of the long defunct Treaty of Tordesillas and their rather more recent interference in local politics. Then, in case nobody found that very convincing, they got the British to back their claim by suggesting it was them or the French, and that with British help they could make it difficult for anybody else to reach the Atlantic. Meanwhile, Leopold persuaded the French to back his own obviously tenuous claims by telling them that if it all went horribly wrong, they'd get first dibs on his territory. Nobody else wanted the French to have it, so this encouraged other powers to start backing Leopold's claim, too. All in all, things had the potential to get very messy, very fast, and still no one had bothered to ask the locals what they thought.

Into this mess stepped a man who, you'll recall, had quite some experience of remaking maps. The German chancellor Otto von Bismarck had little interest in Africa (although the assorted industrialists who were turning the still-new state into a superpower may have felt differently). But he did care about the European balance of power and he wasn't one to miss an opportunity to look like the big man in front of the other leaders. Much of the credit for the last seventy years of relative peace in Europe lay with the Congress of Vienna, the huge post-Napoleon peace conference held in the winter of 1814–15. Why not solidify both his own and the Reich's diplomatic position by repeating the trick?

And so, when the Portuguese called for a summit, Bismarck invited them and a dozen other countries to send deputations to Berlin to sort this whole mess out. To the first approximation, everyone* was there – just so long as they were white.

After several months toiling away beneath a giant map of Africa, most of the powers in attendance agreed the 'General Act'. Slavery, officially at least, was to be abolished; spheres of influence were established to stop troops of armed Europeans from

* The only European countries not in attendance, not counting the microstates, were Greece, Serbia, Romania and Luxembourg.

banging into each other. (This part, at least, was a success: Europe wouldn't explode into war for another thirty years.) To maximise the economic benefits of colonialism for those going to all the trouble of doing the colonising, there would be free trade in the Congo basin, and both the Congo and Niger rivers would be open to ship traffic.

The most damaging thing, though, was the establishment of the principle of 'effective occupation'. For a territorial claim to be valid, a foreign power would henceforth actually have to possess said territory, through military or police control. That possession, however, required little of the state that claimed it; powers like Britain and France, which already had claims, resisted the idea they needed to do more for the locals to retain these territories. All this meant that the Berlin Conference established an internationally recognised regime of colonial power without responsibility. Africa was now a place which things would be done to, not by or with – an entire continent which Europeans could divide up among themselves using suspiciously straight lines, and from which they could export resources while doing little for those who called it home.

On 27 February 1885, the very day after the conference concluded, Bismarck signed a charter with the Society for German Colonisation, allowing it to set up a German protectorate in the African Great Lakes region. Others would follow. Over the next decade, the Italians moved into Eritrea and Somaliland; the French grabbed large chunks of West Africa and the Sahel; the British took Nigeria and a sizable amount of East Africa, and began working their way up from the Cape. In 1890, British prime minister Lord Salisbury summed the situation up in perhaps the most famous speech ever made about colonialism and borders, which I quoted in the introduction but is worth reading again. 'We have been engaged in drawing lines upon maps,' he said, 'where no white man's foot has ever trod. We have been giving away mountains and rivers and lakes to each other, only hindered by the small impediment that we never knew exactly where the mountains

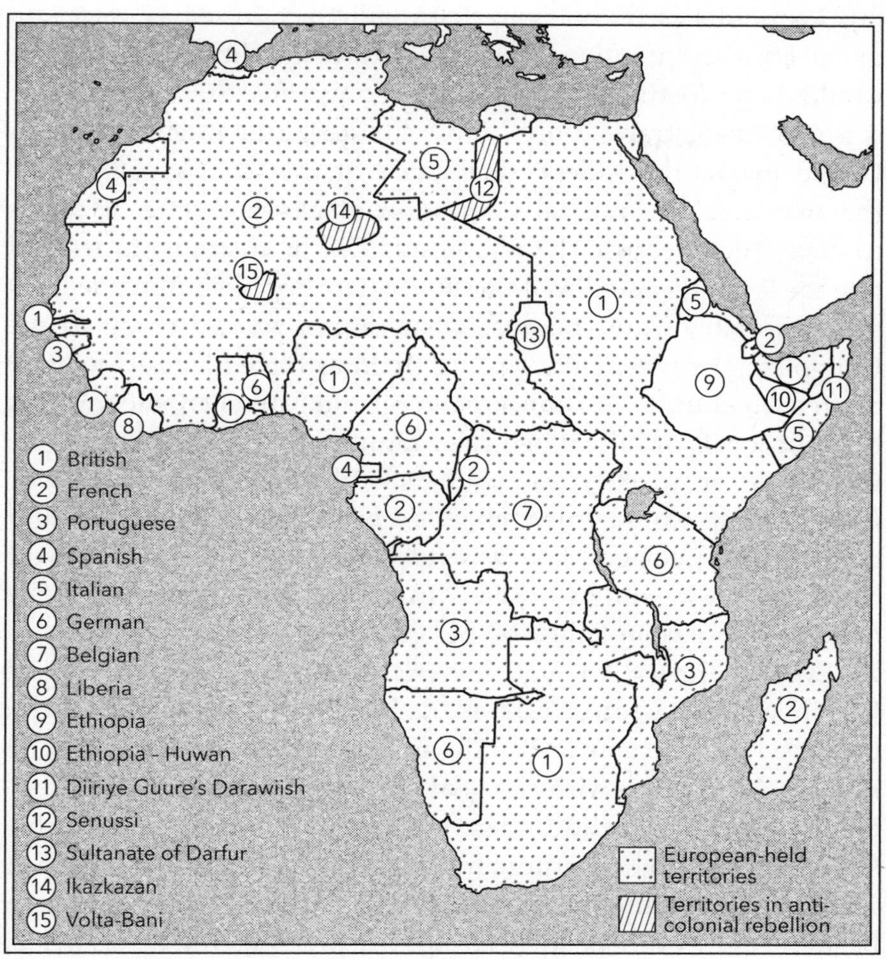

The results of the Scramble for Africa. By 1913, the vast majority of the continent was dominated by a handful of European powers, although some areas were in revolt. (For those wondering, Huwan – today's Ethiopia's Somali Regional State – was in rebellion against Ethiopia.)

and rivers and lakes were.' This isn't one of those bits of history which is only seen as an atrocity in retrospect: those involved knew exactly what they were doing at the time.

The Berlin Conference had one other, more immediate effect: it gave Leopold what he wanted. Belgium still had no empire but Leopold was himself internationally recognised as sovereign of an area seventy-nine times the size of his little kingdom. It would, henceforth, be known as the Congo Free State. This name is a sort of mistranslation – more literally, État Indépendant du Congo means the Independent State of the Congo, somewhere that was not an imperial possession of another state. It seems to have stuck because the region was free of customs duties and free for foreign capital to do with it what they liked. But the label seems horribly ironic because what capital wanted to do to the Congolese, it turned out, was use them as forced labour, so as to drain their country of rubber, palm oil and ivory. Leopold's agents beat the locals or kidnapped their families to force them to work. His private army of African soldiers led by European officers, the *Force Publique*, would crush rebellions by slaughtering families and burning their villages, and was not above cutting the hands off children as a warning to others. In a little over twenty years, the region's population fell by 60 per cent.

Even in the age of high imperialism, this proved too much. Joseph Conrad wrote *Heart of Darkness* to publicise the state's brutality; intellectuals in Britain and beyond founded the Congo Reform Association with the goal of getting the state out of Leopold's sweaty paws and under the control of a more responsible European colonial government. That happened in 1908, when it ceased to be the king's personal property and became, instead, a Belgian colony; independence followed in 1960. Today, what was once the Congo Free State is known by another uncomfortably ironic name: the Democratic Republic of Congo.

The wars that seem frequently to consume this part of Africa today can perhaps be traced partly to the behaviour of Europe's leaders in the 1880s. In 1959, the American anthropologist George P. Murdock attempted to map Africa's internal ethnic boundaries as they had been on the eve of the Berlin Conference; he came up with a map vastly more complex than anything the Europeans ever countenanced, with some areas (Nigeria, Sudan, the Congo basin) broken up into dozens of tiny fragments. Some peoples ended up bundled into countries with others they'd historically seen as antagonists; others found their homelands split down the middle by lines drawn in Berlin.

Half a century later, a pair of researchers at London's Centre for Economic Policy Research overlaid modern national boundaries on Murdock's work and tried to quantify their effects. They found that 'civil conflict intensity, as reflected in casualties and duration, is approximately 25 per cent higher in areas where partitioned ethnicities reside (as compared to the homelands of ethnicities that have not been separated)'. On top of that, 'an ethnic group residing adjacent to a partitioned ethnic homeland is on average 5 per cent more likely to experience civil conflict'. It wasn't merely the fact of conquest and exploitation that damaged Africa; it was the thoughtless way in which the continent was carved into pieces with no natural coherence, creating situations in which many groups would have more instinctive affinity with their neighbours across a national boundary than with their ostensibly fellow countrymen in the national capital.

In other words: careless borders cost lives.

The Sudan–Uganda Border Commission

Captains Tufnell and Kelly go walkabout

There are a couple of especially insidious things about the borders that emerge from the high imperial age of the late nineteenth century. One is the point I've been making for several chapters, and which we will be dancing around for a fair few yet: that, thanks to both improvements in mapping and to the way access to such technologies had reshaped how people conceived of the world, it was now possible for distant powers – normally white, normally European – to carve up territories they had never even visited, through a tool no more substantial than a pen. The other was the fact that even those who had decent intentions and tried to do it the hard way could still ultimately find themselves screwing up the world.

In 1882, in an attempt to stamp on the sort of nationalist instability that might interrupt traffic through the Suez Canal, the British had conquered Egypt, but then, to avoid upsetting the Ottoman Empire of which Egypt was still officially a part, pretended they hadn't. For the next thirty years, Egypt was subject to a form of government sometimes described as 'the veiled protectorate': not officially a part of the British Empire, but in practice governed by a bunch of British administrators who claimed to be merely 'advising' the Egyptian government.

All this gave Britain a geopolitical interest in stability up the Nile. So together, the British and their definitely-not-a-colony Egypt fought a war against Sudan and ruled it as an odd sort of condominium, in which one of the two countries responsible was also a colony of the other. Later on, Britain conquered Uganda, the region to the south believed to contain the river's source, too.

Even though these territories were all British, they were governed by different people using different structures, who needed to know where their domain ended and someone else's began. So in 1912, the governor general of Sudan created a commission tasked with establishing a border between his territory and its southern neighbour Uganda, which would 'not divide any single tribe' between them. Thus it was that, on 15 January 1913, a convoy including over 100 men, 50 camels, 320 donkeys and 20 mules assembled at the South Sudanese city of Nimule, with a view to surveying and mapping the roughly 400 miles of territory between there and Lake Rudolph (today's Lake Turkana).

The team was largely composed of locals but at its head were two British army captains. Running the Sudanese side of affairs was one Captain Harry Kelly, a career soldier and champion heavyweight boxer who had been in the Royal Engineers until being seconded to the Egyptian army in Sudan in 1903. He was excellently qualified for the job, having previously surveyed stretches of Sudan's frontiers with both Abyssinia and Congo. And he was determined to do right by the locals, no matter how long the job took.

Heading up the Ugandan side of the commission, meanwhile, was one Captain Tufnell. The main thing history records about Captain Tufnell is that he was tired. Really, really tired. Now district commissioner of Lake Rudolph Province, he had been working for two years without a break and all he wanted was to go on leave. And this dastardly commission and its stupid boundaries were in his way.

In many cases, we know little of the process by which today's international boundaries were decided. In this case, though, we know rather a lot, because Captain Kelly lovingly recorded the survey team's exploits in his diary. And the main thing he recorded – the single biggest factor in determining the exact course of this boundary – was the slow-motion collapse of his relationship with Captain Tufnell.

The team took just over a month to cover the first 120 miles of the boundary, as far as a place named Madial. That works out to somewhat less than four miles a day, which really isn't that much (though it no doubt feels longer when you have a bunch of camels, mules and donkeys to contend with). But this was through potentially hostile territory – rumours abounded of local conflicts and gun-running – and of course they were surveying the land, so in practice almost certainly covering a lot more ground than those raw numbers suggest. A perambulator wheel in the charge of one of the team showed distances of more like eight to twelve miles each day; Kelly was constantly nipping about the place in search of high ground, so may well have travelled even further.

Just as big a problem as the distances, or the security risks, or the mules, however, was the gulf between the two leaders' approaches to their work. It wasn't merely that Tufnell didn't want to be there and was more than happy to announce the fact; he also thought Kelly's determination to map tribal boundaries and keep on good terms with the locals was silly. Better, Tufnell thought, to let them know who was boss by, in not so many words, beating the living shit out of them at the slightest provocation. Kelly's diary contains endless tales of Tufnell and his men violently disarming local tribespeople or burning their huts to the ground just to assert themselves. This went down about as well with the locals the expedition relied on as guides as you would imagine, and they kept quitting.

And throughout all this, as Kelly did his best to get to grips with the cultural differences and appropriate physical boundaries between the Acholi, the Toposa and the Karoko (who may also have been the Dodinga), and to deal with the fact that the locals were almost certainly lying to him about other locals, he also had to put up with listening to Tufnell constantly bitching about the fact that he didn't give a shit about local tribal boundaries, that he knew perfectly well the best place to put the border without talking to anyone, and that he'd been in this stupid, hot country for quite long enough and why couldn't he just go home.

So eventually, when they reached Madial, he did, taking the entire Uganda team with him. That, Kelly thought, was quite all right with him. Tufnell 'thinks of nothing but getting on leave', he wrote in his diary on 16 February. 'I confess I am glad to get rid of him, as he has been little help and has left all the burden of gaining information to me. I am moreover not at all an admirer of the methods of which he is the chief exponent, of dealing with the natives.' Which is one way of saying you think violently assaulting people is not a recipe for peaceful relationships and good government, I suppose.

Kelly's Sudan side of the commission trundled on for another eighty miles or so, covering perhaps four times that distance in total. But by this point, the remaining team was almost as exhausted and bad-tempered as Tufnell had been from the start: everyone's skin was torn to shreds by thornscrub; the camels were hungry and dying of sleeping sickness. To address the revolving door of local guides, the survey team had tried handcuffing them, to physically prevent them from literally running away. This worked fine up to the point when someone lost the key, forcing one poor soul to do the entire trip with them until they reached a settlement large enough to provide tools to cut the blasted things off.

And so, having climbed Mount Mogila fretting about the rapidly dwindling supplies of food and water and found that he could not see a water source from its peak, Kelly decided it was time to give up. The last third of the boundary between the Sudanese Condominium and the Uganda Protectorate was never surveyed by the British at all. They never even visited it. Just three days after Kelly and his team gave up, the dry season came to an end and the heavens opened. A shortage of water, it turned out, would not have been a problem.

The survey teams reported their findings to their political masters back in London; some of them were taken into account. But for the last third of the boundary they made no recommendations – having never got that far, they couldn't. And so, for all Kelly's good, if rather paternalist, intentions, the result of his failure was made painfully plain on the map. The western end of the border the team 'surveyed' is complex and detailed; the eastern consists of a series of straight lines, up to 100 miles long.

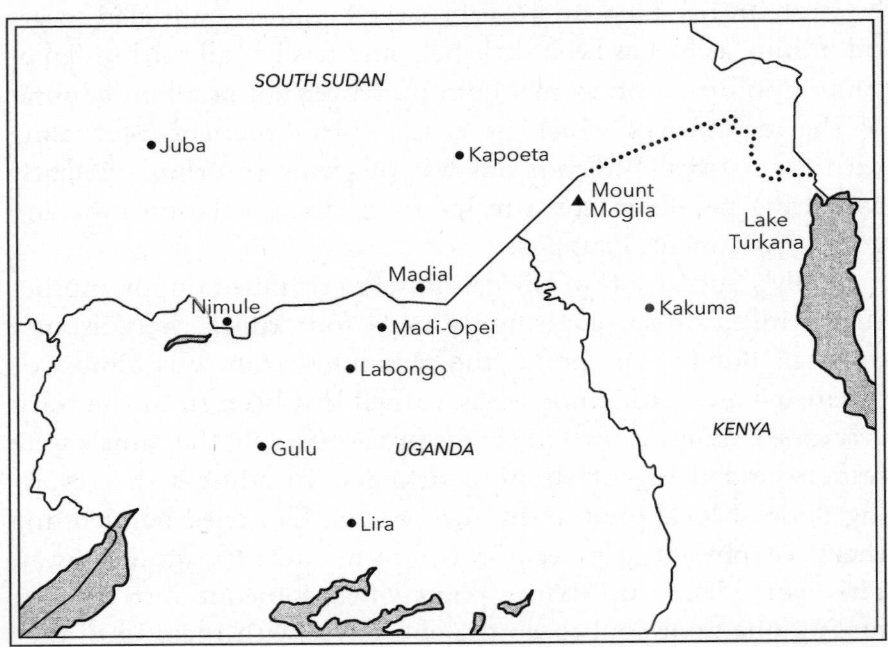

The region surveyed by the Sudan–Uganda Border Commission. Note the striking decrease in the complexity of the border as it moves east.

It's hard to believe that this was the best reflection of the borders between the tribal territories in this part of Africa. One of these straight lines – the one just beyond Mount Mogila in fact, which divides Sudan from Uganda's Rudolf Province, transferred to Kenya in 1926 – marks one side of the 'Ilemi Triangle', which is still claimed by both South Sudan and Kenya to this day. If you don't bother surveying a region, it turns out, you're storing up border disputes for the future.

Sudan won its independence from the British Empire in 1955; Uganda seven years later and Kenya the following year. In 2011, South Sudan broke away from Sudan to become Africa's newest nation. But still, maps of this part of Africa contain oddly straight lines – because some British army officers in the years before the First World War were simply too tired to come up with anything better.

European Nationalism and the United States of Greater Austria

History takes a wrong turn

This story begins at its end: on the streets of Sarajevo, on 28 June 1914, a car took a wrong turn and tens of millions died.

A member of the Serbian nationalist Black Hand group had already made one attempt that morning on the life of Archduke Franz Ferdinand, heir presumptive to the Austro-Hungarian throne. But the bomb he had thrown had hit the wrong car, injuring several people and leaving the archduke himself furious with almost everybody but otherwise unharmed. And that should have been that.*

Later that day, though, the archduke – a Habsburg, in line to rule over a vast chunk of central and eastern Europe – decided to visit one of the injured in hospital. That required a change of route, instructions for which were given in German and not understood by the Czech-speaking drivers. The result was an unnecessary turn onto Franz Joseph Street, where another member of the Black Hand, Gavrilo Princip, was waiting on the motorcade's published route for precisely this moment. He fired two shots. One killed the archduke's wife, Sophie; the other, the man himself.

You know the rest. War between Austro-Hungary and Serbia; Russia, Germany, France and Britain all mobilising as an intricate

---

* The man responsible, a Bosnian Serb named Nedeljko Čabrinović, attempted to kill himself by both swallowing cyanide and then jumping in a river. Rather pathetically, neither worked; he was arrested and died in prison.

system of treaties and alliances built up over nearly a century kicked into gear. The First World War would kill millions, bring down empires and trigger revolutions, reshaping the European map in the process. While some of this would surely have happened anyway – Europe was a tinderbox – you need not even consider the fairly direct links between this and the next major European war to argue that this assassination, those shots and that wrong turn are about the most influential and ruinous events of their type in the whole of human history.

In the face of all that, it's perhaps unsurprising that relatively little attention has been paid to what it is that the ageing archduke was actually planning to *do* when he finally inherited the throne. As it happens, though, he'd planned to do a fair bit of reshaping of the map himself. By doing so, he had hoped to tame the very force which got him killed: nationalism.

Since last we left this part of Europe, the nature of the Habsburg realms had changed rather substantially. The first member of the family had been elected to the throne of the Holy Roman Empire in 1272 as Rudolf I; after 1438, no other dynasty got a look-in. By 1914, that ancient empire had been dead for a century, dissolved as part of Napoleon's reorganisation of Europe. But after 400 years as the world's most powerful family, the Habsburgs had no intention of giving up on power altogether.

One of the things that Rudolf had secured for his descendants all the way back in 1282 was the Duchy of Austria, whose capital, Vienna, had remained the dynasty's home ever since. This had proved useful a century later when they found themselves chased out of their Alpine homelands by the Swiss. Centuries of conquest and clever marriage had added sundry other kingdoms, duchies, counties and margravates to their territories. Some of these had been lost again, of course: the Spanish branch of the Habsburgs had, rather embarrassingly, died out through incest at the turn of the eighteenth century, leaving the vast American and Pacific realms of the Spanish Empire to drop into the hands of some other family. By the time Napoleon was doing his thing, though, the surviving branch still held a swathe of territories, conveniently located in a contiguous block to the south and east of Germany: Austria, Bohemia, Croatia, Transylvania, Hungary. Although these assorted territories bordered the Holy Roman Empire, many of them weren't actually part of it.

So in 1804, with the writing on the wall for the empire, Emperor Francis II took a leaf out of his distant ancestor's book and built the family a lifeboat. Although these territories were a mere personal union, rather than a proper state, why couldn't they become one? Napoleon, after all, had turned the kingdom of France into an empire and appointed himself emperor. Why shouldn't Francis, who unlike that upstart actually *was* a proper emperor, do the same? And in this empire, unlike the creaking Reich, perhaps people might actually do what their emperor bloody well told them to do.

So, when the Holy Roman Empire – a feature of the European map for nearly a thousand years – finally met its end in 1806, Habsburg rule continued unabated: Holy Roman Emperor Francis II simply became Emperor Francis I of Austria instead. He even married his daughter to Napoleon for good measure. All this, one suspects, must have seemed like a tremendous wheeze. Other European dynasts had had to go overseas in search of new, more pliant territory; the Austrian Habsburgs had them already – and they were right next door!

As the century wore on, though, it became clear that creating a new, multiethnic empire inside Europe itself was not going to be quite as simple as it had appeared. For much of European history, much of the continent had put up with being ruled by absentee landlords, often ones who spoke an entirely different language to themselves. But with the American and French revolutions having introduced inconvenient ideas like 'liberty' and 'democracy' into the discourse, new concepts like nationalism were all the rage. The Habsburg Empire, a block of territory covering all or part of thirteen modern European countries, and ruled by a family who spoke a language, German, that three-quarters of their subjects did not, simply didn't match the spirit of the age. During the revolutionary fervour that convulsed Europe in 1848–9, Germans,* Romanians, Ukrainians, Poles and half a dozen other nationalities all attempted to declare autonomy or independence, or at least to crush some other national group which they didn't happen to like. Even the Hungarians, the one group that had been allowed to keep some semblance of their own institutions, a semi-autonomous kingdom in the heart of the empire, rebelled. The *ingratitude* of it.

All this died down, eventually, but not before it had had two big impacts on the court in Vienna. The first was to force the ejection of the emperor. Ferdinand I has often been portrayed by history as an idiot, generally because he is said to have responded to the revolutions by asking, 'Are they allowed to do that?' which is, to be fair, an idiotic thing to say. Even so, his diaries suggest a certain sharpness. The big problem was that, thanks to his epilepsy, he couldn't consummate his marriage without fitting, which meant he couldn't produce an heir – and the Austrian Habsburgs were determined not to go the way of their Spanish cousins. And so, in the midst of the chaos, out Ferdinand went, to live the rest of his days unworried by imperial affairs as a much-loved king of Bohemia. In his place entered a thrusting eighteen-year-old by the name of Franz Joseph. He would occupy the imperial throne, stultifyingly, for the next sixty-eight years.

The other effect of 1848 was that Hungary lost its independence: no longer would it be in a mere personal union with the rest of the empire; now it would be swallowed up by it. That, though, could not hold. The Hungarians were the largest of the empire's many nationalities, after the Germans, and within twenty years they were rebelling again, this time successfully. And so came the great compromise of 1867, and the creation of a state that has been confusing schoolchildren ever since: the Austro-Hungarian Empire, or dual monarchy. The two largest ethnicities of this new

* Confusingly, 'Germans' here doesn't mean German in the sense we're used to the term – that is, someone from what we'd call Germany (hardly any of them were). It means *ethnic* Germans – German *speakers*. Most of these lived in what we think of as Austria; others did not.

state, Germans and Hungarians, were from now on to have theoretically equal status. In the spirit of brotherhood, they would join together, hand in hand, to crush the nationalist ambitions of the other 56 per cent of the population.

One man who would disapprove of all of this was Franz Ferdinand. He would come to believe that many of the empire's problems lay in its elites - more specifically, its *Hungarian* elites - being elevated to a position where they could stamp on other groups. In 1867, though, he wasn't in a position to express his views one way or the other, being only two years old. He was also not yet the heir; that honour belonged to his cousin, Franz Joseph's son, the Crown Prince Rudolf.

But Rudolf, who was either sensitive or insane, depending on which account you read, had been so enthusiastically shagging his way round Vienna that he'd contracted syphilis, given it to his wife and rendered her infertile. Then, in 1889, at the age of thirty, he took himself off to his hunting lodge with his seventeen-year-old mistress, Mary Vetsera, and shot first her, then himself. That left Franz Ferdinand's father, the sprightly fifty-five-year-old Karl Ludwig, as heir - until 1896, when he died, too. And so, Franz Ferdinand began to think about what he might do with his great inheritance. By now, after all, Franz Joseph was nearly sixty-six - how much longer could the emperor possibly last?

Franz Ferdinand was, among other things, one of history's great collectors - of statues, weapons, roses. He was a man who loved nothing more than to sit down and sort things into categories; above his desk, he kept a chart, outlining the 'national characteristics' of the various groups he would be ruling beneficently over, which is an unnervingly 1890s sort of thing to do. To his mind, the thing his future empire really needed in order to stem the constant stream of nationalist rebellions was a good old-fashioned reorganisation.

So in 1906, Franz Ferdinand found himself drawn to a plan proposed by a Romanian lawyer named Aurel Popovici. Out would go the messiness of dual monarchy, in which two peoples tried, hopelessly, to dominate the others; in would come the United

States of Greater Austria, a rational, federal *modern* state fit for the twentieth century. Czechs, Italians, Croatians, Slovenes: each would have their own domain at last, fifteen in total, all under the loving, watchful eye of their thoughtful, caring emperor.

It's tempting to see the good ol' USGA as one of the great roads not taken of history: a glimpse of an alternative timeline, in which twentieth-century Europe had a model for a multicultural, multiethnic state to build on, and did not descend into decades of horrific ethnic war. Even if Black Hand, Gavrilo Princip and war had not intervened, though, it's not clear the plan would ever have got off the ground. In *Dunubia*, his fascinating book on the Habsburgs, Simon Winder argues that Franz Ferdinand may have been motivated not just by modernisation and justice, but by a baser impulse: a dislike of those upstart Hungarians, whose language he'd found annoyingly impossible to learn.

The United States of Greater Austria wasn't, in fact, the only plan Franz Ferdinand took an interest in during his long and disappointing wait for the imperial throne. Another would have created a *triple* monarchy, weakening the influence of Budapest and elevating the Croatians by adding a third capital in Zagreb. Another would have introduced democracy in Hungary – though not, amusingly, in Austria. All of these problems might eventually have run aground on the same practical difficulty: the Hungarians were the Habsburgs' enforcers. Weakening them might have wrecked the whole show.

There were other problems with the fifteen-state plan. As neat as it looked on the map, it ignored the messy realities of linguistic enclaves, German islands in other ethnicities' seas, and it's not clear handwaved references to autonomous regions or cities would have been enough. Come to that, what would have happened to the empire's Jewish populations, who would have found themselves outsiders in newly monocultural regions, without a state of their own? Perhaps this would have been fine. History suggests many reasons to suspect otherwise.

And maybe, as a way of stifling nationalism, it simply wouldn't have worked. The plan, writes Winder, 'assumed that each nation-

Aurel Popovici's proposal for a United States of Greater Austria, c. 1906.

ality would have remained happy and merely *folklorique* within the bounds of Habsburg federalism. [But] why would the Bohemian Germans be willing to keep living in their little woodsy province rather than unite with the Second Reich?' Thirty years later, after all, moves to unite Bohemian Germans with the *Third* Reich would become one of the many milestones on the road to the Second World War.

The Holy Roman Empire over which the Habsburgs had once ruled had kept alive a sort of feudalism long after the rest of Europe had done away with such things. So it's striking that their successor empire ended up an anachronism, too: a state built not on shared institutions or identity, but simply on having the same bloke in a crown at its head. This was its entire *raison d'être*, and the Habsburgs' commitment to their own dynastic territories was why Austria had ended up excluded from the process of German unification. By the late nineteenth century, though, the idea that dynastic concerns might outrank national feeling was starting to look increasingly weird. Perhaps, even without the war and everything that followed, after all those centuries, the Habsburgs' time was simply done.

We'll never know for sure. Franz Ferdinand had been waiting nearly twenty years to become emperor when his car took that wrong turn and he was shot dead, aged just fifty. His inheritance, on the losing side in the resulting war, did not long outlast him. The Europe of the twentieth century would not be multicultural or federal after all.

Britain and France Carve Up the Middle East

Sykes–Picot, 'the line in the sand'

In October 1916, with the Great War raging and the world in chaos, a man named Hussein proclaimed himself king of the Arabs. The sharif and emir of Mecca, a member of the Hashemite line descended from the prophet Muhammad, Hussein bin Ali had as good a claim to the role as anyone. And if there was ever a year in which it seemed worth declaring yourself king of something on the off chance you'd get away with it, surely 1916 was it.

Hussein, though, was not simply chancing his arm; so far as he was concerned, he'd been given the go-ahead by the great superpower of the age. He had, after all, kept his side of the bargain, set out in correspondence with the British high commissioner in Egypt, Sir Henry McMahon himself: he'd led an Arab revolt against Ottoman rule. Now it was time to reap the rewards and establish a new, independent state consisting of all the Arab lands east of Egypt.

It didn't come off. The plan set out in the McMahon–Hussein correspondence, you see, wasn't the only territorial agreement the British made in 1916. There was another, secret one, with France, an ally they were minded to treat with rather more respect, which would still be haunting the region a century later: the Sykes–Picot agreement.

We often think of the First World War, as its participants thankfully did not then know to call it, as the beginning of the twentieth century, setting the stage as it does for fascism, communism and everything that followed. By doing so, though, we sometimes miss that it was also the belated end of the nineteenth

– the sudden, explosive conclusion to a century of relative peace – and that the goals being pursued by the great powers were often those they'd been nursing for decades.

Top of the list was the so-called 'eastern question': the widespread belief that the Ottoman Empire, which controlled a vast chunk of the eastern Mediterranean from its capital in Constantinople/Istanbul, was weak, decadent, bureaucratic and on the path to inevitable collapse. When hostilities broke out, the question of whether the 'sick man' of Europe's demise was inevitable began to matter less than the fact the Entente powers were now in a position to help finish it off. And so, after decades of talk, Britain, France and Russia had the opportunity to redraw the map. The only thing standing in their way was the tiny matter of winning the war.

The people whose names ended up on the secret 1916 Anglo-French plan were relatively low-ranking bureaucrats compared to the sorts who'd, say, carved up the map of Africa in Berlin three decades earlier (see page 114). François Georges-Picot was a diplomat and lawyer, at the time serving as consul in Beirut. Mark Sykes – or, to give him his full title, Colonel Sir Tatton Bienvenuto Mark Sykes, sixth Baronet – was a Boer War veteran and Conservative MP, working for Lord Kitchener at the War Office. Some sense of how arbitrary was the agreement they would between them cook up can perhaps be gleaned from the fact Sykes is said to have told Prime Minister Herbert Asquith at a preliminary meeting in 1915: 'I should like to draw a line from the "E" in Acre to the last "K" in Kirkuk.'

Broadly speaking, he did just that. The allied power of Russia was promised Istanbul, the Dardanelles strait and much of Anatolia. The core of the agreement, though, was that France would run the coast of the northern Levant (today's Lebanon and Syria), an area already home to plenty of French money, while Britain would take oil-rich southern Mesopotamia, around Basra and Baghdad. In between would lie a zone not directly colonised but divided into French and British spheres of influence by a long, straight border through the desert. The proverbial 'line in the sand' would

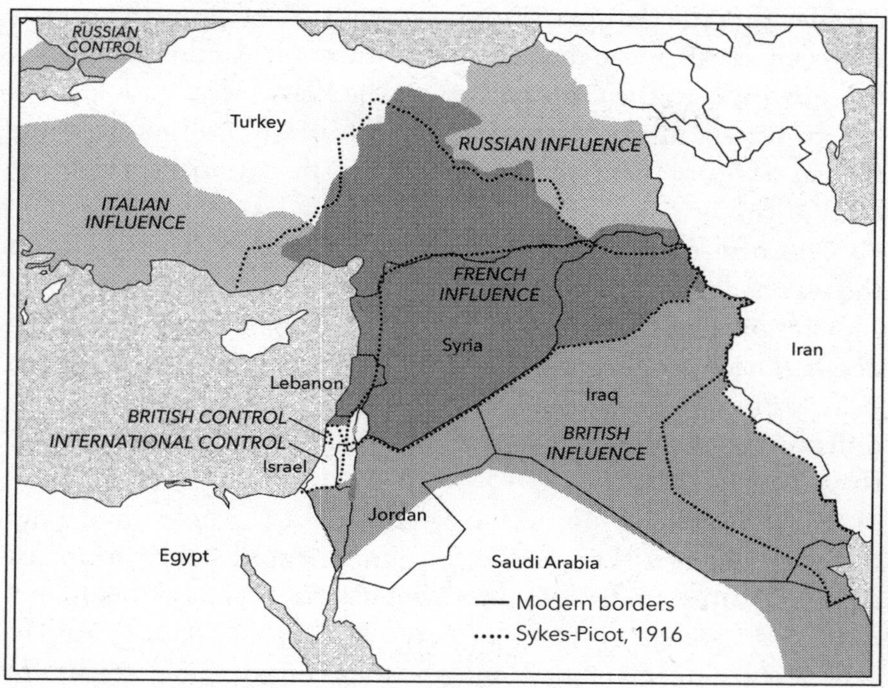

The various spheres of influence set out in the Sykes–Picot agreement and associated agreements of 1916, overlaid onto modern boundaries.

inevitably cut any proposed Arab state in half, and divide peoples like the Kurds and the Druze, too.

Sykes–Picot wasn't the first plan the Triple Entente made to divide up the Ottoman Empire during the course of the war, nor would it be the last. Much of the agreement was foreshadowed in the Constantinople Agreement of April 1915, which would have given Russia control of Constantinople and the Dardanelles, providing naval access from the Black Sea to the Mediterranean. Later on, the Agreement of Saint-Jean-de-Maurienne – negotiated by British, French and Italian leaders in a train in southeastern France – denied the by then revolutionary Russia its share of the spoils, instead handing Italy a large chunk of Anatolia.

The Central Powers (Germany, Austro-Hungary and the Ottomans themselves) were hardly averse to a spot of creative cartography, either, although since their proposals were premised on the idea that the Ottoman Empire would *not* be falling, their plans were necessarily more modest: Constantinople would take back a few provinces in the Caucasus or on the Black Sea that had been lost to Russia in the Russo-Turkish War of 1877–8, regain some Balkan territory that had recently caught the nationalist bug, that kind of thing.

The new map of the region that ultimately emerged from the war had only a loose resemblance to the one agreed in 1916. The notion that there should be a long, straight line through the desert, dividing a French mandate (which became Syria) from a British one (Iraq) survived. So did the idea that there should be different political arrangements on the Mediterranean coast to those further inland.

But the precise borders created were not those drawn up in Sykes–Picot. Although the Ottoman Empire fell, nationalist troops fighting under the man who'd later be known as Kemal Atatürk succeeded in retaining Anatolia for a new nation, Turkey. Where the agreement had imagined an international status for the region around Jerusalem, a city at the heart of multiple religions, the 1917 Balfour Declaration saw the British government throw its support behind the idea of a Jewish state. Three decades on, that would come to pass in the form of Israel (more on this on page 192). And where the 1916 agreement had put the land around Mosul in the French sphere of influence, it ultimately ended up as the northern part of Iraq, in the British one. Today's line in the sand, controversial though it is, is not a line that Sykes, Picot and their teams ever drew.

And yet, Sykes–Picot is still the label attached to a whole basket of historical grievances, not all of which have anything to do with the agreement that actually bears that name. When the militant group calling itself Islamic State swept across the region in 2014, it tweeted pictures of its bulldozers levelling the border, along with a statement from its 'caliph', Abu Bakr al-Baghdadi, that 'this blessed advance will not stop until we hit the last nail in the coffin of the Sykes–Picot conspiracy'. The border in question was probably several hundred miles from the line proposed by Picot and

Sykes. Nor is it just militants who talk this way. In 2016, Massoud Barzani, president of Iraq's autonomous Kurdistan region, told the BBC: 'It's not just me that's saying it, the fact is that Sykes–Picot has failed, it's over.'

It's unsurprising that a people whose land was cut in two by treaties agreed between Western powers should resent either those treaties or those powers. To many, it's a genuine injustice; to others, it offers useful propaganda, a way of framing existing states as illegitimate and the West as conspirators determined to keep the region divided. To those same Westerners, it provides an original sin, something to blame for the region's instability that's rooted in a helpfully distant past, rather than any foreign policy choices they may have made more recently. But why Sykes–Picot? Why not any of the other agreements that came before or after?

One reason is perhaps the way it was revealed to the world. Although the Russian Empire had signed the agreement and stood to profit from it handsomely – Constantinople was no small prize – no Russian negotiator's name was attached to it. More than that, in late 1917, the newly established communist government washed their hands of the previously secret agreement by publishing full details in its newspaper, *Pravda.* This was obviously a shock to the Entente's Arab allies who were, even then, in the midst of their anti-Ottoman rebellion. This was the moment at which Britain's betrayal of its promise of a pan-Arab homeland became apparent. Whatever treaty it was that eventually went into effect, Sykes–Picot was the moment they *knew.* (Sir Henry McMahon and his colleagues may not have felt they had made any such promise but they must surely have known that the Arabs had *understood* there to be one. That was, after all, a big reason why they were rebelling against Ottoman rule in the first place.)

I think there are two other reasons why the region should hate Sykes–Picot specifically. One is that, unlike so many of the other stories in which European empires screwed others over in their own self-interest, this one came reasonably recently and still pops up on the news. 'All borders, not just those in the Middle East, are, of course, artificial,' the UCLA historian James L. Gelvin noted in a 2016 article to mark the agreement's centenary. 'If you choose to worry about the durability of states whose borders were drawn by far-off diplomats, worry not just about Syria and Iraq but about Belgium as well.' Perhaps if the Flemings and the Walloons went to war we would.*

The other reason is because, well, it has a name. As we've seen again and again in this story – from the Peace of Westphalia to the Berlin Conference via the Mason–Dixon line – a synecdoche, a label into which you can subsume several decades of complicated diplomatic process, can make that process easier to talk about. The British had betrayed their Arab allies. Sykes–Picot turned that fact into a story.

What happened to the various characters involved in that story? Sir Mark Sykes died in the flu pandemic of 1919, aged just thirty-nine, and didn't live to see what he'd wrought. François Georges-Picot was high commissioner in Palestine and Syria from 1917 to 1919, but then moved on to other posts in other regions; he lived until 1951 but his career doesn't trouble history again.†

The family of Hussein bin Ali had more of an impact. Though his claim to be king of the Arabs was all but universally ignored, he was recognised as king of Hejaz, a region of western Arabia, from 1916 until 1924, when he was forced to abdicate by the Wahhābī invasion that was to lead to the creation of Saudi Arabia. He died in 1931 at the court of his second son Abdullah, who was by then the king of Transjordan (the 'trans' was dropped on independence in 1946). His third son, Faisal, was reigning next door in Iraq.‡

---

* In the same article, Gelvin noted another reason why the obsession with Sykes–Picot might seem, from some angles, a little strange. 'For all the talk of artificial borders in this particular corner of the Arab world, it is easy to forget one essential fact: the state system in the Arab world has been remarkably stable for almost three-quarters of a century,' he wrote. 'It has been more stable, in fact, than the European state system.'

† His great-nephew did, however: Valéry Giscard d'Estaing was president of France from 1974 to 1981.

‡ His first son Ali succeeded him in Hejaz for a year before he was chased out, too.

It was Faisal who had established a short-lived Arab kingdom in Damascus after it fell to Western troops in October 1918, and who represented his family and his people at the peace conference at Versailles the following year. But the French didn't want a new Arab kingdom in their sphere of influence, and the British listened to the French. The Arabs refused to ratify the resulting treaty as a protest against the regimes it imposed on the Middle East. It made no difference, in the end.

The Partition of Ulster

Or: why is there a Northern Ireland, exactly?

So how, you may be wondering, did Anglo-Scottish attempts to resettle the entire east of Ireland lead ultimately to a border between the modern Irish Republic and the United Kingdom of Great Britain and *Northern* Ireland?

Plans to push the entire Catholic population of Ireland west into Connaught and replace them with pliable Protestant Brits proved unworkable – not because of any outburst of morality but because there simply weren't enough settlers willing to do the job. Perhaps 10,000 men settled on the confiscated land, out of around 100,000 British settlers who arrived in Ireland in the century and a half between the beginning of plantation and the end of the seventeenth century. But while the Cromwellian wars saw Catholic land ownership in Ireland reduced from around 60 per cent to perhaps as little as 10 per cent (estimates vary), the population in many areas remained, predominantly, Irish.

The result was a culture of absentee landlords, in which a stubbornly Catholic Ireland was ruled by a relatively small number of Protestant families, a period known as 'the Protestant ascendancy'. The security problem that plantation had been intended to solve didn't merely persist, it was actively fanned by resentment of oppressive minority rule. So when the end of the eighteenth century again saw Irish rebels working with Britain's enemies, this time in the form of revolutionary France, Britain – by now it definitely *was* Britain – panicked and tried a new strategy. Under the Act of Union 1801, the Dublin parliament was swallowed by the Westminster one; Ireland ceased to be a colony and became, instead, a part of the imperial heartland itself, which would now go by the new name of the United Kingdom of Great Britain and Ireland.

This variation on 'if you can't beat them, join them' seemed, for a time, to be working: the Irish played a disproportionate role in building and governing the British Empire, while Irish nationalists began worrying about the phenomenon of the 'West Briton', a type of Irishman unnervingly comfortable with being British. But there were signs that the British did not entirely accept the Irish as kin. Popular cartoons depicted them as wild bog creatures. Although most of the laws discriminating against Catholics were repealed around the turn of the nineteenth century, some remained on the books into the modern era. (One, preventing anyone who married a 'Papist' from inheriting the crown, was not repealed until 2013.) Far worse was that, between 1845 and 1849, the government in London failed abysmally to provide relief from the famine brought upon Ireland by the potato blight and allowed thousands to simply die by the roadside.*

By the end of the nineteenth century, the size of the Irish voting bloc in Westminster meant that domestic British politics was increasingly dominated by rows over whether or not to grant Ireland 'Home Rule' – not full independence but something closer to the Austro-Hungarian dual monarchy, or the devolution of domestic powers granted to Scotland and Wales since 1999. Even this limited change proved contentious, to put it mildly. On the British side of the Irish Sea, the landowner-dominated House of Lords repeatedly blocked the bill; on the Irish one, by the early

---

* I'm skipping over the Great Irish Famine rather because it's not directly connected to maps or borders, although the consolidation of land ownership into the hands of roughly 5,000 mostly absent landlords certainly didn't help. But the atrocity remains inescapable in Irish history and a significant blot on the British conscience. Not only did this help create a diaspora that, not entirely unreasonably, hated the perfidious Brits who had failed to save those they claimed were their countrymen, it also meant that Ireland, which had nearly half the population of England on the eve of the famine, saw its population decline in a period in which that of essentially every other country in western Europe boomed. This was largely due to emigration but it remains a shocking fact nonetheless that Ireland's population is still lower than it was in 1841.

1910s, the descendants of those English and Scottish Protestant settlers had begun signing oaths, forming paramilitary groups and smuggling in weapons from the German Empire. If the First World War hadn't intervened, University College Dublin historian Paul Rouse has argued, there was a real chance the British Isles would have dissolved into civil war.

Eventually, though, despite such opposition, Home Rule passed: the Government of Ireland Act finally received royal assent on 18 September 1914. By then, however, the British government had other things on its mind and so the bill was never implemented.* And with London distracted by a world war, a group of Irish nationalists saw the perfect opportunity to move for something more radical. On Easter Monday 1916, the Irish Republican Brotherhood seized control of several strategically important buildings in Dublin and declared an independent Irish Republic. In theory, they had some support from the German Empire, which – stealing an idea from revolutionary France and the Spanish Empire before it – had spotted an opportunity to destabilise the British on their home ground, and promised to send the rebels guns. (The shipment, intercepted by the imperial authorities, never arrived.) What they did not have was significant support from the people of Ireland.

Right up until the British government defeated the revolutionaries, rounded them up and shot them.

The resulting outrage turned into a growing resistance to wartime conscription, a majority for the Irish nationalist party Sinn Féin in Irish seats in the UK general election of December 1918 and a boycott of the UK parliament in favour of a new Irish one, which promptly declared independence. There was still a war to be fought to make this a reality but, nonetheless, Ireland was to be independent at last.

But not the whole of Ireland. The Protestant unionist population, which was especially concentrated in the northeast, had seen

---

* Technically, it was passed on the same day as the Suspensory Bill, which delayed its effects. Six rather busy years later it would eventually be repealed.

themselves as British in Ireland for three centuries. They didn't want to be a minority in a new country.

So, as the Great War drew to a close, the UK government appointed a committee to rethink Home Rule. Its plan had been to partition the island, whose domestic affairs were to be managed by *two* parliaments: one covering the nine, largely unionist counties of the northernmost province of Ulster; another, the other three provinces. That was not enough for the unionists, however. Concerned about nationalist sympathy in the west of Ulster, they persuaded the government to cut the three most Catholic counties – Cavan, Donegal and Monaghan – out of the plan.* This meant that the new Northern Ireland would contain six counties, not nine; and its population was two-thirds Protestant and only one-third Catholic. This would, it was assumed, effectively create a permanent Protestant majority and a region loyal to the United Kingdom. And so when Ireland became independent in 1922, it had a northern border: one that didn't just partition Ireland but Ulster, too.

However far from Belfast you are as you read this, you almost certainly have some sense of how that went. The unionist majority didn't just run Northern Ireland but dominated it. Its leaders were drawn from the ultra-Protestant Orange Order; the Catholic minority were discriminated against and shut out of government, police, legal system and jobs. In 1969, the 800th anniversary of Henry II's first arrival in Ireland, civil rights marches led to riots, which led to intercommunal violence, which led to the rise of both nationalist and unionist paramilitaries. That meant a sizable British military presence, which was rarely even-handed, and which meant more oppression, more targets and more violence –

---

* One aspect of the English/British occupation that has shown remarkable persistence, incidentally, is the 'shiring' of Ireland: the division of the land into thirty-two counties, beginning with Dublin in the twelfth century and ending with Wicklow in 1606. This was a tool of colonial administration, not to mention the imposition of a type of land division invented in early medieval Wessex. But it's one that remains strong in Irish local identity in everything from sports to politics today.

some officially sanctioned. By the time 'the Troubles' ended, with the Good Friday Agreement of 1998, over 3,000 people were dead and 50,000 injured.

That conflict is, thankfully, history. But one thing that helped drain the poison was the decreasing relevance of the border. The fact that the United Kingdom and Ireland had both joined the European Union did not just make it seem less important whether Northern Ireland was British or Irish: it removed the need for border posts that could become targets. In practice, if not in theory, the border slowly ceased to matter.

And then, in 2016, the British people voted to leave the European Union, thus raising the need for a managed border between the two countries once again. What this might mean for the people of Ireland was, after eight centuries of interference in the island's affairs, barely even discussed.

That carefully gerrymandered permanent majority, incidentally, is these days not looking so permanent. The UK's 2021 census found that, for the first time, those in the province who identified as Catholic outnumbered those identifying as Protestant. Two years later, Sinn Féin, the nationalist party which had backed the IRA throughout the Troubles, won the highest share of votes in local elections for the first time. The reunification of Ireland is unlikely to be imminent – it would require a referendum and involve a lot of upheaval, not to mention significant problems to be overcome in the Republic of Ireland itself – but it feels significantly more plausible than it did before 2016. This is a story that may not have reached its end.

The Partition of India

The biggest and deadliest migration in history

Every sunset, along the line that carves up Punjab, two rival border forces perform a ritual that looks unnervingly like something out of Monty Python's Ministry of Silly Walks.

There are several sites at which members of the Indian Border Security Force and Pakistani Rangers conduct such ceremonies, in uniforms covered in medals and with what appear to be fans on their heads. The famous one, though – the one for which the authorities on each side have built viewing platforms to hold the tourists it attracts from across South Asia and far beyond – takes place between the villages of Attari in India and Wagah in Pakistan. There, the two militaries, dressed in outfits that don't quite match but nonetheless mirror, perform an elaborate drill, involving lots of high kicks and furious synchronised staring. Then, once each side has lowered and folded its flag, they turn away from one another and close the gate across the Grand Trunk Road.*

This display of synchronised intimidation manages, somehow, to encapsulate both cooperation and rivalry all in one go. This shouldn't be a surprise: this is one people, who share language, culture and cuisine, but were divided less than a lifetime ago into two countries that have more than once since gone to war. In a 1997 documentary for the BBC World Service, produced to mark the fiftieth anniversary of partition, journalist Andrew Whitehead summed the ceremony up: 'In unison but not in harmony'.

---

* If you aren't planning to visit the Lahore/Amritsar border region anytime soon, you can watch all this on YouTube.

The Indian subcontinent has long been a patchwork of languages, cultures and religions. By the time the Europeans started poking around in significant numbers after 1500, Hinduism and Buddhism had been around for millennia, and an upstart new creed named Sikhism was winning converts in Punjab. The region's dominant power, though, was the Mughal Empire, which began in Kabul and gradually expanded southwards, spreading Islam as it went.*

So rich was the region in spices, textiles and other luxuries that all sorts of colonial empires established trading posts. First on the scene were the Portuguese, whose interest in India was what led them to be so blasé about handing the western hemisphere to the Spanish; they were followed by the French, the Dutch and even, unexpectedly, the Danish. But it was the British East India Company that gradually came to control the subcontinent – an area nearly as big as the non-Russian bit of Europe and with significantly more people, all in the hands of one extremely dodgy company. That only changed after 1857, when the war euphemistically known as the 'mutiny', 'rebellion' or 'insurrection' led the British state to assume full colonial control, in a period known to history as the British Raj.

Campaigners fought for independence throughout the early twentieth century and by the mid-1940s, the British – physically, emotionally and financially exhausted by war – were ready, even eager, to oblige. The only problem was that the region's leaders disagreed about how many countries it should be. The Indian National Congress, the leading independence movement, was determined that there should be a single India. This, its leader Jawaharlal Nehru was convinced, was the best way of bringing socialism to his country and thus addressing its poverty.

But one of the tricks the British had found helpful when ruling an area the size of Europe with just a couple of thousand

* The founder of this empire, Babur, claimed descent from Genghis Khan on one side and Timur/Tamburlaine on the other. Quite the pedigree for a would-be conqueror.

staff had been 'divide and rule': building caste and creed into the very structures of empire; setting the various communities to compete against one another to ensure they could not unite against the colonial rulers; even, when a measure of democracy was introduced, creating separate communal electorates in which, say, the Muslim minority would vote for their own bloc of candidates to ensure Muslim representation. Recent events in Europe had, what's more, brought home quite how dangerous it could be to be a member of an ethnic or religious minority.

So by the time the British were seriously discussing withdrawal, the leader of the All-India Muslim League, Muhammad Ali Jinnah – a man who had once firmly believed in Indian unity – was convinced that the only way to protect the interests of the one in five Indians who were Muslim was for them to have their own state. In the Muslim-dominated areas, during the national and provincial elections of 1945–6, the League swept the board. Now their goals, too, needed to be taken into account.

So in 1946, the British government sent a deputation to India, in an attempt to find a roadmap acceptable to both sides. The 'Cabinet Mission Plan' was a complicated three-tiered system with a weak federal government at the top and powerful provincial governments at the bottom. In between would sit three groups of provinces: one in the largely Muslim areas of the northwest including Punjab; another in the largely Muslim areas of the east including Bengal; and a third covering the vast, mainly Hindu area in between. (The 40 per cent of the subcontinent made up of 'princely states', governed by local rulers directly answerable to the crown, was excluded.) This, it was hoped, would square the circle: one India, with protections for Muslim areas.

It didn't work. Despite misgivings, both parties seemed, at first, to accept the plan. But Nehru worried that it would mean a weak central government unable to modernise India – and on 10 July, he gave a speech making clear his party did not feel bound to follow it. Panicking that Congress's opposition would make the creation of Pakistan through constitutional means impossible,

Jinnah withdrew his support and named 16 August as a day of 'direct action'. He did not explain what this meant.

Calcutta, once the capital of British India, was a Hindu-majority city in Muslim-majority Bengal. Which of those communities began the riots that day is unclear – accounts differ and there probably wasn't a single inciting incident anyway. Whatever the truth, though, peaceful protest and counter-protest soon spiralled to violence, arson, then murder in the streets. Many on both sides seem to have believed that they were acting in self-defence.

All this, of course, was horrifying. So is the fact the British authorities saw it coming but, aside from declaring a national holiday in the hope of keeping the city shuttered, did little to prevent it. By the time Direct Action Day was over, there were perhaps 4,000 dead, 100,000 homeless and an untold number radicalised. In the months that followed, both Congress and the League used the memory of Calcutta in an attempt to drum up support; there were more riots and more deaths as Hindu and Muslim alike looked to take their revenge.

In March 1947, a new Viceroy of India arrived from Britain, with a mandate to make himself redundant. Louis Mountbatten was a war hero and, in a distant sort of way, a member of the royal family. He hoped to keep India in one piece, if possible; but his job was to get Britain out by the end of June 1948 at the latest, while doing the minimal amount of reputational damage in the process. That, he almost immediately decided, was too long: with his arrival greeted by yet more riots, Mountbatten decided that the situation was too volatile to prolong British engagement. To prevent civil war – or, at least, Britain's involvement in civil war – India was to have independence as soon as possible.

There are a number of ways in which Mountbatten was perhaps not ideally suited to the job with which history had presented him. One is that he seemed obsessed with maintaining the dignity of empire – wearing full dress uniforms covered with medals and unselfconsciously sitting on a throne at precisely the moment when it would have been politic to play these things down. Another is that he had a chummy approach to negotiation, a belief that the solution to difficult problems was for chaps to come together and work through them over a whisky. With Nehru, this worked brilliantly: the two rapidly became firm friends. Jinnah, though, was cooler and determined to keep relations strictly professional. 'I regard Jinnah,' Mountbatten wrote in his notes one day, 'as a psychopathic case.'

There was another factor that would prevent Mountbatten from being an honest broker between the two leaders. For some years, he and his wife Edwina had been in an open marriage, and while in India, she and Nehru began an affair. Surprisingly, perhaps, this seems not to have poisoned the viceroy against him: rather, this closeness with the family, as it were, gave the Congress leader an early insight into what the British were planning. Given the speed at which events were moving, this was no small advantage.

The nature of Mountbatten's first proposal, drawn up in four weeks without input from India's leaders, can be gleaned from its name: Plan Balkan would have divided the subcontinent into as many as a dozen countries. This was, of course, the diametric opposite of what Nehru wanted and, shown the plan at the viceregal lodge in the Himalayas where he was staying, bizarrely, with the Mountbattens, he hit the roof. So a political advisor by the name of V. P. Menon suggested an alternative: instead of a dozen pieces, why not two? Creating a new nation of Pakistan in the Muslim-dominated regions of the east and northwest would satisfy Jinnah but it would also allow Congress to keep together the vast realm in between. Nehru, terrified by the alternative prospect presented by Project Balkan, agreed.

A few weeks later, on 2 June, the leaders gathered at Viceroy's House in Delhi to examine yet another plan for Indian independence. Nehru had seen it weeks ago; Jinnah, unaware of the extent to which he had been kept in the dark, was seeing it for the first time. Despite this disparity, Mountbatten set a deadline of midnight, giving them just a few hours to consider it.

The plan was not ideal. Pakistan would consist of two pieces, separated by 1,500 miles that were to remain Indian. Two provinces were to be split down the middle, with the exact borders yet to even be determined. But it was the Muslim homeland Jinnah had campaigned for. And so, he agreed.

Two days later, Mountbatten gave a radio broadcast, announcing the plan to the world. The decision to divide the country was to his 'great regret', he said – but, 'There can be no question of coercing any large areas in which one community has a majority to live against their will under a government in which another community has a majority. And the only alternative to coercion is partition.' Independence would take place on 15 August. There were less than ten weeks to build two new nations.

It's worth pausing at this point to consider just how few people come out well from this story. Nehru, who would later describe himself as 'the last Englishman to have ruled over India', comes across as cynical and duplicitous, Jinnah as inflexible and stubborn. Both Congress and the League were more than willing to drum up conflict to forward their goals, and there are seemingly endless stories, from both before and after independence, about Hindus attacking Muslims, and Muslims attacking Hindus or Sikhs.* V. P. Menon, the civil servant who proposed the plan to divide India, would later reject an honour, asking, 'How could I accept a knighthood for being the man who devised the partition of my country?'

But Mountbatten surely comes out worst of all. It may have been his bosses in London who made the decision to cut and run, and many in the imperial hierarchy held patronising, if not outright racist, attitudes towards people they'd been colonising for over 200 years. (A sample quote, from a BBC radio report of the violence in Calcutta: 'Whether they're Hindus or Muslims I cannot tell you . . . Nothing that I can see except a very good hard smack on the nose will stop them.') But it was Mountbatten who was in a position to affect events on the ground, who failed to

* I've largely left the Sikhs out of this story, for reasons of length and clarity, but for the record: they were largely aligned with Congress as part of the more pluralist India.

act as an honest broker and who decided to rush independence through. It was Mountbatten who chose not to announce the details of the new borders until the countries they divided already existed, leaving millions of people – Hindu, Muslim, Sikh – uncertain whether they'd have to abandon their homes. And it was Mountbatten who decided to keep the tens of thousands of British troops in their barracks, even as militia began to spring up and intercommunal violence broke out yet again. As riots rocked Lahore, Jinnah and Nehru alike begged the British to impose martial law. Mountbatten, concerned primarily with protecting British lives and keeping British hands clean, refused. With the chaos unfolding, he seemed instead more concerned with matters of protocol, such as when exactly the union flag should fly over the newly independent dominions.*

In mid-July, with just six weeks to go before independence, the British decided that now would be a good time to work out where the new boundary should run. Most provinces were easily allocated into one or other of the two countries by virtue of their demographics, but two were not: Bengal in the east and Punjab in the west. The governor of the latter felt strongly that the ideal person to divide the two provinces would be a High Court judge† but none was available, so instead, the job fell to the nearest equivalent: Sir Cyril Radcliffe, a barrister and civil servant who had never set foot in India or, come to that, anywhere east of Paris. In theory, Radcliffe was simply the leader of a commission, backed up by two advisors from Congress and two more from the League. In practice, though, the effect of this was not balance but deadlock,

* A 'dominion' was a self-governing nation within the British Empire, implying that a country has not *really* left because it retains the monarchy (making it a sort of successor to 'personal union'). India ceased to be a dominion in 1950; Pakistan in 1956.

† The nature of this story means that this entry has fewer comic asides in it than almost any in this book, but can we pause just a moment to consider the absurdity of the belief that an expertise in the British legal system and a stupid wig would make you ideally qualified to cut countries into pieces on the other side of the planet? *These* are the people who ruled the world?

meaning all the really tough decisions were left to Radcliffe himself. With no previous experience, he had just over a month to divide territory the size of Sweden and home to more people than the modern UK, and thus create a viable new country in two halves, a thousand miles apart. After that, he insisted, he would be back on a plane and out of the country before his proposals could be announced. 'There will be roughly 80 million people with a grievance,' he wrote to his stepson. 'I do not want them to find me.'

Thus, it came to pass. On 14 August – Jinnah had requested he go first – Mountbatten was in Karachi to swear in the League's leader as the first governor general of the new dominion of Pakistan. After midnight, on 15 August, he was in New Delhi to offer India's new leader, Nehru, the same oath. Two days later, details of the borders between the two new countries were finally published. And millions of people found themselves on the wrong side of the line.

And so, they began to move, at least 12 and perhaps as many as 18 million of them – Muslims towards Pakistan, Hindus and Sikhs towards India, abandoning all possessions except those that they could carry. For some, this may have been a matter of wanting to stay with those who shared their faith but for many more it wasn't a choice: it was a way of escaping the militias, made up of people who had been their neighbours but who now wanted this land for themselves. Those who did not move were raped or killed; some committed suicide, or were slaughtered by their own family to escape the dishonour of forced conversion. Eyewitness reports tell of mass graves, of death squads boarding trains in search of people from the other side, of being part of a miles-long column of refugees crossing the border, passing another line of people who'd lost everything going the other way and feeling a strange sense of camaraderie.

Just a few days before, that border had not even existed. Not so long ago, the people on either side had been neighbours and friends.

Mountbatten would later claim that under 250,000 people died. That would be horrifying enough, more than eighty 9/11s in a single event, but even conservative estimates put the real figure closer to 1 million, and others at three times that. Although Jinnah had called for a homeland for Muslims, he doesn't seem to have expected mass migration. But the violence, and the British decision not to intervene to prevent it, made it inevitable. Just thirteen months later, incidentally, Jinnah was dead of tuberculosis. If he had known the Muslim leader was dying, Mountbatten later claimed, he would never have let partition go ahead.

All this, like the other horrors of that blood-soaked decade, is still shockingly recent. Perhaps that's why it still feels so unfinished. In the decades since, the two new countries have fought four wars over the region's borders: three over Kashmir, which as a former princely state had been left out of the settlement; the other, in 1971, over East Pakistan's bid for independence as yet another new nation, Bangladesh.* (This means, bizarrely, that millions of people were citizens of British India, then Pakistan, then Bangladesh, without ever moving an inch.) Now both India and Pakistan are nuclear powers, we must all hope they don't find cause to go to war again.

It's unfinished in a different way, too. The previously mixed Punjab may have ended up almost perfectly segregated by the Radcliffe line. But partition was a largely north Indian phenomenon and, as late as the turn of this century, India still contained more Muslims than Pakistan. Since 2014, though, the country has been in the hands of Prime Minister Narendra Modi and the Hindu nationalist BJP. Looking at a country that's increasingly unfriendly to religious minorities, it's hard to escape the feeling that the events of 1946–7 still haunt the Indian subcontinent.

---

* Another country, often forgotten in this story, actually came out of the Raj: Lower Burma was already a part of British India in 1858, Upper Burma was added in 1886, and the two were later merged into a single province which became a separate colony in 1937 and independent in 1948. In 1989, Burma changed its name to Myanmar.

The Iron Curtain and the Division of Berlin

The train via Friedrichstraße

West Berlin, sometime in the 1970s. Your plane touches down at Tempelhof Airport, to the south of the city centre, but your final destination is Wedding, just to the north. So you descend into the bowels of the earth, to board a U-Bahn train: line 6, coloured purple on the map.

At first, the train seems little different to those you're used to from back home. The adverts on the carriage walls and the newspapers people hide behind are all in German, of course. But the tense, bored lack of conversation, the way no one meets each other's eye – you could be on any subway, metro, tube.

But after Kochstraße, something changes. The train doesn't stop at the next station, or the one after that, but merely slows. Through windows sliding past stations at little more than walking pace, you can see darkened platforms patrolled by shadowy uniformed figures, their hands clenched round things you'd rather not think about. Beyond them on the walls are peeling hoardings, advertising products from a half-remembered past. At Friedrichstraße, the train does stop but announcements remind you it's for interchange only. Those without papers should make no attempt to leave the station.

And then, a few stops later, all is normal. The train stops; passengers disembark to be replaced by others. You are safely back in the West. For a few moments, though, you passed beneath a border not merely between nations but between two worlds. You've travelled beneath Soviet East Berlin; you've crossed the Berlin Wall.

The division of Berlin/Germany/Europe/the world into two rival blocs that spent half a century unnervingly close to nuking each other is arguably the most important border of the twentieth century. In 1945, as the Second World War wound down, the Allies divided both Germany and its capital Berlin into four zones of occupation: American, British, French and Soviet. As victory gave way to suspicion and Cold War, the three western zones gradually consolidated, by 1949, into the Federal Republic of Germany. The fourth, meanwhile, became the German Democratic Republic (never a *great* sign when they put the D-word in the name of a country, is it?). The two states would soon become known by other names: West and East Germany.

In March 1946 – before either new state had been established, a sign of how clearly the writing was on the wall – the once and future British prime minister Winston Churchill gave the speech which defined the line between the two camps in the world's imagination. 'From Stettin in the Baltic to Trieste in the Adriatic,' he told the audience at Westminster College, Missouri, 'an iron curtain has descended across the continent. Behind that line lie all the capitals of the ancient states of Central and Eastern Europe. Warsaw, Berlin, Prague, Vienna, Budapest, Belgrade, Bucharest and Sofia; all these famous cities and the populations around them lie in what I must call the Soviet sphere.'

Churchill's 'Iron Curtain' caught on as a label for the thousands of miles of fences, walls, minefields and watchtowers, the heavily patrolled new division between East and West that would last for most of the rest of the century. There was, however, one slight error in that famous quote:* Berlin may have been behind the curtain, in a physical sense; but three-quarters of it were still held by the West.

---

* Actually, there were two. Austria had been divided up in the exact same manner as Germany, and Vienna like Berlin: the parallel even extended to the Austrian capital lying deep inside the eastern, Soviet zone. But neither city nor country ever became a flashpoint in the way Berlin and Germany did; they remained jointly occupied until 1955 when, with participants in the Cold War enjoying one of its periodic thaws, everyone agreed Austria should be allowed unification and independence, just so long as it remained neutral. There was thus never any Vienna Wall, and nightlife in the Austrian capital remains disappointingly pedestrian to this day.

And the Western powers made it very clear that, despite being surrounded, they weren't going anywhere. In early 1948, when the Allies announced plans to merge the economies of their three zones, the Soviets responded by blockading Berlin. If the residents were denied food and fuel, the theory went, the Allies would come under pressure to pull out. Instead, they responded with the eleven-month Berlin airlift, flying 2.3 million tonnes of goods into the city on 270,000 flights. Some planes even dropped candy for kids. Not only did the Soviets fail to dislodge the Allies, they accidentally turned Berlin into a symbol. In May 1949, the blockade was lifted; four months later, the airlifts stopped.

For the next few years, Berlin remained divided and the Western presence continued to niggle the Soviets. It wasn't just a problem of optics, either: millions of East Germans used the West German enclave in their midst as their way of defecting. West Berlin was like a great big exit sign in the heart of the GDR.

So, in 1961, sick of this brain drain, the government of Nikita Khrushchev issued an ultimatum: all Western forces out of Berlin, or else. When they declined to leave, the Soviets walled them in. On the night of 12–13 August, the parliament of the Soviet satellite of East Germany passed a decree ordering construction of a physical barrier around the enemy within. At first, it was a makeshift structure of barbed wire and cinder blocks, running for 45km (28mi) through the city and another 120km (75mi) around its edge. Later, it became something more complex and more imposing: two walls of concrete slabs up to five metres (about 15ft) high: one on the border itself, another several metres into East German territory. In between lay the 'death strip', a sandy no man's land of watchtowers and signal fences. In the event that anyone managed to scale one fence, they would leave footprints in the sand or accidentally touch two wires on the fence and sound the alarm. Either way, they would alert armed guards to their presence.

The resulting scenes are familiar from countless spy films. At least 2.5 million East Germans had defected via West Berlin over the previous twelve years; just 5,000 managed to cross the Berlin

Wall over the next twenty-eight. Thousands more were caught in the attempt; nearly 200 didn't live to tell the tale.

Let's take a moment here to think about quite how odd this is. Many civilisations have built walls around themselves to keep the enemy out or around others to keep them in. What was unique about the Berlin Wall, for nearly three decades the most famous border in the world, was that it didn't do either of those things. The world the East Germans and their Soviet paymasters enclosed, the people it imprisoned, were their own. It was the people inside who were actually free to leave.

One of the less familiar aspects of this story concerns what the wall did to Berlin's railway network. It wasn't a historic city that was being cleaved in two but a modern one, with the transport infrastructure that comes with it. Overground railway lines presented no challenge to the wall builders: lines could be severed, track pulled up, the wall driven on through. Some parts of the eight-line U-Bahn system could be easily segregated, too: the U2 line, for example, which crossed the city for 20km (12mi) from east to west, was split into two segments that operated independently of each other. Three routes, however – two U-Bahn lines and the north–south tunnel used by the S-Bahn – proved more difficult. Each passed under the wall twice, linking northern and southern areas of West Berlin, but passing briefly through the East in the city centre.

So a compromise was reached. West Berlin would be allowed to run trains under the other side's territory – in exchange for a fee, of course. To make sure this didn't undermine the border guards, however, East Berlin closed the stations those trains passed through on its own side of the wall. They became *Geisterbahnhöfe*, 'ghost stations', their doorways sealed and their platforms, like the wall above, patrolled by armed border guards. These worked in pairs, to reduce the chance either would feel the urge to catch a train.

The only exception to this – the only point of contact between East and West Berlin metro networks – was the central station of

Friedrichstraße. This lay beneath the East but remained open as an interchange for use by Western passengers, and doubled, too, as a portal for Westerners with the correct papers to enter the East. No such option was open to East Berliners; the station was even redesigned, with corridors strategically blocked off to keep East and West apart at all times.

The inescapable nature of both the division of Berlin and the politics that lay behind it is perhaps best summed up by the two sides' attitude to cartography. Contemporary West Berlin U-Bahn maps show the stations in the East but mark them as closed; they don't feature the S-Bahn, even where trains were available and useful, because it was still run by the East German authorities and their counterparts in the West preferred that passengers spent their fares with them. That's nothing compared to what the East German maps did, however. Earlier ones labelled the two halves of the city as, respectively, 'Democratic Berlin' and 'West Berlin: The area of the occupation regime of the United States, Great Britain and France'. By 1988, the maps had gone further, reducing West Berlin to a gap in the fabric of the city. It was as if it simply didn't exist.

Although the people who made that map didn't realise it, they were among the last to whom 'East Berlin' would be a meaningful concept. In 1989, Eastern Europe was hit by a wave of revolutions, as government after government began to liberalise and move away from the Soviet Union. On 9 November, after weeks of unrest, the East German government announced it was opening the border and the city's residents began to tear down the wall. Two days later, Jannowitzbrücke became the first of the ghost stations to reopen. In August 1990, what had been East Germany joined the Federal Republic, and in June 1991, the Bundestag voted to return the capital to its historic home. You can now move around Berlin, above ground or below, and not even realise it used to be two cities, not one.

I didn't visit Berlin until more than fifteen years after the wall came down but this story, unlike most in this book, feels personal to me all the same. I was nine years old when it fell and, even at that age, it felt like the end of an era. The wall had stood my whole life: the division of Germany into East and West felt as natural a feature of the world as the division of Italy and France. It was nothing of the sort. The wall hadn't even stood for that long: less than thirty years, less time than has now passed since it fell. If you grow up with a border, it's easy to assume it's as natural and eternal as the mountains or the seas. That it was consciously and deliberately designed – perhaps only a few years before you first entered the world – does not easily occur to you.

Yet the Berlin Wall and East Germany were no more natural than the other borders or states which fell over the next few years, no more eternal than Czechoslovakia or the USSR, or, come to that, the successor states that replaced them. Borders can be erased, states can die; this too may one day pass.

That doesn't mean their effects will vanish with them, though. As late as 2012, the Dutch astronaut André Kuipers could take a photograph from the International Space Station of his view of Berlin from space. More than two decades after the wall came down, the two halves of the city were still clear in the slightly different colour of the street lights they used. Meanwhile, the path of the Iron Curtain is still visible at ground level as the 'European Green Belt': a strip of land thousands of miles long where the decades-long lack of human activity has allowed rare plants and animals to thrive. Even out of evil, sometimes, can come some good.

PART TWO

LEGACIES

Some lingering foreign policy problems – some odd places to draw the line – some problems with defining cities – some problems with modern maps

Königsberg/Kaliningrad, Eastern Germany/ Western Russia

The city at the edge of the world

In the summer of 2022, one of Europe's smallest countries introduced sanctions which genuinely infuriated its biggest. That June, Lithuania, a nation of 3 million people in an area not much bigger than West Virginia, announced that it would no longer allow Russia to transport metals across its territory. The following month, the measures, a part of the European Union's programme of sanctions to protest the war in Ukraine, were extended to include concrete, wood, chemicals and alcohol.

Even though the sanctions did not affect all goods, or actual people come to that, Moscow was furious. One statement warned of 'harsh measures' if the ban was not lifted. Meanwhile, Nikolai Patrushev, chief of the Russian security council, threatened a 'serious negative impact on the population of Lithuania'.

The reason a minnow like Lithuania had been able to so upset the Russian bear – if we can imagine, for a moment, a situation in which minnows and bears actually interact – is because Lithuania isn't just any chunk of land only slightly bigger than West Virginia. It's a small-ish chunk of land which lies between the vast, Eurasian bulk of Russia and its vital Baltic exclave of Kaliningrad: a sovereign Russian territory surrounded by EU states where its residents, in the normal course of things, might take their holidays or do their shopping. When Moscow said the sanctions were effectively a blockade on sovereign Russian territory, it was not entirely wrong.

Named for the city which holds roughly half its population, Kaliningrad Oblast is a block of territory which, to stick with

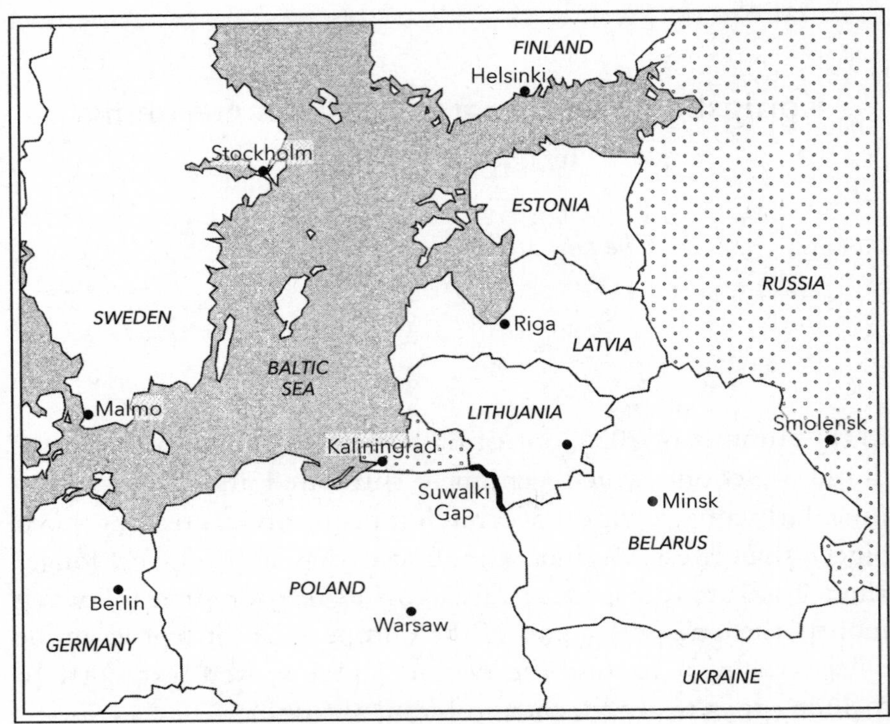

The lands around the Baltic as they are today.

our theme, is not much bigger than Connecticut. It lies at the southeast corner of the Baltic, with Poland to the south and west, Lithuania to the north and east, and the southern tip of Sweden nearly 300km (186mi) away across the sea. The key point, though, is that it's an exclave of Russia, an area completely separated from its mother country, which, at its closest point, is still over 350km (217mi) away.* Not all of the land in between is hostile to Russian interests – much of it is held by its last remaining European ally, Belarus – but there is no way of reaching it by land without going through Poland, Lithuania or both.

To explain how Russia ended up with a chunk of Baltic coastline which, unlike certain other bits of territory it holds, no one seriously argues is *not* Russian, we need to start with – this'll

* Technically a semi-exclave because part of its border is sea.

throw you – the Germans. Until the Middle Ages, the area was home to a people known variously as the Prussians, Old Prussians or Baltic Prussians, a non-Christian tribe who have very little to do with the more familiar Prussians who played a starring role in assorted wars later.

Sometime in the thirteenth century, though, a bunch of German-speaking knights showed up, fresh from the Crusades and looking for a new way in which they could be outstandingly violent on behalf of the church. In 1226, a Polish duke helpfully suggested that conquering the godless lands of the Baltic north-east might be a good project for a nice bunch of lads like this. Thus it was that the Teutonic Order launched the decades-long Northern Crusade, wiping out the Prussians and conquering their lands. Along the way, they levelled their existing city and built a new, more German one in its place. They christened it Königsberg: 'king's mountain'. Then, just to add insult to injury, they stole the Prussians' name as well.

These lands went through a number of incarnations. They started out as the 'Deutschordensstaat' – literally, the state of the Teutonic Order. Then, when the thirty-seventh Grand Master, Albert, fancied giving up the whole warrior-monk thing in favour of a spot of Lutheranism, they became the rather more secular 'Duchy of Prussia'. Later still, they became the Kingdom of Prussia, and merged with the neighbouring Electorate of Brandenburg. At some times, these territories were close allies of the Poles; at others, their sworn enemy. But despite being hundreds of miles to the east of the area Germany occupies today, what had once been the lands of the Old Prussians were absolutely, undeniably German.

This wasn't some backwater, either. Under Otto von Bismarck (see page 112), Prussia became the key driving force in the unification of the new German Empire. Königsberg, meanwhile, had been a part of the Hanseatic League of trading cities and had grown into a major Baltic port. Thanks to the university that Lutheran Albert had founded in 1544, what's more, the city was also a major intellectual centre, whose most famous alumnus was

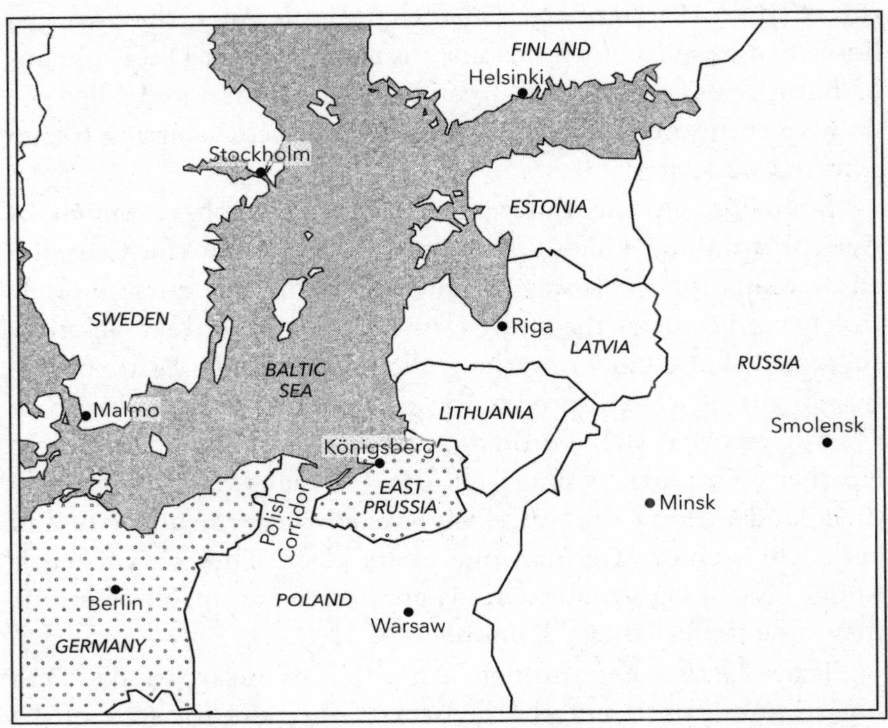

The lands around the Baltic between the world wars. Königsberg/ Kaliningrad has since gone from being the easternmost outpost of Germany to the westernmost oblast of Russia.

the philosopher Immanuel Kant. Even the city's seven bridges were clever, inspiring a world-famous maths puzzle. Königsberg may have been 500km (311mi) northeast of Berlin and nearly 1,000km (621mi) from the Rhine, but it was important, it was intellectual and it was German.

And then the twentieth century happened.

The first big territorial change came after the First World War. One of the Allies' peace terms was that the Poles should have a state again, for the first time since their last one had been carved up between Prussians, Russians and Austrians around a century and a half before. More than that, it should have secure access to the sea, which meant the creation of a 'Polish Corridor' through what had previously been West Prussia. This wasn't crazy – the area had historically been Polish; many of its inhabitants still were – but the way it turned East Prussia into an exclave, an island of German territory cut off from the rest, was a sizable source of resentment, which the Nazis seized on as a potential driver of support.

All that helped contribute (I'm simplifying a bit here) to the Second World War, which, by 1945, it was fairly clear the Germans were losing. With the Red Army approaching, preceded by rumours of anti-German atrocities – revenge for those the Nazis had inflicted themselves – the German state moved to evacuate East Prussia.* After seven centuries, Königsberg was German no longer.

At that summer's Potsdam peace conference, Soviet control of East Prussia was confirmed. It was far from the only part of eastern Europe forced into that empire during the war – the Baltic states and parts of Poland were all swallowed up too – but what made the lands around Königsberg unique was that their previous population had already left. (Those few who hadn't could be kicked out.) That meant the area could be repopulated with existing Soviet citizens. In 1946, the USSR renamed both city and region – an *oblast*, as it was now – in honour of the recently deceased chairman of the presidium of the Supreme Soviet. His name had been Mikhail Kalinin.

---

* Not for the first time, I am conscious of breezily throwing out a sentence about an event that deserves an entire book in itself. Operation Hannibal was a 115-day operation to evacuate an entire German province by boat. It was commanded by Grand Admiral Karl Dönitz, who briefly served as führer after Adolf Hitler's suicide, and it included four sinkings in which more lives were lost than in that of the *Titanic*. Those included that of the horribly overloaded cruise ship *Wilhelm Gustloff*, on which more than 9,000 people are believed to have died. These were not classed as war crimes because the Nazi state deliberately mingled military personnel and civilians in the hope they'd act as human shields. More than that, the entire purpose of the evacuation seems to have been less about saving civilians than about bringing forces west for military operations. Nonetheless, Operation Hannibal managed to evacuate six times as many people as the much more famous seaborne evacuation of Dunkirk and would probably be much better known if it hadn't been one of the last acts of the horrific Nazi state.

For the second time in its history, in other words, the city had been levelled by an invading force, who now set about replacing the previous population. Königsberg had once been the easternmost outpost of Germany; now Kaliningrad became the westernmost edge of Russia. For security reasons, the city, home to the Baltic fleet, was kept closed to visitors. But both its physical location and the fact a large chunk of its population were sailors left it more open to outside cultural influence – Western music, Western fashions – than the rest of the country. Its population, Oleg Kashin, a Kaliningrad-born journalist told the *Guardian* in 2018, 'have always likened themselves to Americans – our families all came here from different places across the Soviet Union and created a melting pot with what was practically a new ethos'.

When the USSR began disintegrating in 1991, Kaliningrad presented a problem. The Soviet republics to its east could become independent, as either resurrected nation states like Latvia or Lithuania, or brand new ones like Belarus. Kaliningrad, though, wasn't a republic in its own right and it didn't have its own people. More than that, as the only Russian port on the Baltic that didn't spend part of the year frozen over, it was a vital military base. So it remained part of the new Russian Federation – one separated from the motherland by several hundred kilometres of other people's land.

This has made the Suwalki Gap, the sparsely populated land on the Polish side of the border with Lithuania, a surprisingly important bit of territory. If Russia were to close access to it, it could cut overland communications between the Baltic states and their allies. By the same token, though, if the *West* were to close access to it, it could cut communication between Russia and Kaliningrad. It was to forestall the latter that, in the relatively happy times of the 1990s, the Russian government called for an extraterritorial link – a road or railway through Polish territory but administered separately. The Poles, reminded that the Nazis had asked for much the same through the Polish Corridor almost immediately before invading, were not keen. Since then, Poland and the Baltic states have joined both the European Union and

NATO, which provides them with added security against Russian aggression, but leaves Kaliningrad more cut off than ever.

And so Russia has been left with a semi-exclave in the far west that remains vital to its national security but which is completely surrounded by NATO countries. The relative ease with which its residents have been able to cross the border to Poland or Lithuania, moreover, means that they've become more sceptical of the Kremlin's anti-Western propaganda. There's even talk of 'Germanisation': reintroducing Prussian street names or rebuilding Königsberg castle (little of it survived the war; what was left was destroyed in 1968 on the orders of Leonid Brezhnev). In Kaliningrad today, there is little evidence of the city's once proud German history, except for the odd manhole cover which still says 'Königsberg'. Yet souvenir stalls sell fridge magnets reading 'Kant touch it' and 'Yes, I Kant'.

What Russia can do about any of this is unclear. It has occasionally threatened to site nuclear missiles in Kaliningrad, effectively placing devastating weapons behind enemy lines – but since Western security services have long assumed they're already there, this feels like an empty threat.

There is another option. Since 2003, Lithuania had allowed people and goods to travel across its territory between the two bits of Russia; what imperilled this wasn't a change in Lithuanian policy but the war in Ukraine and the sanctions that followed. So perhaps, if Russia really wants to maintain links between Kaliningrad and the motherland, the best thing it could do would be to end hostilities towards its eastern European neighbour. It's surely worth a shot.

The Strange Case of Bir Tawil

No man's land

Bir Tawil, a small patch of desert on the Egypt–Sudan border, is often described as the last unclaimed land on Earth. This is wrong, at least twice. For one thing, Marie Byrd Land – an entire ninth of Antarctica, an area three times the size of France – is also unclaimed, a matter we'll be returning to later (see page 299).

Secondly, Bir Tawil is not unclaimed at all. Those who have claimed this chunk of northeastern Africa from behind the safety of their keyboard include the Kingdom of the State of Bir Tawil (whose website discusses the civil war between former co-rulers Adam I and Kieran I, the latter of whom 'now rules West Bir Tawil as a dictator, styling himself "General Binns"'); the Kingdom of Bir Tawil (which in 2010 was claimed 'by a group of responsible citizens who aim to make it a glowing example of peace and justice in the world'; the number of registered citizens it claimed was fourteen and growing, though clearly, given that 2010 was quite some time ago now, not growing that fast); and the Emirate of Bir Tawil (established, according to a 2011 press release, by one Sheikh Andrew S. Edwards of Louisville, 'using International Law, Religious Law, and Historical Records'. The laws in question include the 1933 Montevideo Convention and the 1856 US Guano Islands Act). Then there are 'the Grand Dukedom of Bir Tawil, an Empire of Bir Tawil, a United Arab Republic of Bir Tawil and a United Lunar Emirate of Bir Tawil'.

Most of these claimants have never even set foot in Bir Tawil, of course. Someone who has is the *Guardian*'s former Egypt correspondent Jack Shenker, who visited in 2011 with a notion of claiming it himself, but, on arrival in what was clearly a real place with its own history and not just an amusing footnote in the annals of human folly, thought better of it. (He did at least get a *Guardian* long read out of it; this is what I'm quoting at the end of the previous paragraph.)

Last but not least, there's Jeremiah Heaton, a farmer from Virginia, whose daughter Emily had told him she wanted to be a princess. 'So be it proclaimed,' Heaton wrote on Facebook, after visiting and planting a flag, 'that Bir Tawil shall be forever known as the Kingdom of North Sudan. The Kingdom is established as a sovereign monarchy with myself as the head of state; with Emily becoming an actual princess.' From one perspective, this story is rather sweet. From another – the one from which you've perhaps had rather more direct experience of white people showing up with flags – it was a little bit close to the bone.

At any rate, Bir Tawil is not unclaimed. It is very, very claimed indeed. But it has not been claimed *by a state*. In fact, two of them have specifically renounced their claim to it, which is how it became so infamous in the first place.

Bir Tawil lies in the Nubian desert on the border between Egypt to the north and Sudan to the south. At 2,060km^2 (795mi^2) it's quite a lot smaller than Marie Byrd Land – rather than 'three times the size of France', we're talking 'a little less than twice the size of Los Angeles' – and frankly, there is not a lot there. The territory contains no cities or other permanent settlements, and indeed no permanent inhabitants, although local tribes do on occasion pass through to graze their crops in its more fertile corners. Look it up on Google Maps and you'll see nothing but a featureless, beige trapezoid. To the extent that this can be said of anywhere, Bir Tawil is empty.

That has never stopped anyone from claiming other bits of largely uninhabited desert, of course, and, inaccessible as it is, down the centuries Bir Tawil has been a distant outpost of assorted empires: Egyptian, Nubian, Ottoman, British. It was the latter's taste for drawing lines across the map of Africa that led to the territory's unwanted status. Because the British weren't content with just one line – they insisted on drawing two.

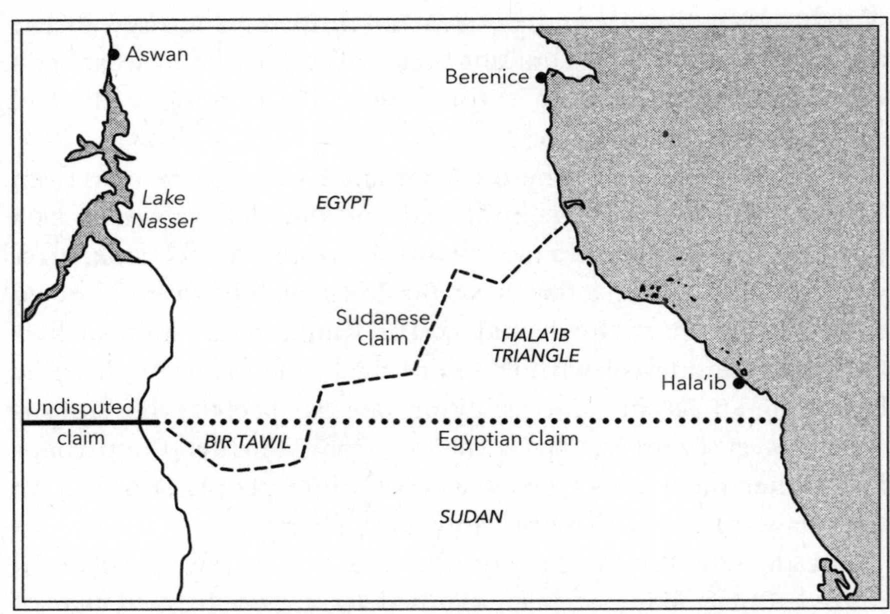

The clashing Egyptian and Sudanese definitions of their border. Both claim the Hala'ib Triangle; neither wants Bir Tawil.

The first came as the result of the eighteen-year war between Britain and its definitely-not-a-secret-colony Egypt, on the one hand, and Sudan, on the other. This ended in 1899 with Sudanese defeat, and an agreement that the planet's oldest civilisation and the largest empire the world had ever seen would henceforth team up and run the conquered territory together. (This, you may recall, was the background to captains Kelly and Tufnell's 1913 walkabout, discussed on page 122.) The agreement placed the 'political boundary' between really-we're-honestly-not-colonised Egypt and the condominium of Anglo-Egyptian Sudan at the twenty-second parallel.

Generally speaking, it's still there: look at a map of northeast Africa, and you'll see that the border between the two countries is a 1,200km (746mi) straight line, running east to the Red Sea. Only the westernmost 850km (528mi) of that are uncontested, however: the last 450km (280mi) will be shown in the dotted line used to indicate a dispute. Accompanying them is an alternative border, which first detours south into the Sudanese desert before recrossing the twenty-second parallel and wobbling its way up to the Egyptian coastal town of Shalateen.

That is the second line created by the British, the 'administrative boundary' drawn up in 1902. The imperial authorities had noticed that Bir Tawil, the trapezoid-shaped area south of the parallel, was mainly used as grazing land by the Ababda tribe, who were based to the north near Aswan. Further east, however, the much larger area *north* of the parallel – the 20,580 square kilometre (7,946mi^2) Hala'ib Triangle; roughly the size of New Jersey – had more links to those who lived to the *south*, in Sudan. It thus made sense to administer Bir Tawil from Cairo and the Hala'ib Triangle from Khartoum. Nobody, it seemed, thought to do anything as useful as countermand the previous border.

For a while, this didn't matter, because – whatever language was used to half-heartedly disguise the fact – both territories were outposts of the British Empire. By the 1950s, though, both states were independent, and both – not unnaturally – decided they preferred the interpretation which gave them the larger territory. In other words, Sudan favoured the 1902 agreement as a correction of an earlier mistake; Egypt dismissed that as a mere administrative document and claimed that *sovereignty* was still as defined in 1899. Both wanted the Hala'ib Triangle; neither wanted Bir Tawil.

This would have stayed a mere academic debate, except that in 1992 the Sudanese government granted exploration rights to some Canadian oil prospectors. And, realising the Hala'ib Triangle was actually worth something, the Egyptians sent in the army. After a few years of relatively low-level conflict, the Sudanese pulled out. The triangle was de facto Egyptian.

But Sudan has not renounced its claim. And since both countries' claims to the larger, more valuable territory rest on a treaty which cedes the smaller, emptier one to their neighbour, neither can touch Bir Tawil without effectively surrendering their claim to the Hala'ib Triangle. That is something which neither wants to do. And so, both have renounced their claim to that double Los Angeles–sized patch of Nubian desert.

Another way Bir Tawil is frequently described is as '*terra nullius*', nobody's land, an ancient concept much used during the latter stages of European imperialism, when the notion that ownership of territory required not merely habitation but legal title was a rather useful fiction.* But what does it mean to describe Bir Tawil as nobody's land? The Egyptian and Sudanese governments may make no use of it, but the same could be said of plenty of other desert territory they do claim. And even if nobody lives there, those Ababda tribespeople still visit to graze their livestock. Perhaps, under the circumstances – instead of assigning it to Cairo or Khartoum or to any one of a dozen internet mischief-makers – it should be considered theirs.

* The doctrine of *terra nullius* lasted in Australia until the unnervingly recent year of 1992. That was when Eddie Mabo, an Indigenous Australian man, brought a case against the state of Queensland and successfully argued that British settlers had deprived the Indigenous people of the Murray Islands of their property rights. The High Court agreed that *terra nullius* should no longer be seen as part of Australian common law. The following year, the Labour government of Paul Keating codified the doctrine of native title in its place.

The Dangers of Gardening in the Korean DMZ

The thirty-eighth parallel and the two Koreas, 1945–present

The first thing worth knowing about the border between the two Koreas – the increasingly affluent K-pop and *Squid Game*-producing South, and the weird, isolationist, sort-of-communist, sort-of-theocratic North, the only country in the world whose constitution names a couple of dead guys as president* – is this: it does not run along the thirty-eighth parallel north.

The name of this line – which at other points on its journey around the globe visits such places as Lexington, Kentucky and Murcia, Spain – is still closely associated with the border between the two zones of the peninsula, and was indeed the boundary for a brief period between 1945 and 1950. Then there was a war and now it isn't. Since then, the boundary and the demilitarised zone (DMZ) surrounding it has actually run from south of the thirty-eighth parallel, in the west, to north of it, in the east. This

* Seriously. In 1998, Kim Jong-Il, second supreme leader of North Korea, changed the constitution to name his father Kim Il-Sung, the founder of the nation and originator of its state ideology of '*juche*', as 'eternal president'. At the time, Kim Il-Sung had been dead for four years. The post of president as a role for actually breathing politicians was abolished at the same time. After Kim Jong-Il too died in December 2011, the country's third and current supreme leader, his son Kim Jong-Un, amended the constitution again, to name his late father 'Eternal General Secretary of the Workers' Party of Korea and Eternal Chairman of the National Defence Commission'. This was quite wordy, so in 2016 he changed it *again*, this time to name both Kim Il-Sung and Kim Jong-Il as 'eternal leaders of *Juche* Korea'. This, if it continues, could grow to become a problem – the US has at the time of writing racked up thirty-nine dead presidents; imagine what a pain it'd be to list all of them in the preamble to the constitution. It also seems to make a mockery of the word 'eternal'.

worked out great for counties like Goseong and Cheorwon, which would have been in the North but actually ended up in the South; it's gone less well for cities like Kaesong, which went the other way.

The other thing worth knowing about the border between the Koreas is that it's one where a minor skirmish could plausibly result in large chunks of the planet burning to a crisp in nuclear fire. It's thus one of those lines it's worth considering relatively carefully.

Korea has been divided before: as with many of today's nation states, its earliest history is one of unification. It began as a whole series of tribal regions, which gradually merged into three warring kingdoms in an era known, with great originality, as the 'Three Kingdoms period'. Then, after some more shuffling of territory, for a couple of centuries there were just two – Unified Silla in the south and Balhae in the north – which has led the eighth and ninth centuries to be referred to as the 'Northern and Southern States period'. It's tempting to look for parallels with the modern situation here, not least because one of these kingdoms seems to have been a lot friendlier with Tang China than the other. But since the border then was some way north of the border now, and since it was in fact the *southern* Silla that had the pro-China policies, it doesn't quite fit.

At any rate, in the late ninth century, Silla collapsed and the Northern and Southern States period was followed by a brief and excitingly war-y interlude, until the appealingly named Wang Kŏn managed to unify the lot under the Goryeo or Koryŏ dynasty in 936. Despite all the challenges you'd expect an Asian kingdom to face in this period – Mongol invasions, an occasionally over-mighty China, a change of dynasty and possibly also of name in 1392 – the resulting kingdom lasted for the better part of 1,000 years, which is not bad going. Then, in 1897, Kojong, the last king of the Chosŏn, declared his realm an empire, partly because empires were very much the thing in 1897 but also to emphasise that his people were no longer going to be pushed around by China, thank you very much. The Empire of Korea lasted all of thirteen years because, in 1910, it was annexed by the bigger, scarier and better-armed Empire of Japan. This period of imperial domination lasted another three and a half decades, until the end of the Second World War, the surrender of Japan and the end of its empire in August 1945.

Which is where all the trouble started.

One problem was that, unlike many territories that had been occupied by Japan or its allies, there was no one obvious waiting in the wings to resume government: it had been occupied too long and many of those keen to take on the job were in exile, in China, the US or elsewhere. The other problem was that the peninsula was divided between the increasingly misnamed 'Allies', with the USSR occupying the North and the Americans the South. The division, at – we got there eventually – the thirty-eighth parallel was originally meant as a mere temporary administrative convenience. But as the anti-Nazi alliance soured into the Cold War, neither side was much in the mood for letting the other get their hands on the lot, and so the division remained. (This was basically, you may recall from page 156, what was happening in Germany at around the same time.)

There followed a few years of scuffles and rearmament on both sides. Until, in the early hours of 25 June 1950, the North, under the leadership of a former Soviet army major by the name of Kim Il-Sung, invaded the South.

At first, it looked like a walkover. Tacitly backed by both the USSR and China, troops reached Seoul in three days and pushed the defending forces back as far as the city of Busan in the far south. 'For almost eight weeks,' military historian Allan R. Millett has written, 'near Osan, along the Kum River, through Taejŏn, and south to Taegu, US soldiers fought and died – and some fled.'

In September, though, US and South Korean forces, under the joint banner of the UN Command, mounted a seaborne invasion of Incheon, just outside Seoul, cutting the North Korean forces in two. The counter-invasion briefly looked to be going just as decisively as the invasion, with much of the northern force pushed back to the Yalu River, which divides Korea from China. But at that point, the Chinese invaded to assist the North and the battle lines went into reverse *again*. Then things escalated, with troops from countries including Colombia, Thailand, Ethiopia, the Philippines and a large chunk of Europe all joining the UN forces on the side of the South.

By the autumn of 1951, the lines, which had moved so rapidly during the early weeks of the war, had all but ground to a halt: Korea was divided along a line which ran from south of the thirty-eighth parallel, in the west, to north of it, in the east. As armistice negotiations began, President Harry Truman's priority seems to have been to extract the US from a horrible war that had achieved almost nothing. The US was committed to there being *some* kind of democratic Korea; but that didn't mean there couldn't also be another, deeply undemocratic one, just so long as US forces got to go home. For their part, it wasn't clear that Chairman Mao's China was that bothered about ending the war at all. 'The Koreans,' Millett notes grimly, 'were not a factor for either side.'

And all the while the talks went on, even though the front stayed put, people continued to die. By the time the fighting was over, around 3 million people were dead; most Korean cities had seen significant destruction and atrocities had been committed on both sides – the South murdering suspected communists, the North torturing prisoners of war and then starving them to death. Measured by proportional civilian death toll, the Korean War was worse than the Second World War.

It took the death of Stalin to unblock the stalemate. As long as Uncle Joe had lived, even though the USSR never fought directly, it had been happy to let the Chinese and North Koreans get on with it, and to aid their war effort. With Stalin dead, though, the Politburo wanted out. In the spring of 1953, all the issues which seemed to have been blocking a peace settlement were swiftly and miraculously solved. On 27 July, generals from the US, North Korea and China signed the armistice, and, as agreed, pulled their forces 2km (1.2mi) back from the front line. The fighting was over.

An armistice, though, is not the same as a peace treaty: it's merely an agreement to stop fighting while peace terms are agreed.

In Korea, they never have been. So the demilitarised zone remains, a largely empty buffer zone between the two Koreas: 4km (2.5mi) wide, 250km (155mi) long, and – ironically, given its name – surrounded by some of the scariest military hardware the world has ever seen.

Officially, there are now, still, two Koreas, with their border running down the middle of the DMZ. In practice, though, there are three: the North, the South and the empty strip that divides them. The DMZ contains one village apiece for each of the two nations, plus the Joint Security Area, half a mile south of the largely demolished 'truce village' of Panmunjom, which occasionally plays host to peace talks* and remains the only point at which the two sides' troops stand face to face. Other than that, though, the DMZ is empty: former farmland that's reverted to a natural state, full of forests and wetlands and even endangered bird species like the white-naped and red-crowned cranes. If you can discount the fact it also contains roughly a million landmines, it almost sounds peaceful.

But not that peaceful. For more than half a century after the armistice, each of the two sides used giant loudspeakers to broadcast propaganda at the other (the North favoured martial music and praise of the country's rulers; the South K-pop and lectures on freedom and democracy). They agreed to pack it in in 2004, although on more than one occasion following an incident (some South Korean soldiers wounding themselves after stepping on a landmine; the North successfully testing a hydrogen bomb) they've turned the speakers back on. Which is, to be fair, a fairly modest sort of an escalation.

---

* One of the most difficult topics during the armistice talks, incidentally, was what to do about prisoners of war. The standard assumption, stemming from the Geneva Convention, is that such people will be repatriated to the side that they fought for. But for those in the South, that raised ethical issues, since it meant returning people to a totalitarian state which had forced many people – including many southerners – to fight. When an agreement was eventually reached, prisoners were allowed to make their own choice – but whatever they chose, they could not change their mind. To this day, the bridge inside the JSA, on which released prisoners could move from one side to the other, is known as the Bridge of No Return.

At other times, the propaganda effort has involved launching balloons laden with leaflets at one another or – my personal favourite – the 1984 Flagpole War, in which the South raised a big flagpole in sight of the border, to which the North responded by putting up an even *bigger* flagpole. The latter stands at 160 metres (525ft) tall, flies a 270kg (595lb) North Korean flag and is thought to be the world's fourth tallest. It is certainly bigger than anything South Korea has to offer – its own effort had been a titchy 94 metres (308ft) – so yah boo sucks to you.

Much less amusing are the violent flashpoints which could have escalated into full-scale war but, thankfully, thus far, have not. Each side has attempted incursions or assassinations; North Korea has dug at least four tunnels under the border which it claimed were for coal mining, although the complete absence of coal made some suspect they might possibly serve some other purpose. In 1966, while US president Lyndon B. Johnson visited Seoul, North Korean agents ambushed an American ship. For the next three years, a thing euphemistically referred to as the 'Korean DMZ Conflict', or less euphemistically as the 'Second Korean War', raged. This mainly took the form of low-level skirmishes, although in 1968, the North did raid Seoul's Blue House – the equivalent of Washington's White House – in an attempt to assassinate the South's president.

And then there's the incident involving the tree.

The tree in question was a poplar, thirty metres (about 100ft) tall, which stood in the Joint Security Area and which the North claimed – citation needed – had been planted by its glorious leader Kim Il-Sung. On 18 August 1976, concerned it was blocking a line of sight between a UN Command checkpoint and an observation post, the UN sent out a joint US–South Korean detail of fourteen men to prune it. Around fifteen North Korean troops appeared, watched them in silence, asked them to stop, went for reinforcements, asked them to stop again and, on being ignored, began attacking them with their own equipment. Two American soldiers were killed.

A few days later, the UN forces were back, in force. Operation Paul Bunyan – the name, in North American folklore, of a giant lumberjack – involved more than 300 troops, some of whom had mines strapped to their chest, protected by air cover from B-52 bombers, fighter aircraft and dozens of attack helicopters. The tree didn't stand a chance, and ended up as little more than a stump. The whole thing sounds ridiculous, until you remember that this, too, nearly resulted in a full-scale war, and also that two Americans had been axed to death.

Nothing on that scale has happened since, which is lucky, because in 2006, North Korea became a nuclear power. Peace talks have been tried; peace talks have failed. As recently as July 2022, the country's leader Kim Jong-Un has appeared on television to remind the world that he has nukes and that, if it came to it, he would use them, too. Seven decades after the Korean War ended in armistice, a peace treaty has yet to be signed and the border remains one of the most dangerous in the world.

One last thing about this bit of the world that feels of note from an international perspective: the two resulting countries use entirely different names for 'Korea'. Both, to be clear, agree that there *is* such a thing as Korea and refer to it as such internationally – this isn't one of those cases where ignorant foreigners have simply bunged together two neighbouring but largely separate places and pretended they're parts of the same thing – they simply use different words for it. And their names are drawn not from geography but from history: they refer not to different regions but come from different times.

North Koreans call it Chosŏn, a name derived from the Joseon dynasty, which ruled the country from 1392 until 1910. South Koreans call it Hanguk, which means, roughly, 'land of the Han'; the Han in question is a word denoting 'great' or 'leader' and has absolutely nothing to do with the Han people who have long dominated the various empires across the Yellow Sea in China. Neither of these words, you will note, are 'Korea', which derives from Goryeo or Koryŏ, the name of the kingdom that once occupied the peninsula but stopped doing so sometime in the fourteenth century. It's as if everyone else in the world still insisted on referring to England as 'Wessex'. (Or, I suppose, if people insisted on referring to the Deutsch by the Roman name of 'Germans'.)

The idea that one 'nation', albeit one split into two states, would have two entirely different names for itself feels weird because it's hard to think of Western equivalents. But I suppose this is a result of chance and contingency, rather than an inevitable result of anything much: alternate histories in which one half of France calls itself Gaul or one half of Scotland calls itself Alba are entirely possible and wouldn't dent the notional existence of France or Scotland.

So why shouldn't the two Koreas use different words that have been used at different times to mean Korea? That, at least, is not doing anyone any harm.

China's Nine-Dash Line and Its Discontents

Of competing claims to the South China Sea

Abominable is a 2019 animated adventure film in which a trio of winsome Shanghai teenagers have to save a yeti named Everest. The lead teenager is voiced by Chloe Bennet, the evil foreigners intent on capturing and dissecting her furry friend are voiced by Eddie Izzard and Sarah Paulson, and the film has been banned in three countries because of claims it endorses Chinese expansionism in the South China Sea.

It's perhaps easy for me to say this, over 5,000 miles away at the other end of Eurasia, but this seems like an over-reaction. The controversy stemmed from the fact the movie briefly shows a map of Asia, including nine dashes in the aforementioned sea, each of them marking the Chinese claim on another far-flung but strategically useful island group. It's true that most of China's neighbours don't recognise these claims – view them, indeed, as an act of aggression. But while it's hard to be certain, the decision to show the nine-dash line seems unlikely to be the work of Chinese foreign policy operatives who've cleverly infiltrated the halls of DreamWorks Animation. More probable, surely, is that the film simply copied maps actually available in China because the animators didn't want their cartoon about a lost yeti to be unrealistic. It didn't matter; ten days after its release, Vietnam banned it. When the distributors Universal refused to cut the scene, Malaysia and the Philippines followed suit.

This is not the only such controversy. The 2021 Netflix series *Pine Gap* appalled one reviewer with its 'great amounts of yakkety yak interspersed with occasional scenes of bonking' (one star, the *Guardian*). But the thing that really caused problems was the accusation that, by showing the controversial map, it had 'violated Philippine sovereignty'. Then there was the 2022 film *Uncharted*, banned both there and in Vietnam after featuring a treasure map which showed the dreaded dashes. Or 2023's *Barbie*, which featured a momentary glimpse of a childish map of the 'real world', including some unidentified dashes beside a shapeless blob labelled 'Asia' (that also caused a ruckus in Vietnam). American broadcaster ESPN and a publisher of Australian school textbooks have come under fire, too. 'I'd planned to watch this film,' one Hanoi student told Reuters when *Abominable* was banned, 'but after having heard about that maritime sovereignty issue, I think I shouldn't.' Stop smirking, this is a serious business.

There's another thing that makes those dashes seem ever so slightly absurd: nobody seems exactly certain how many of them there are. Although everyone calls it the 'nine-dash line', the original version of the map which caused all the trouble actually included *eleven* dashes: two were quietly removed in the 1950s after Chairman Mao abandoned Chinese claims to the Gulf of Tonkin, in what *Time* magazine has called 'a moment of socialist bonhomie with Vietnam'.* In the last few years, Beijing has begun including a version of the map in Chinese passports that includes *ten* dashes: the extra one sits to the east of Taiwan, to remind anyone who cares to notice of the People's Republic's long-standing hope of reincorporating the *de facto* independent island.† In 2016, Vietnamese officials refused to stamp those passports, instead issuing separate visas, just to be really, *really* clear that their government didn't recognise the claims shown in this map.

All this might seem ridiculous. What it isn't, though, is trivial. Because, I'm afraid, there's a non-zero chance that this story, too, could end in nuclear conflagration.

The dispute dates to the years immediately after the Second World War. With the Japanese Empire finally defeated, the

---

* This was eventually formalised by a treaty in 2000.

† This had apparently been on the map since sometime in the 1980s but no one outside China noticed until the passport thing.

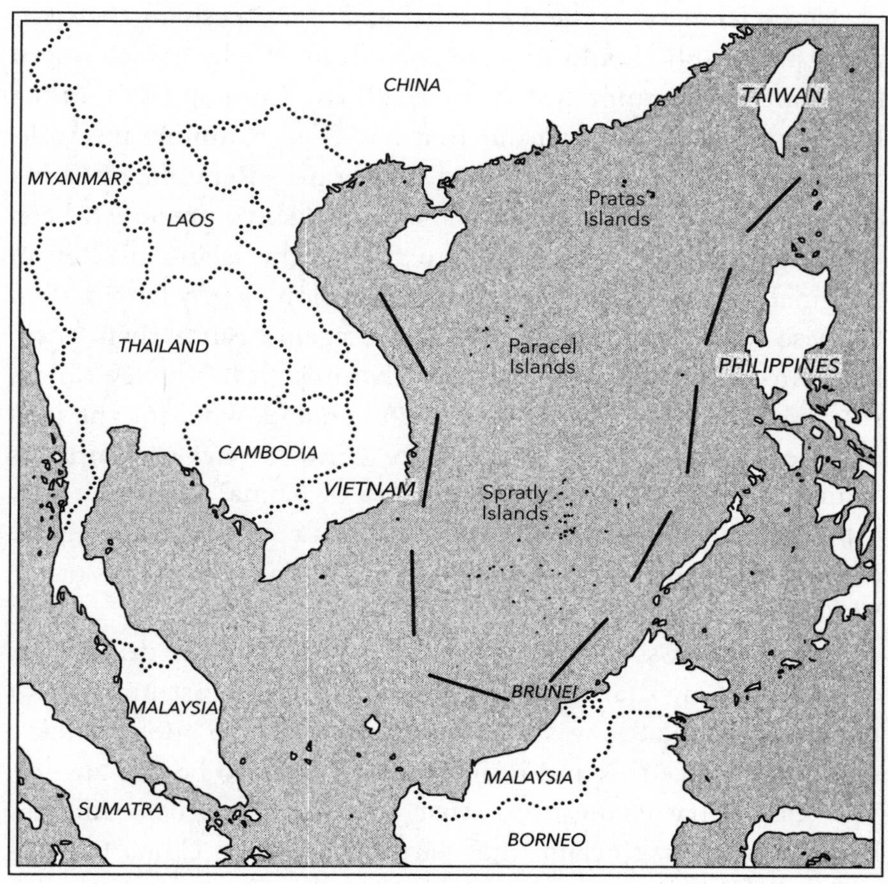

The 'nine-dash line', through which China lays claim to most of the South China Sea.

Republic of China was determined to take control of three sets of islands in the South China Sea: from north to south, the Pratas, Paracels and Spratlys. To support its claim, the government did what governments had been doing to support territorial claims for at least 400 years by then and published a map, including the aforementioned eleven dashes. According to both the Chinese and Taiwanese, Robert Kaplan explained in *Asia's Cauldron*, 'each of the dashes . . . represents the median line between the islands within the South China Sea and the large landmasses comprising the sea's littorals'.

The references to the 'Republic' and 'Taiwanese' in that previous paragraph should provide some hint of why things might be about to get complicated. In 1949, the Chinese Communist Party finally won the civil war that had been rumbling intermittently since 1927 and established the People's Republic of China (PRC). The leaders of the nationalist forces who'd previously been running the show were forced to flee to the island of Taiwan (originally home to an indigenous population, briefly Dutch, then Chinese, then Japanese, then Chinese again). Since then, there have effectively been *two* countries claiming to be the legitimate rulers of all China: the PRC on the mainland, who, for the purposes of keeping things simple, I'm going to refer to simply as 'China', and the Taiwan-based *Republic* of China, with their new capital at Taipei ('Taiwan'). Helpfully for our story, both recognise the nine-dash map. Unhelpfully, they do not recognise each other. We'll be coming back to this.

For the next sixty years or so, the map was no big deal. It was officially Beijing's (and Taipei's!) policy that the vast majority of the South China Sea was actually Chinese, but no one was doing much to enforce this and it didn't much seem to bother anyone. The reason that changed was that, in 2009, two other countries had the audacity to claim that part of the South China Sea was theirs: both Malaysia and Vietnam lodged official requests with the UN to claim sovereignty over their continental shelves.

China objected, on the grounds it had 'indisputable sovereignty over the islands in the South China Sea and the adjacent waters . . . and jurisdiction over the relevant waters as well as the seabed and subsoil thereof'. It also attached a map, with some dashes on it. Malaysia and Vietnam responded by objecting to the objection; so, over the next couple of years, did Indonesia and the Philippines.

This should not have been a surprise. The map of the South China Sea is a mess of competing claims, with Philippine and Vietnamese claims overlapping, and Malaysia seeming a bit iffy about Brunei. But China's claim is by far the most extravagant, unless you count Taiwan's, which is identical but a bit quieter. (One particular patch of the Spratlys is claimed by all six countries, which bodes well.) China's claim goes as far south as James Shoal, a submerged bank around 1,000 miles from the Chinese coast but a mere fifty from Malaysia, and thus well within the area it might expect to be its exclusive economic zone. (More on maritime sovereignty on page 288.)

This is obviously absurd, so it's worth asking *why* the Chinese claim is so expansive. The boring, predictable, *realpolitik* answer is almost certainly exactly what you think: the US Energy Information Agency has estimated that the South China Sea contains up to 33 billion barrels of oil and 14 *trillion* barrels of natural gas. Those numbers are not as big as they sound – the oil is apparently around a year's supply for China – but, nonetheless, you can see why everyone might be getting territorial.

No one is saying that out loud, of course. Beijing's line is instead, simply, that it has a historic right to these islands because its sailors explored and claimed them centuries ago. Whether that's true, or whether it's unique if it is, is unclear – but that doesn't necessarily matter because historic claims not backed up by any form of occupation don't count for much in international law. In 2013, the Philippines initiated arbitration against China under the UN Convention on the Law of the Sea. When the results finally came in, three and a half years later, the tribunal ruled in the Philippines' favour: China had not exercised exclusive control of the region within its claim and thus its 'historic rights' had no legal basis.

China responded in the same way great powers have pretty much always responded to UN rulings – by ignoring them. 'China's territorial sovereignty and marine rights in the South China Sea will not be affected by the so-called Philippines South China Sea ruling in any way,' said President Xi Jinping. What it did do, though, was step up its PR campaign, using state-owned press and, rather more surprisingly, Chinese K-pop artists to push the map, accompanied by the slogan, 'This is China, not one bit less.'* It's tempting to read another reason for China's intransigence into this, to imagine that it's not just about economic or security gains, or historic occupation, but is simply about pride in its millennia-old standing as regional hegemon. That is also, of course, a very good reason for its neighbours to resist.

Even if the reasons for China's claim are understandable, however, the map it uses to back them up is anything but. Dashed lines count for about as much in international law as unverifiable historic tourist trips, and Beijing has anyway declined to explain exactly what they represent: it's not clear how the dashes might be joined, or whether it is claiming the islands, or exclusive rights to all waters between them and the mainland, or something else entirely. In 2016, the marine geographer Wang Ying told *Time* magazine that the reason for a broken line was simply that it was a *maritime* boundary. 'It's not like a fixed borderline on land,' she explained. 'As a scientist, I'd say it's impossible to have a fixed border on the sea . . . the waves in the ocean move.' Lucky we have scientists to help us with such things, isn't it?

This strategic ambiguity is probably deliberate, an attempt to maximise China's room for manoeuvre by not tying it to a specific policy. But it has been attempting to change the facts on the ground, as it were, by building what United States admiral Harry B. Harris has called the 'great wall of sand': a vast land reclamation project, extending previously uninhabited islands in the Spratlys, reinforcing them with concrete and then sticking military bases on top.† This, in an area vastly closer to Vietnam, Malaysia, the Philippines *and* Brunei than it is to China, is a little unnerving. Nor is it the only way the PRC has been attempting

* So far as I can tell, the reports suggesting the slogan was 'not one *dash* less' were a mistranslation. Which is disappointing. What does seem to be true, however, is that the Chinese authorities sometimes refer to the sea as their 'blue national soil'. Cool.

† Fun fact! The state-owned Chinese company that did much of the work on the Great Wall of Sand was advised by the American consultancy firm McKinsey & Company. Small world!

to – this pun is deliberate – shore up its claim. In 2012, its boats were to be found cutting cables laid by Vietnam as part of its energy exploration efforts. They've also been travelling the region with TV crews, to give the Chinese domestic audience a tour of what the resulting programming suggested was Chinese territory.

In 2011, Robert Kaplan wrote a much-discussed piece for *Foreign Policy* under the headline 'The South China Sea is the future of conflict'. The region, he suggested, would be the 'twenty-first century's defining battleground'. Most of the reasons why – competing territorial interests, a superpower beginning to throw its weight around, oil – don't need spelling out: Chinese policy in the region clearly puts it at odds with most of its neighbours.

But there's one thing that could plausibly turn a regional conflict into something even more frightening. China's position remains that, at some point, possibly quite soon, it will reintegrate Taiwan; it's widely understood it will use force, if necessary. The main guarantor of Taiwan's security is the US, which – in an attempt to discourage an invasion – has followed a policy of 'strategic ambiguity' regarding whether or not it would fight to defend the island.

The risk with ambiguity, though, is that, sometimes, it leads your opponents to misunderstand your intent. What if instead of tricking Beijing into thinking that a gun-shy US would fight to defend Taiwan, it fooled them into thinking that a gung-ho US would not? What if the deliberate ambiguity of China's claim to those far-flung island chains had roughly the same effect?

In 1914, a tinderbox of long-standing resentments, rival territorial claims and defensive alliances dragged Europe into war. Kaplan's argument was that the South China Sea poses much the same risk. There is, however, one crucial difference: this time, some of the participants have nukes.

The Uncertain Borders Between Israel and Palestine

The vanishing green line

In 1949, the war between them finally over, representatives of the recently independent Kingdom of Transjordan and the newly formed state of Israel sat down around a map and used a green pencil to mark the border between their countries. The line they drew was narrow – perhaps a millimetre or two wide, narrow enough on that scale to be barely there at all.

The problem, of course, is that the world did not exist on that scale but on one thousands upon thousands of times bigger. There, a line supposed to have no thickness at all was many dozens of metres wide, perhaps sixty at its narrowest, as much as 250 elsewhere. For nearly twenty years, the thickness of that line would create uncertainty about whether the villages, fields and orchards it divided were a part of Israel or the West Bank.

That, it turned out, would be the least of the trouble.

I'm going to confess something at this point: I've been dreading this bit. More than any of the chapters about European colonialism messing up the world, more than any of the other chapters at all.* Stories of territory and borders are always messy and complicated, and I've often had to simplify both geography and history, no doubt opening myself up to angry letters in the process, just to make them fit within the confines of the book. This one, though, is something else. The history of this part of the

* This is of course why I've begun by writing about a cock-up involving a pencil.

Middle East is a morass of competing rights and clashing grievances, of peoples who've been mistreated and mistreated others in return, and leaders who've often found it more convenient to stoke conflict than to work towards peace. The involvement of outside powers hasn't helped much either. The more I've read about this region, the more sympathy I've had for its people and the greater the contempt I've felt for its politicians. It'd be extremely easy to get this one wrong and offend one side or the other. Nevertheless, here goes.

The core of the problem is that this is a region containing two nations – one a sovereign state, one a sort of shadow of one that exists to some extent upon the sufferance of the other. Each contains significant numbers of people who think its entire land should be theirs; each is seen, by some sizable share of the world's population, as less a nation than a problem. And each believes its claim to have roots which are very, very old indeed.

Judaism first emerged in the Levant, probably in the second millennium BCE, and one of the faith's founding myths is the story of the Exodus, in which the Jewish people were enslaved in Egypt until led to their freedom by Moses. The historicity of this story is unclear, to put it mildly, and its importance may lie less in its literal truth than in its resemblance to the Babylonian captivity: the period of imperial domination which followed the destruction of the First Temple around 600BCE, when a large chunk of the ruling class was forced to live in exile until the rather more accommodating Persian Empire came to the rescue in the 530s. (The resonances of this in everything that comes later rather jump out at you.) Other empires came and went, until the rebellion against the Romans in 69CE, which led to the destruction of the *Second* Temple. After that, the Jewish people were scattered the length and breadth of the empire and beyond. The land they'd left behind them became first Christian, when the Romans converted, then Muslim, with the Arab conquests of the 630s.

I'm ducking the issue, aren't I? It's so much easier when dealing in ancient history. Don't worry, I'll get there.

In Europe, where large numbers of Jews had settled, pogroms – violent antisemitic attacks, in which communities were forced to abandon their homes and move on – had been a feature of Jewish life for centuries. By the late nineteenth century, though, the continent was in the grip of nationalism, with peoples beginning to sort themselves into relatively homogeneous nations. Theodor Herzl, an Austro-Hungarian Jewish journalist, who had grown up believing that assimilation with Western secular culture would be the best path for his people, began to fear that rising antisemitism would make this impossible. Instead, he began to campaign for Zionism: the idea of creating a Jewish nation in a homeland of its own.

To that end, in August 1897, he convened the first Zionist Congress in Basel, Switzerland. In his diary afterwards, he wrote that he had just 'founded the Jewish state': 'In five years, perhaps, and certainly in fifty, everyone will see it.' He himself wouldn't live to see it – he died in 1904 – but, as it turned out, that latter prediction would be out by just nine months.

In other ways, though, Herzl proved rather less prescient. For one thing, having come from a largely secular background, he had no particular attachment to the idea of a return to Palestine. He'd considered Argentina as a possible site for a Jewish homeland; at one point, he presented a plan by the British colonial secretary Joseph Chamberlain to base it in Uganda. Many of those who joined his movement, though, were less flexible: it was Palestine or bust.

The only slight difficulty with this plan was that Palestine was not empty: it was home to a group of (mainly, though not exclusively) Muslim Arabs, who by 1897 had been there for a very long time. It was also part of the Ottoman Empire, widely believed to be on its last legs, and if that were wishful thinking before the Great War it certainly wasn't afterwards. In November 1917, the British government issued the Balfour Declaration in support of 'the establishment in Palestine of a national home for the Jewish people'. It added the phrase 'nothing shall be done which may prejudice the civil and religious rights of existing non-Jewish communities' in literally the same sentence, but nonetheless, the line had been crossed: a major power now supported Zionism.

After the war, the region passed into the hands of the British Empire, which governed it under a League of Nations mandate. So the Jewish migration, which had begun as a reaction to pogroms of the 1880s, began to accelerate; after the Nazis took power in Germany in 1933, and European antisemitism approached its horrifying new heights, the numbers grew even bigger. From 1936, the Arab population of Palestine revolted against the British mandate – partly because of fairly standard economic or anti-imperialist grievances, but partly, too, because of the region's changing ethnic mix and fears their country could become the Jewish national home. In 1939, in an attempt to restore peace, the British authorities promised temporary limits on Jewish migration to Palestine – but they also reiterated their commitment to a Jewish state. After the next war, as the full horrors of the Holocaust became known and those who'd survived it continued to migrate, and Zionist paramilitaries began their own campaign against British rule, pressure to create that state was looking increasingly unstoppable.

So in February 1947, the British referred the brewing crisis in Palestine to the UN, essentially admitting that the now exhausted empire couldn't fix it. The following September, the UN proposed two plans. The minority report proposed a binational federal state, a sort of Levantine Belgium. But this, it was feared, might not entail adequate protections for the Jewish community, which was still outnumbered.

So instead, the majority plan was adopted: partition. Slightly over half the land in what had been the Mandate of Palestine would form a new Jewish state; slightly under half would form a new Arab one. Jerusalem, a holy city to several major religions, which both groups saw as their capital, would be run by a special international regime. This did not go down well with the local Arab community, who were still a two-to-one majority, and rejection of the plan soon spilled over into strikes and riots. Before the year was out, in a story that'd seem familiar to anyone who'd been following events in India, Britain – having abstained on the vote to create Israel – announced it would be ending its mandate in the summer of 1948, come what may.

What came was war between the two communities, and ultimately a Jewish victory. The winners were rewarded with the state of Israel; the losers with the Nakba, or 'catastrophe', the destruction of the existing Palestinian society and the expulsion of hundreds of thousands of Palestinians. Some emigrated and became a diaspora; others remained and became effectively stateless.

Let's pause here for a moment to note both how many reasonable grievances and genuine historical tragedies have so far featured in this story, and that the state of Israel has only just been created.

It was that last war which resulted in the 1949 armistice agreement, and the set of borders for Israel still colloquially referred to as the 'Green Line' after that pencil mark. In practice, though, that line is fairly theoretical: while its meaning has often changed, and it's been taken more seriously at some times than at others, it's never really been Israel's border.

At first, the demarcation represented by the Green Line was seen as provisional: an armistice, after all, is not a peace treaty. Israel maintained a distinctly uneasy relationship with its neighbours, including those who'd occupied the two Palestinian territories, the West Bank (Jordan) and Gaza Strip (Egypt). That finally boiled over into the violence of the Six Day War in June 1967. But decisive Israeli victory in that war gave what had previously looked like a pretty vulnerable state control of not only those two territories but also the Sinai Peninsula, Jerusalem and a strip of Syrian land known as the Golan Heights.* Before, the Green Line had not officially been a border; now, with Palestine under

* One of the less traumatic subplots of this period concerns the seaside town of Taba. A reasonably detailed map of the Israel–Egypt border through Sinai, drawn up at the end of the 1967 war, ended in little more than a black splodge of disputed territory where the line met the beach. The Israelis promptly built a hotel in it. The confusion on this occasion seemed to stem less from politics than from penmanship, or lack thereof, but it did mean that, when – one peace

Israeli control, it was no longer a border at all. As early as October 1967, Israel began omitting the Green Line from its maps.

Control, though, wasn't the same as annexation: the populations of Gaza and the West Bank may have had military occupation to deal with, but they were not citizens of Israel and were not especially welcome in the democracy's public life. In 1967, the plan had been to trade the captured land for peace but, as the decades wore on and Israel's neighbours remained hostile, and its politicians won elections by campaigning on the idea of 'greater Israel', and more and more Israeli settlers moved into Palestinian land, occupation gradually morphed into something that looked more like colonisation. In 1987, the war's twentieth anniversary, the disenfranchised Palestinians responded with the protests, riots and other forms of violence known as the first intifada. After seven years of US-led peace talks collapsed in 2000 with no Palestinian state in the offing, a second intifada began – one that involved more terrorist attacks on Israeli civilian targets and came with a significantly higher death toll.

So in 2002, the Israeli government began constructing a new dividing line between it and the Palestinians: this one a barrier of concrete and metal. The Israelis called it the 'Separation Wall'; many Palestinians and human rights activists preferred 'Apartheid Wall'. This was not merely a much more physical barrier than what had come before but a more intrusive one, running far into the West Bank, cutting Palestinian settlements off from one another and adding to the effective territory of Israel. Even so, this was nothing as simple as a new national border. 'Rather than conceiving of it as a political border to solve the conflict,' the Israeli journalist Meron Rapoport wrote for the *Nation* in 2022, 'Israelis understood it as a line of defence against the Palestinian suicide bombing attacks of the time.'

By the 2020s, Western politicians could often still be heard calling for a 'two-state solution', with Israel and Palestine as two

---

treaty and an international court case later – the dispute was finally settled, Egypt gained not just some land but a luxury resort and a $37 million bill.

nations divided by the Green Line. On the ground, though, that line barely existed any more. Israel may have pulled out of the narrow Gaza Strip in 2005, but the real division between Israel and the West Bank no longer followed the 1949 borders; and it was, in any case, a sort of permeable membrane, which, thanks to the Israeli military, was much more of a barrier to one side than the other.

That's not to say that Palestinians couldn't cross it at all, of course. During the Covid pandemic of 2020, Israeli news website *Local Call* reported that the Israeli government went so far as to deliberately breach its own barrier to provide access for the Palestinian workers its economy could no longer do without. (The same article claimed some Palestinians now saw the wall as a way of keeping the virus out.) A return to the pre-1967 borders might require disentanglement of two economies and would certainly require Israeli settlers to give up their homes in the hundreds of thousands.

The government's lack of enthusiasm for such measures is clear not just from its behaviour in Palestine, or its occasional attempts to legislate Greater Israel into existence, but in its behaviour within its own borders. In the autumn of 2022, the city council of Israel's capital Tel Aviv-Yafo began distributing maps marked with the Green Line to its schools and was promptly rebuked by the national ministry of education for using unofficial maps that placed the settlements outside of Israel. (That same body has been rather less keen on the complete absence of Israel in Palestinian textbooks.)

The result of all this has been a growing cynicism that a two-state solution is even possible any more. 'In many ways, the refrain, "I support a two-state solution" from Democrats functions much like "thoughts and prayers" does from Republicans each time a mass shooting reignites the American debate over gun control,' the Palestinian-American Yousef Munayyer wrote in 2021. For his part, the Israeli journalist Meron Rapoport has noted that his government's policy seems almost intentionally vague. 'In many ways, the present deadlock – no Green Line yet no formal annexation – works for Israel,' he argued: it allows control over the whole of Greater Israel without the inconvenience of needing to extend political rights to Palestinians.

And then, in October 2023, as I was finishing this book, the Hamas terrorists who control the Gaza strip launched the largest attack on Israel in the country's history, and the Israeli government responded with one of the most vicious attacks in Palestine's history. At time of writing, nobody can be sure what will come next. Far from this conflict, in the city from which the Balfour Declaration was issued, it's easy to pontificate on a situation of which my knowledge and experience are inherently limited. But it seems to me that any solution has to take account of a number of conflicting facts. After centuries of mistreatment, the Jewish people had as much right to create their own state as any nation, and after nearly eight decades of existence, Israel isn't, and shouldn't be, going anywhere. Neither, though, are the Palestinians; they too have a right to a state and everything that comes with it. Israelis are entitled to security; Palestinians to protest and political rights and not to live under a hostile military occupation. Both peoples have a claim to the land between the Jordan River and the Mediterranean Sea, and any solution that doesn't work for both is no solution at all.

There are options. A one-state solution may not be workable but some kind of confederation, of the sort pushed by the Israeli-Palestinian campaign group A Land For All (Rapoport is a member), might. That would mean two sovereign states based on the Green Line borders but with freedom of movement and shared institutions governing certain policy areas. Israeli settlers would be allowed to remain in their homes but would need to accept Palestinian sovereignty. The plan was inspired by the European Union – but it's also, as it happens, not a million miles away from the UN's minority report of 1947.

Whether this could ever work remains to be seen. The events of autumn 2023 hardly seem likely to help. But it surely couldn't make things any worse.

The Siamese Twin Towns of Baarle-Hertog and Baarle-Nassau

The border as tourist attraction

There is, in most senses, nothing especially noteworthy about the village of Baarle. It's home to a little shy of 10,000 people, which is hardly anyone, in the scheme of things. It's around fifty miles from the sea and thirty from the nearest big city, Antwerp. And, despite sitting atop one of Europe's main political fault lines, the break between the French and German worlds that's been troubling European history for much of the last 1,200 years (see: a lot of the first half of this book), few things of note seem ever to have happened here. It's not even especially accessible to travellers: the motorways bypass it; the railway station closed in 1934, and the line has been pulled up and turned into a cycle path, which is an adorably Dutch thing to do.

And yet, this nondescript village attracts thousands of visitors every year. In 2017, Willem van Gool, chair of the Baarle tourist office, told the BBC that his home had a 'number of shops, hotels and cafes . . . more suited to a town of 40,000 rather than 9,000'. The very existence of a tourist office in a town this size, come to that, feels like a telling thing in itself.

The reason all these people descend on this nondescript town, the thing all those tourists come to see, is a sort of geopolitical freak show. Because Baarle isn't one village but two, a Belgian one surrounded by a Dutch one, and with yet more parcels of the Netherlands buried within it. Baarle-Hertog and Baarle-Nassau – so intertwined that in places the border literally runs through the middle of buildings, so that you can be in bed in one country while the partner beside you is asleep in another – are home to one of the stupidest international borders in the world.

This situation can be traced, as can so many in this part of the world, to a combination of medieval posh people and the Holy Roman Empire. In the late twelfth century, this entire region was the fief of an emperor who was more often than not a very long way away. On a day to day basis, though, things were in the charge of assorted smaller, more local lords and bishops, and by 1198, two rival groups – the counts of Holland, to the northwest, and those of Brabant, to the south – were having a row about which of them owned the area around Baarle.

Such rows had a nasty tendency to end in bloodshed (see: all European history, 476 to date). On this occasion, though, Hendrik I of Brabant found a way out: by fair means or foul, he got the even more local power, Godfried van Schoten, the lord of Breda, to acknowledge him as his superior, effectively granting him rights to the territory, but then immediately loaned it back. Godfried, in effect, got to keep everything that belonged to him anyway, with all its lovely tax revenues, plus some more bits of land to say thanks; Hendrik got the rest of the land, with *its* lovely tax revenues, while getting the count of Holland off his back as well. If the resulting map of the territories around the village of Baarle looked like a jigsaw, well, that didn't really matter because Baarle wasn't anywhere to speak of and nobody in the late twelfth century was much in the business of making maps anyway.

This is the sort of feudal wheeling and dealing that was going on constantly in much of medieval Europe and most of it doesn't matter a damn today. The reason this bit did is because, four and a half centuries later, after the Habsburg family had started passing bits of Europe around its members like Christmas presents, the Netherlands' eighty-year war of independence from the Spanish Empire ended with a peace treaty that put the two lots of feudal territories on opposite sides of a line. Those belonging to the lords of Breda, by now in the hands of the counts of Nassau, would be part of the independent Dutch Republic to their north; those belonging to the dukes of Brabant would remain part of the Habsburg Empire, like those to their south. They were briefly united in a single polity, the United Kingdom of the Netherlands, in 1815; but in 1830, the Belgians fought their own war of independence and the area around Baarle was divided once again. Baarle itself, in fact, proved such a contentious matter that the 1843 Treaty of Maastricht which delineated the border divided it up into more than 5,000 discrete packages of land.*

A number of commissions have since been tasked with simplifying the border, most recently in 1995. But while they've succeeded in cutting the number of parcels of land into which the town is divided by a couple of orders of magnitude, it remains, by any sensible standard, a mess. The Dutch town of Baarle-Nassau, named for its former owners, contains two-thirds of the area's population and 90 per cent of its land. But that still leaves approximately 3,000 Belgian citizens in the Belgian enclaves of Baarle-Hertog, several miles north of the Netherlands' border with Belgium.

You'll notice I said 'enclaves'. That's because Baarle-Hertog is not a single territory but a couple of dozen discrete patches of land, the largest roughly 1.5km² (0.6mi²), the smallest equivalent to a square just 50 metres (164ft) on each side. Exactly how many of these there are is surprisingly hard to pin down: different sources claim anywhere between twenty-two and twenty-six, which tells you something in itself. There's more agreement on the number of Dutch enclaves within these patches of Belgian territory, of which there are eight (though some sources seem to have forgotten the one across the border inside Belgium proper and only count seven).

So messy is this arrangement that the border, marked on the ground by lines of neat white crosses and by plaques showing Dutch or Belgian flags on the fronts of houses, frequently divides buildings in half. In one place, it enters a block through a gift shop and leaves it by a supermarket; in another, it runs through

---

* This is not to be confused with the 1993 Treaty of Maastricht, which had little effect on the Dutch–Belgian border but has been dividing British Eurosceptics from their sanity for much of the last three decades.

the middle of a bathroom, dividing toilet from bath. In most cases, this is less of a pain than one might imagine – however the land a property sits on is divided up, it is treated as belonging to that territory which contains its front door. But in some places the border runs through the front door itself. The town deals with that by giving said buildings two different addresses, one for each nationality.

Messy as the border is, it has not, in recent history, been particularly consequential: the two countries are as close as two sovereign states can be. Although the existence of free Belgian enclaves inside the neutral Netherlands may have acted as a beacon for refugees and thus annoyed the Imperial German forces occupying Belgium during the First World War, Baarle has never really bothered the realm of international relations.

That does not mean that this unusual situation has had no effect more locally, however. Those located on the right side of the border have historically benefited from Belgium's more permissive trading laws, opening on Sundays when good, Protestant Dutch shopkeepers were supposed to be at church. Apocryphal stories abound of restaurants asking their customers to move to the more liberal Belgian side of the room at the hour when Dutch law required them to close up shop, or of banks pushing paperwork from one end of the building to another to avoid tax inspectors.

These may or may not be true – everyone includes them in their write-ups but, well, they would, wouldn't they? What definitely *is* true, though, is that Dutch town planning laws are more restrictive than their Belgian equivalents, something still visible now in the more architecturally diverse Belgian parts of the town. Property owners have also genuinely moved their front doors across the border to take advantage of Belgium's more liberal regime. Those in the Belgian parts of the town have been able to take advantage of more permissive laws concerning selling fireworks, and drinks to teenagers, too.

As fun as all this is, though, it is also a pain in the backside: you try properly maintaining a road or a sewer that switches countries multiple times along its length. It also means that what is, let's remember, one town needs to maintain two police forces and two mayors, one of whom – the Belgian one – is based in a town hall they're not allowed to extend without planning permission from a foreign government. In the 1960s, the mayors even agreed to stagger the time that their two towns' schools ended for the day, to reduce the chance that marauding gangs of Dutch and Belgian schoolkids would spend their afternoon merrily beating the crap out of each other in a cheerily patriotic manner.

The greatest recent absurdity came in June 2020, when the Netherlands decided to reopen after the first wave of the Covid pandemic, even as its southern neighbour continued lockdown. That meant that the bars of Baarle-Nassau reopened but it was illegal for any resident of Baarle-Hertog to set foot in one, even if they lived on the same street, potentially leaving them open to a €250 fine. (The latter's mayor said he would not be enforcing the law.)

On the other side of the balance sheet, though, Baarle-Hertog and Baarle-Nassau have shown that, with the right attitude, it's possible for two nationalities to share a single town, and to do so basically happily, a feat so unusual that occasional Israeli prime minister Benjamin Netanyahu has discussed sending researchers to find out what lessons it might hold for the Middle East. And it does attract a lot of tourists. So, even if the arrangement is very silly indeed, who's to say whether it's good or bad?

The US–Canada Border, and the Trouble with Straight Lines

Northern exposure

The 5,525-mile border between the United States and Canada is famously the longest undefended border in the world. Less famously, perhaps, it's the longest border in the world of any sort. This is a bit of a cheat – it's actually *two* borders, one between Canada and the lower forty-eight states (3,987 miles), the other between Canada and Alaska (1,538 miles) – and if you want a single *continuous* border the Russia–Kazakhstan one, at 4,750 miles, is rather longer. But America likes to have everything bigger, so let's just count both bits and say it's the longest one.

As to it being undefended – that rather depends on what kind of defence you're imagining. It's true that it's not defended by any military forces. And it's certainly a far less intense line to cross than the US's southern border, which is actively patrolled by the good and terrifying people of US Customs and Border Protection, whose job it is to prevent the trafficking of both people and drugs (or, at the very least, to give the impression that someone's doing that).

That is not the same as being unguarded, however. A crossing in inhabited regions will still generally involve showing someone an ID and offering at least some explanation of why it is that you happen to fancy switching countries today. In uninhabited ones, you may be able to avoid the border guards, but

a) who, really, is going to bother trekking miles through rural Alberta just to cross to Montana undetected, and

b) even there, the border is hardly invisible: for around 1,349 miles, it is marked by 'the Slash', a twenty-foot-wide area of deforestation so different to the lands to either side that you can see it on satellite photographs. (Seriously, check your mapping app.)

The US's northern limit was also, it's worth noting, not always a peaceful border. The territories that would one day become Canada were those, by definition, that remained British during the American War of Independence – indeed, became more so after 1783, when British forces evacuated thousands of loyalists from New York to new homes in sunny Nova Scotia. The two territories went to war again in 1812, in an event sometimes known as the Second War of Independence but more often known as, well, the War of 1812.*

For its first few decades, then, the border between the United States and British North America was as contentious and as prone to being both cause and site of conflict – or, to put it another way, as 'defended' – as any other. Defining it thus required multiple treaties.

The first attempt to agree the border came in the Treaty of Paris of 1783, which ended the Revolutionary War. This ruled that the new, international boundary would run along the forty-fifth parallel north, thus following an already established colonial one between Quebec and the bit of New York that was starting to think of itself as 'Vermont'. After that, it would continue along the St Lawrence River, through the helpful natural barrier of the Great Lakes, then along assorted smaller rivers to the smaller Lake of the Woods, 'to the northwestern-most point thereof, and from thence on a due west course to the River Mississippi'. No one involved had actually visited this land. This was to become a problem.

All this gave the US surprisingly generous boundaries, given that it was a tiny, scrappy start-up sort of a thing and the empire

---

* The one when the British managed to burn down the White House.

on the other side of the table was on the verge of becoming a superpower. The new nation included a vast stretch of territory beyond the Appalachian Mountains to which the thirteen colonies on the eastern seaboard did not have an obvious claim. (Nor, to be fair, did the British.) Britain's thinking seems to have been that, having lost the war, it really might as well create a new market for its merchants, by helping the US to boom: as the French foreign minister, the count of Vergennes, is reputed to have put it, 'The English buy peace rather than make it.'

More agreements followed. The Jay Treaty of 1794 established an international commission to survey and map the boundary. The Treaty of Ghent of 1815, which concluded the War of 1812, established that – despite what either side may have felt during any fit of enthusiasm over the previous couple of years of waving guns at each other – the boundary was exactly where it had been to start with. In 1817, the Rush–Bagot Treaty agreed that, despite those earlier bouts of ill-feeling, the boundary would be demilitarised; in 1818, the London Convention extended it, ruling that it would run along the forty-ninth parallel as far as the Rockies.

That's not to say there was no further conflict. The unclear boundaries of the newly independent state of Maine, until relatively recently a part of Massachusetts, caused tensions in the 1830s and led ultimately to the event known variously as the Aroostook War, Madawaska War or Pork and Beans War (a reference to the terrible diet frontiersmen were forced to live on). But despite these names, it consisted almost entirely of rival posses growling at each other: no actual fighting occurred, and a compromise was reached in 1842.

Around the same time, there was some mild disagreement about where the border should run through the vast, northwestern area known as Oregon Country, joint control of which had been established in 1818. The British wanted it to run far enough south that what is today Washington state would be a part of Canada; the Americans wanted it to run far enough north that, though they wouldn't acquire it from the Russians until 1867, Alaska would have ended up attached to the rest of the United

States. In the event, a hugely unexciting compromise was reached: why not just . . . keep following the forty-ninth parallel? Peace had broken out.

You might imagine that, having been drawn up in a rational, post-Enlightenment era, the US–Canada border would be free from the kind of irrationalities we've sometimes come across in the Old World. You would, of course, be wrong.

One problem is that many of these boundaries were poorly surveyed: often, the Slash marking today's border only *roughly* follows the forty-ninth parallel, actually running a few hundred feet to either north or south. (You try walking in a perfectly straight line for a thousand miles and see how *you* get on.) Worse, in a by now familiar story, they were drawn up without anybody actually bothering to visit them. The forty-fifth parallel, agreed as the boundary between Vermont and Quebec, turned out to be some way south of where everyone had always assumed. This caused some problems for those American authorities that had already started building things in what turned out to be Canada (more on this on page 255).

Then there was that whole bit of the Treaty of Paris which talked about a line running west from the northwesternmost point of the Lake of the Woods till it hit the Mississippi. This ran into two problems:

a) No one had surveyed the Lake of the Woods, which turned out not to be a helpful, vaguely round shape of which the northwesternmost point would be obvious, but a jagged thing with lots of inlets, where it was very much not, and
b) the Mississippi didn't actually run west of the Lake of the Woods: its source was almost directly south of it. Oopsie.

The second problem meant that the original treaty couldn't be read literally – a line west from that point in search of the Mississippi would simply run round and round the Earth forever, which was not much use as a border. Instead, in 1818, everyone agreed that the border would simply run south to the already agreed upon forty-ninth parallel, and then turn sharply west.

This was all very well. But when, in 1825, a German astronomer named Johann Ludwig Tiarks solved the first problem by taking it *extremely* literally – drawing lots of southwest–northeast lines on maps until he'd found the outermost, and thus northwesty-est – it turned out that a line running from the newly established northwesternmost point of the lake south to the forty-ninth parallel caused another problem: it left two patches of land now defined as Minnesota attached to Canada instead of the rest of the United States. One of these is a tiny, uninhabited cape known as Elm Point. But the other, the Northwest Angle – or Angle Township, as it's also known – contains roughly 120 residents, not to mention the northernmost road in the contiguous United States, which at time of writing has five stars on Google Reviews. Those entering or leaving the territory must alert the relevant border authorities via videophone booths because it's not really worth having a proper customs post. Of course they must.

The reliance on straight lines has caused similar oddities elsewhere on the border. The parallel which divides Vermont from Quebec runs through Province Island, in the entertainingly spelled Lake Memphremagog. Most of it is in Canada but its southernmost tip is technically in the United States. (Nobody seems especially concerned about this: online discussion instead obsesses over the fact it's roughly the same shape as Taiwan.)

Then there's Point Roberts, the end of a peninsula in the suburbs of Vancouver, which, inconveniently for local administrative purposes, is south of the forty-ninth parallel and thus part of Washington State.* This is especially inconvenient for any American children who happen to live there because the nearest American high school is in the city of Blaine, a forty-mile drive

---

* This, like the Northwest Angle, is a pene-exclave: a territory that's an exclave for practical purposes – because there's a bloody great body of water in the way – even if it doesn't technically meet the criteria of being separated from the motherland by another state.

away. (Any Canadian neighbours who live in the territory have far more convenient options available.)

Given that this is the very last point at which the border follows the forty-ninth parallel before diverting for the last stretch of its journey west, and given that there are plenty of places where it only roughly follows that parallel anyway because of those long-forgotten survey errors, there have been numerous discussions about whether it might make more sense for everyone to simply agree that Point Roberts is Canadian. This would seem, especially after incidents like the 11 September attacks of 2001 and the Covid pandemic of 2020, which meant it suddenly became a lot harder to just nip across even an un-militarised national border, like by far the sanest thing to do. So far, though, discussions have come to naught.

Maybe that doesn't matter. At the other end of the country, a mere six miles east of Province Island, you'll find the town of Stanstead, Quebec (population 2,800). Across the border, and contiguous with it, lies the Vermont town of Derby Line (population 700). Along Canusa Street (geddit?), the border runs down the middle of the road, meaning that neighbours live in entirely different countries.

This has sometimes annoyed US border officials, who worry the town could become a hotspot for illegal immigration (a lot of Quebecois are desperate to get to the US, obviously). So far, though, the two remain essentially a single settlement – residents can even make a local phone call between the two – and their unity is symbolised by a single building. Opened in 1904, Haskell Free Library and Opera House is almost certainly the only opera house ever deliberately built to straddle a national boundary. While the entrance and most of the seats are in the United States, the books and stage are in Canada.

It would perhaps be impolite to read too much into that.

Some Places That Aren't Switzerland

A couple of enclaves in Europe's most baffling country

Switzerland, even more than Belgium, is a challenge to the mainstream European conception of How Nations Work. Much of the continent consists of countries made up by particular national/religious/language communities and even where it isn't, it's generally a fairly easy matter to explain. 'Belgium is the Catholic bits of the Low Countries that didn't win independence in 1648.' 'Austria was kept out of Germany by its own empire and Bismarck's jealousy.' 'Luxembourg just really hates taxes.'* And so on.

Switzerland, though: what the hell? It's got a lot of Catholics but a lot of Protestants too; most people speak German but a sizable minority speak French, and a fair few speak Italian or even the highly localised language of Romansh. Even its sense of being 'The Alpine Nation' rather ignores the fact that there are eight Alpine nations† and that most of its population lives not in the mountains but on its northern plains, which isn't really surprising because people don't generally like to live at the top of mountains.

The full name of the country offers some clue as to how Switzerland happened. Officially, it's the Swiss Confederation, a union of twenty-six 'cantons' (essentially, member states). It traces its origins to the 1291 Federal Charter, in which the rural areas of Uri, Schwyz and Unterwalden agreed to work together to defend

---

* This is not the real reason Luxembourg exists but I have never got over the fact that the Luxembourg City History Museum has an entire room dedicated to the importance of a competitive tax regime.

† Monaco, France, Switzerland, Germany, Liechtenstein, Austria, Slovenia, Italy.

their common interests against those who threatened them.* This being medieval Europe, that tended to mean noble families with imperial ambitions. As the confederation grew, the powers which it defended its members' interests from included the Habsburgs (local lads either thrown out or who moved to Vienna of their own accord, depending on who you ask), the dukes of Burgundy (spent the fifteenth century trying and failing to relaunch Lotharingia) and Napoleon (successfully invaded but lacked staying power).

So Switzerland is, by definition, the bits that the confederation succeeded in keeping out of the hands of bigger powers and whose independence was formally recognised in the Peace of Westphalia of 1648. Long before the map of Europe we're all familiar with began to solidify in the nineteenth century, both the idea of Switzerland and its approximate modern boundaries had been established for centuries. If they appear a little twiddly in places to the distant observer, well, that's sometimes an artefact of local history (Geneva was a tiny Protestant republic that joined the confederation in the nineteenth century to escape the embrace of Catholic France). Often, though, the blame lies with Alpine geography (peninsulas of Swiss territory poking into other countries, such as that around the Bernina Pass, are often actually low-lying land with mountains on either side).

This does not mean that those boundaries are free from absurdities, however. Take the existence of Campione d'Italia, a town of 2,000 souls which remains an exclave of (this'll shock you) Italy, despite being less than 3km^2 (1.2mi^2) in extent and entirely surrounded by one of those sticky-out bits of Switzerland we just talked about. Although it lies under a kilometre from the Italian border to its east as the crow flies, the inconvenient presence of an Alp means it's well over 10km (6mi) by road. And, of course,

---

* The widely used abbreviation for Switzerland – 'CH' – stands for the confederation's Latin name *Confoederatio Helvetica*. This was mainly a way of finding an abbreviation that everyone in a country with four national languages would be happy with, but nonetheless it is very funny that there's a country code used in internet domain names which is taken from a language that went out of fashion over a thousand years before anybody invented the internet.

as your mapping app will remind you, you have to pass through Switzerland to make the trip.

The origins of this exclave of Italian territory are nearly 1,100 years older than the existence of Italy. In 777, a local landowner died and left his inheritance to the archbishop of Milan, which meant the area ended up in the hands of the Papal States. And there it remained, even after the surrounding area was annexed by the Swiss Confederacy during the War of the League of Cambrai in the 1510s. The territory that developed into Ticino – the southernmost, sunniest and most Italian of Switzerland's cantons – attempted to address the anomaly through either land swaps or referendums. The residents of Campione were having none of it.*

If the mysterious workings of the Catholic God explain the existence of the exclave, those of Mammon carried it through the twentieth century. During the First World War, the Italian government licensed a casino in the town, hoping foreign diplomats might helpfully give away state secrets at the gambling table. This clearly went down well because, with another war looming in the 1930s, Mussolini repeated the trick, adding 'd'Italia' to the town's name just to clear up any potential misunderstandings about whose territory exactly this was.

By the century's end, nightlife was the town's main business, local government was funded by the municipal casino rather than the more usual 'taxes', and the town abounded with stories of intrigue and glamour. In one, Mussolini's rival Cesare Rossi was lured from the safety of neutral Switzerland by a mistress promising a fun night. Once there, her handlers in the Italian government promptly arrested him. More recently, celebrity drugs smuggler Howard Marks spent some time on the lakefront; before being forced to flee, he buried a passport in a public garden where

---

* Actually, this may have been a source of regret: in the *New York Times* 'Borderlines' column, Frank Jacobs has written that the town, unnerved by the year of revolutions of 1848 and the growing chaos that would, eventually, lead to the creation of Italy, begged the Swiss for annexation. The locals were keen but the national government, committed as it was to neutrality, declined. I have not been able to find a second source for this story.

it was later found by an excitable German tourist. Throw in the beautiful ambience provided by its setting on the shores of Lake Lugano and it's all very James Bond, only with slightly more fascists and celebrity Welsh cannabis dealers.

The people of Campione d'Italia had, in other words, a pretty nice time of it: officially they were Italian but in practice the Swiss provided most of the services a thriving town needs (clean water, empty bins, working telephones and so on) because it'd be too big a pain not to. What's more, they were welcome to use both Swiss francs or euros, depending on what was most convenient. It was the best of both worlds.

In 2018, though, the casino went bankrupt, which meant a loss of 500 jobs in a town of just 2,000. Less than two years later, against howls of derision from the locals, Campione was forced out of the Swiss customs territory so that it could, like the rest of its country, join the European Union. That meant border posts conducting customs and immigration checks. For a time, it forced the locals to leave the country if they wanted to buy cigarettes, too, because nobody in town had an Italian tobacco licence. In a warped mirror of what Brexit has done to Northern Ireland, after decades in which it could pretend to be in whichever country was most convenient, EU customs status means that Campione d'Italia is now very definitely Italian and thus inside the EU. The casino has since reopened but still, the disadvantages of being surrounded by Switzerland are suddenly very, very apparent.

The decision to reintegrate Campione into Italian territory came, it's worth noting, from Rome. (It seems to be something to do with VAT, possibly a result of the hole in the budget left by the casino's collapse.) One sign it didn't come from Bern or Brussels can be found 200km (124mi) away on the other side of Switzerland. There, you'll find another enclave of an EU member's territory – and this one has been able to remain outside the union.

Büsingen am Hochrhein – Büsingen, to its friends – is a 7.6km^2 (2.9mi^2) chunk of the German state of Baden-Württemberg, where 1,500 people live entirely surrounded by Switzerland. Like Campione d'Italia, it is barely any distance from its nation state, just 700 metres (about 2,300ft). Unlike that territory, though, there is no inconvenient Alpine geography keeping the two apart because the Alps are fifty miles away. The reason this enclave exists is sheer bloody-mindedness.

In the late seventeenth century, you'll recall, maps of this bit of Europe were beginning to look a bit untidy. Swiss independence had been confirmed by the Peace of Westphalia. So had the ability of every prince in the Holy Roman Empire to impose whatever religion they felt best, which formalised the change in the balance of power between states and emperor, and set the empire on the road to that annoying Voltaire quote.

At that time, Büsingen was held by the Habsburgs, a part of the scattered south German territories by the name of 'Further Austria'. The next town up the Rhine, Schaffhausen, was part of the Swiss canton of the same name. The former was Catholic, the latter Protestant, and the same family held many influential positions in both. Which is how it was that, in 1693, Eberhard Im Thurn, the lord of Büsingen, was kidnapped by members of his own Protestant family, who believed him to be hiding the fact he was Catholic. They handed him over to the Schaffhausen authorities, who promptly threw him in jail. Six years and one nasty threat of Austrian invasion later, they grudgingly released him, but by then it was too late, and he was a broken man. (Also, to be fair to his traitorous cousins, a Catholic.)

More importantly, from the point of view of our story, the Austrian authorities stubbornly declared that, as repayment for this affair, Büsingen must never be Swiss. In the decades that followed, Austria sold nearby territory to another Swiss canton, Zurich, leaving Büsingen encircled, but it insisted on hanging onto the town itself, ostensibly out of spite. In 2019, three and a quarter centuries since Eberhard Im Thurn emerged blinking and, presumably, gibbering into the daylight, the town's deputy mayor Roland Güntert was still telling news reporters that, 'They said it would never go back to Switzerland. Never, ever, ever.' That is quite the grudge.

The town has not been Austrian for a long time, of course: in 1805, it became part of the Kingdom of Württemberg, from whence it became German. In 1919, with the Habsburgs without an empire for the first time in nearly half a millennium and thus, finally, in no position to object, the town held a referendum on joining Switzerland. Some 96 per cent of the residents voted yes. Now, though, the problem was that the Germans didn't want to give up territory without getting something in return and the Swiss didn't want Büsingen enough to give anything else up. And so, German it remains.

This has not always made life easy. Soldiers from Büsingen returning home on leave during the Second World War had to leave their weapons at the Swiss border and cover up their uniforms – although, since the people we are talking about here were literally Nazis, it's difficult to feel too sad. Later, shopping trips to nearby towns could involve an annoying amount of form-filling; today, although the town's residents often earn Swiss-level salaries, higher than their compatriots, they also have to pay German-level income taxes, higher than their neighbours. Hmm, this has turned out to be quite a 'tiny violin' paragraph, sorry.

But some of the problems that come from being an enclave have been solved in recent years. In 1967, Berlin and Bern agreed that the town would be included in the Swiss customs area, thus removing the need for border checks. Today, it's politically German but economically Swiss – a model that in 2019, at the height of the Brexit talks, a number of Irish politicians suggested as a model for Northern Ireland. Whether this could work as well in a region of nearly 2 million as it does in one of less than 2,000 isn't entirely clear but, nonetheless, Büsingen's successful status as a German town outside the EU shows exactly the spirit of compromise from which politicians in eighteenth-century Vienna and twenty-first-century London alike could learn.

Some Notes on Microstates

A sort of sovereignty

In 1783, in a development which, by this point, you will no doubt find truly shocking, a treaty included some vague and unhelpful language about a border. The Treaty of Paris, which you'll recall concluded the American Revolutionary War, placed the boundary between New Hampshire and what was then British Lower Canada along a stretch of highlands 'to the northwesternmost head of the Connecticut River'. The problem was that there were several possible watercourses to which this phrase might have referred. So, true to form, the British chose the easternmost option, which gave them the most land, and the Americans chose the westernmost option, which gave *them* the most land.

By 1832, all this had ceased to be fun for those who lived in the contested area, who were paying taxes to both sides. So on 9 July, they held an assembly, organised a government and declared independence. The Constitution of the Republic of Indian Stream stated that the area would 'exercise all the powers of a free, sovereign and independent state . . . till such time as we can ascertain to what government we properly belong'.

Such time duly arrived on 4 August 1835, when the sheriff of Coos County, New Hampshire, pulled together the local militia and mounted an invasion. The good people of Indian Stream invited the government of Lower Canada to protect them; when the British failed to respond, they cheerily agreed to their annexation by New Hampshire, where the town of Pittsburgh, as it is now, remains to this day. The Republic of Indian Stream had been an independent state for a little over three years.

You could write an entire book of such stories – people have – because history is absolutely littered with them. There's Jaxa, a Russian–Chinese border territory founded by an exiled Pole, who responded to the rape of his daughter by murdering the local bigwig, building his own town, and playing the Romanov and Qing empires off against each other for the next nine years. Or consider Cospaia, a small strip of land in what was then the Papal States, accidentally left out of a 1440 treaty selling the area to the Republic of Florence, which nobody thought worth annexing for nearly 400 years. You can find dozens of these things without even needing to consider the madness that was the Holy Roman Empire.

The weird thing is not that such states existed. The weird thing is that some survive. Why, for example, should Andorra, a tiny mountain enclave on the border between France or Spain, have never been swallowed by either? It's all very well saying you were granted your independence by Charlemagne; Charlemagne did a lot of things in his time and most of them aren't still bothering us twelve centuries later. So why did this one, specifically, survive? By the same token, why was Monaco, a small Mediterranean resort town ruled over by the Grimaldi family since 1297, never absorbed during one of France's numerous expansionary periods? Why are these things still there?

There's no universally accepted definition of a microstate but it's generally understood to mean 'very, very small indeed'. Luxembourg, which at 2,586km^2 (998mi^2) is over five times the size of Andorra and 1,200 times the size of Monaco, does not generally make the list. A population measured in thousands, not millions, helps. So does being reliant, to some extent, on another state: although microstates are officially classed as sovereign, they often outsource their foreign or defence policies, even basic infrastructure, to larger neighbours. This surely raises questions about whether they have quite the same sovereignty as, say, Indonesia.

Microstates used to be a lot more common – any independent city state, county or principality in existence before the rise of the modern state system would be a microstate by modern standards.

Today, though, most of the planet is covered in territories of a scale that would have seemed like empires to the ancients, and most of the remaining microstates are island nations, which are obviously a special case. That leaves five continental European microstates which require some explaining.

A 2021 op-ed column by the head of a Monaco-based investment firm – an industry, it must be admitted, with more experience of microstates than most of us – credits 'their ability to reinvent themselves over the centuries'. That may be true, in so far as any state that's survived for 700 years will have reinvented itself a few times, but I'm sure there were plenty of equally inventive microstates that were still screwed the moment Napoleon appeared on the horizon. In the same way, there's clearly political skill in the way Andorra used a thirteenth-century quarrel between the Spanish bishops of Urgell and the French heirs to the counts of Urgell to become a condominium, sort of jointly ruled but also sort of independent of both.* The same could no doubt be said of the way Monaco periodically used the threat of Spain to prevent its annexation by France. But playing bigger powers off against one another is a foreign policy tactic as old as foreign policy itself, and most of those who employed it still ultimately found themselves swamped. Luck clearly played as big a role as judgement.

An explanation that's harder to dismiss is geography. Several of the five European microstates are located in mountainous regions. Travelling to and from such places can be difficult, even impossible at certain times of year, which makes them more likely to develop highly localised cultures and less likely to get invaded. They were often also, historically, poor – mountains are not great for either agriculture or industry – so to some extent they survived because their conquest simply wasn't worth the hassle.

Then there's the power of sheer longevity. Even when these places were rolled up into neighbouring empires, as Monaco

---

* This arrangement persists to this day, with the president of France and the bishop of Urgell being joint head of state. This means, bizarrely, that one of Andorra's two co-princes is elected – just not by the people of Andorra.

was during the Napoleonic Wars, they had long histories and misty-eyed founding myths of the sort that made it sound like they *should* exist. They also had rich rulers with powerful friends who could show up at diplomatic jamborees like the Congress of Vienna and ask, in not so many words, for their countries back.*

But again, there were other mountain fastnesses or ancient principalities which were swallowed by a larger state during one of the periodic redrawings of the map and never managed to get out again. At some point, it becomes hard to escape the conclusion that there isn't a single, all-encompassing explanation for why these microstates persisted when so many others didn't. It's simply survivor bias: the ones we're looking at exist because they survived. Partly because they were allowed to; partly because they just weren't worth the trouble. But also, perhaps, because they were lucky.

The fact that microstates have survived thus far, however, is no guarantee that they always will. They all, to some extent, exist on the sufferance of larger states. For obvious reasons, none of them have significant military capacity and instead rely on treaties with countries that do. (An example, from well outside Europe: a number of Pacific Island nations, such as Palau and Micronesia, outsource their defence to the US through the Compact of Free Association.)

That's one obvious vulnerability. The European microstates may have another, less obvious one. Generally, their economies are built on four things: tourism (people love saying they've been to them), banking secrecy, low taxes and duty-free trade. This reliance on slightly iffy financial transactions has made many of these states extremely rich, but it also leaves them vulnerable to political pressure from distant capitals to deal with tax evasion

* San Marino claims not only to be the oldest microstate but the oldest *country* in the world, tracing its origins all the way back to a Christian colony founded in 301. What Diocletian, who as Roman emperor at the time was under the impression all of Italy was his, might think of this we will sadly never know.

or smuggling: they can be buffeted by expensive scrutiny or regulatory change over which they have no control. Using a foreign currency, which all the European microstates do (Swiss franc for Liechtenstein, euro for the rest), also leaves a state vulnerable because in the event of a liquidity crisis the relevant central bank has no legal responsibility to bail them out. The idea that a country could be destroyed by a banking crisis seems unlikely but it would also, to be fair, be quite funny.*

A couple of tiny states that don't fit this pattern seem worth noting, if only because I find them interesting. First of all, eagle-eyed readers will notice that I said there are *five* European microstates, yet only mentioned four. The fifth is the Holy See, better known as the Vatican, which is neither up a mountain nor, primarily, a tax haven. Its special status obviously descends from being the personal realm of the pope: it is, sort of, the descendant of the Papal States, once the main power in central Italy. In 1870, however, the city of Rome chose to join the newly unified country. The popes spent the next fifty-nine years sulkily refusing to leave the Vatican, until the government of Benito Mussolini granted them their own tiny sovereign realm in exchange for their support for fascism.

Then there's Malta, the smallest country in the European Union. Back in the 1950s, however, it was hoping to be part of a different union entirely, when its people voted overwhelmingly (77 per cent to 23) to join the United Kingdom. When it came to it, though, the authorities in Malta baulked at the required financial reforms. And the UK, which was winding up the whole empire thing and losing interest in stuff like strategic Mediterranean

* This seems as good a place as any to note that the UK's crown dependencies, such as the Channel Islands and the Isle of Man, look extremely similar to the microstates: tax havens with small area and small population, using a foreign currency to go about their business. They do not have full sovereignty and are instead possessions of the British crown. Otherwise, though, they seem just as rich, successful and tax haven-y as the proper microstates. This to me raises questions about whether the full sovereignty of a UN seat is actually worth the bother.

naval bases, decided it'd rather not set a precedent for former imperial territories to join the metropole. So it never happened.

Last but not least there's Singapore, a microstate in area (around 730km^2, or about 282 mi^2) if not in population (it's currently heading for 6 million). The unusual thing about that is that it spent two years joined to other former British colonies in Southeast Asia as part of Malaysia. Then it was expelled, for reasons involving economics, cultural differences and race, and forced to go it alone.

With Singapore now ranked alongside Monaco, Liechtenstein and Luxembourg as one of the richest countries in the world, it's hard to think this has gone badly for the city. And given that the cultural differences between liberal metropolitans and conservative provincials seem to be a growing feature of politics these days right across the democratic world, the city state might well be the model to watch.

City Limits

Some notes on the problem of knowing where to draw the line

The hamlet of Sewardstone in the county of Essex, in the East of England, does not, it must be said, look like an outpost of one of the world's most famous or important cities. A scattered landscape of garden centres, equestrian centres and parks, not to mention the global headquarters of the Scout movement, it looks more like country than city and would struggle to rise to the level of urbanisation one might expect from a half-decent suburb. Yet according to the British Post Office, this is London E4 – the only place to fall outside the city limits yet to have a London postcode.

By contrast, there are vast swathes of suburbia, mile upon mile of semi-detached brick houses, which are, in every political or official sense, in London, but which surveys have repeatedly found people don't think of as such – because they don't have the coveted London postcode; because they feel a long way out and are more easily associated still with one of the ancient counties they were carved out of; because their residents' parents paid good money to leave the dirty streets of the capital and move to Surrey, so they're not going to accept they're still there now, thank you very much.*

* At least part of this, I think, is down to our changing sense of what is cool or aspirational. For much of the twentieth century, the city – any city – was a dirty place associated with smoke and slums; a house in the suburbs and a car in the drive was what counted as making it. That flipped sometime around the turn of the millennium, as the economic shift from manufacturing to services meant cleaner cities, and a generation who'd grown up watching sitcoms set in Manhattan while bored out of their mind in suburbia decided that, actually, sprawl and driving were out, and the real good life was to be found in an apartment convenient for the subway. This is a trend I find fascinating for all

My point is that London is a city with a very clearly defined border. Live inside that line and you are a Londoner, can vote for the London mayor, can access subsidised London transport and so on. Live outside it and you are not a Londoner, and cannot do any of those things. Where the city ends, and something else begins, is well-defined and entirely clear. It's just that it has remarkably little to do with where anybody on either side of it *thinks* that border is.

(All this is without even getting into the role played by the 020 London telephone code, the M25 orbital motorway or the Tube map, that latter of which has long defined Londoners' mental geography of their city but extends much farther to the north and west than to east or south. Best not to even mention the existence of an area called the City of London, which is actually only a square mile of central business district and excludes most of the places that people generally associate with the British capital. There are a lot of possible Londons, is what I'm saying here.)

There are plenty of other examples of places that everyone would assume were inside a particular city – that, to some extent, *define* a city in the public mind – but which are not in fact in that city at all. Officially speaking, Old Trafford isn't in Manchester and the arch at La Défense isn't in Paris. Across the Atlantic, the Las Vegas Strip isn't in Las Vegas, while Miami Beach is not in Miami. The way we imagine a city and its actual, official limits diverge with unnerving frequency.

Until the arrival of planes, trains and automobiles, determining what was city and what was not was pretty straightforward. There might be extramural suburbs, places that lay outside the defensive walls that enclosed a settlement and protected it from passing marauders – but if there were a large number of buildings clustered together, you could be pretty confident that this was a city; if there was nothing but fields, you could be equally confident that it was not. Easy.

---

sorts of reasons but it has very little to do with borders, which is why it's in a footnote.

Even in ancient times this was arguably a bit on the simplistic side. The words 'city' and 'civilisation' have the same root for a reason; the latter is essentially a combination of political organisation, economic surplus and planning, all phenomena generally tied to urban forms of living. From the emergence of the earliest cities onwards, urban dwellers have always been dependent on things that happened elsewhere, not least the vast tracts of farmland which grew their food. From one perspective, in fact, the earliest empires – Akkadian, Babylonian, Assyrian and so on; places I largely skipped over in the history section because we don't know enough about their borders – were really just an attempt to ensure their metropole had a large enough hinterland to draw its resources from.

Today, though, it isn't merely that cities rely on the world beyond them; it's that it isn't clear what a city actually *is*. The area that *looks* like a city, the area governed as such, and its actual, functional geography simply don't line up.

Consider some examples. Paris started out as a Gaulish settlement and/or the Gallo-Roman city of Lutetia, probably either on the Île-de-la-Cité where Notre Dame sits today or possibly just across the river on the Left Bank. Over the next 1,500 years, its inhabitants built at least five sets of walls, each slightly further out than the last, in an attempt to defend their expanding settlement. The last and by far the most expansive of these were the Thiers Walls, proposed by Prime Minister Adolphe Thiers in 1840 and built under his successors to encircle the city approximately three miles from Notre Dame.

These walls were demolished in the 1920s, half a century after the last invasion of Paris and even longer, I fear, after walls ceased to be a significant impediment to military technology. But unlike their predecessors, the Thiers Walls still shape perceptions of Paris. For one thing, their path is marked by the Boulevard Périphérique motorway, as well as the more welcoming Boulevards des Maréchaux which sit just inside it. More than that, though, aside from the two great parks just outside the ring, the Bois de Boulogne in the west and Bois de Vincennes in the southeast, the Thiers Wall still marks the official boundary of the city. Look up the population of Paris and you're likely to get an answer of just over 2 million, less than a quarter the apparent population of London. That's because that is the number of people who live inside this ring.

This is, of course, absurd: Paris is not a quarter the size of London; the two cities are basically the same size. The only difference is that the British authorities count most of their capital's suburbs as a part of the city, while their French equivalents do not. If you look at a picture taken from space when it's nighttime in Europe, you will be able to identify Paris as a single patch of lights. But so far as the people within it are concerned, most of those lights aren't Paris at all.

New York City has a similar problem. The Big Apple started out as the Dutch colony of New Amsterdam, a settlement at the southern tip of Manhattan where the financial district now stands, and gradually expanded northwards. In the early 1800s, with the city growing rapidly in a manner perfectly designed to produce open sewers and a public health crisis, the city council and state government worked together to plan the city's future development. That, if you've ever wondered, is why the tangle of streets in Lower Manhattan gives way to an orderly grid north of 14th Street.

By the end of the century, though, the city was breaking out of Manhattan altogether, swallowing first the western half of the Bronx (the 'annexed district', as it was known), then the eastern half. But the big bang came in 1898 when, following a series of referendums, New York expanded to include the wilderness of Staten Island, the semi-rural Queens County and, most importantly, Brooklyn, the third largest city in the country. The result was the five boroughs familiar today and a New York that included its entire urban area, plus plenty of room to grow.*

Soon enough, it wasn't the entire urban area, though: within a few decades, the conurbation was breaking out of those boundaries too, spreading east up Long Island and north into

* In 1993 Staten Island voted to leave the city again. Everyone ignored it.

Westchester County. What's more, there are places like Jersey City and Hoboken, which lie barely a mile or two west of the original New Amsterdam but which have never been – could never be – incorporated into the city because they lie in a different state, New Jersey instead of New York. They are no less New York City suburbs for that.

Once again, the city's boundaries have simply not kept pace with its actual growth. So while New York, too, has an official population (around 8.4 million) on a par with London, by any definition based on common-sense approaches, like 'counting the number of people who live in this big urban blob thing', it's at least twice the size.

This is all very interesting. (At least, I find it so; if it isn't, my editor will have words.) But does it actually matter? Over and over again, we've seen how borders and the identities they create can lead to conflict and atrocities. A city being slightly the wrong size is not going to do that. The people of London are not going to fight a war over the annexation of Sewardstone.

And yet, these oddities do have an effect, all the same. In NYC, as noted half a book back, the subway system stops dead at the city limits; the quality of transport available is determined not by population density or physical geography, but by arbitrary political boundaries. In the same way, the Paris metro stops inside or just beyond La Périphérique. The *banlieu*, the ring of suburbs beyond, have made do with worse connections to the booming city and thus been cursed with isolation, poverty and crime. In 2016, the French government established the Métropole du Grand Paris, today one of twenty-one metropolitan authorities intended to handle matters that don't stop at the city limits. Transport and planning were top of the list.

Perhaps the rise of these and similar structures, like the 'combined authorities' popping up across the Channel in England, show that many modern cities just won't fit into the sort of neat boundaries we imagine they should. Thanks to modern transport and the rise of commuting, cities' economic footprints often don't look anything like their physical ones. We've talked about two ways of defining cities, the municipal boundary and the urban area, but many urban theorists prefer to focus on a third: the metropolitan area, essentially its commuting zone. There is, after all, functionally little difference between a suburb directly attached to a city and a commuter town with a decent transport connection at some distance from it. Metro areas are thus generally much larger than other definitions of city limits – by some measures, the London metropolitan area consists of much of the southeast of England.

This is all very helpful to those planning a city region's housing or infrastructure needs, but it's not clear it counts as a *boundary* in any meaningful sense. For one thing, it's ever-changing, as new transport arteries open or ever sillier house prices push people to commute from ever farther away. For another, the results may sometimes stretch the definition of the word 'city' beyond usefulness. Every few years, the Western press runs a flurry of stories about Chinese plans for a 'mega-city larger than Britain, with 100 million people'. Closer examination, though, will show that this isn't a city at all but a *region*, its cities linked by high-speed railways and motorways. It has less in common with London, Paris or New York than it does with a 'megalopolis' of overlapping metropolitan areas – like that which runs down the US east coast from Boston to Washington, or the Randstad, which contains the Netherlands' largest cities, or the Rhine-Ruhr conglomeration in Germany. This isn't a city, it's just a container for them.

Oh – and then there's the fact that, just as New York City has refused to be caged by the boundaries of New York state, other cities have the same attitude to national boundaries. And while a Belgian woman working in Lille or a Frenchman commuting to Geneva may be able to nip over the border at will, a Mexican who lives at the southern end of the San Diego–Tijuana conurbation may find there are barriers, possibly literally, to accessing the myriad economic opportunities that lie a few miles to the north.

So are those one city, as they'd appear from space? Or two, as they'd appear to those who live and work in them? Which matters more, physics or politics? While we're at it, the South Florida urban area, what one might term Greater Miami, is 100 miles from north to south – is that really one city, just because there's no break in the urban form, even though no one in their right mind is commuting from one end to the other? If not, where do you draw the line?

The boundaries of empires or nations may at times be hard to define. But perhaps those of cities are impossible.

The Curse of Suburbia and the Borders of Detroit

How badly drawn boundaries can murder a city

Detroit, Michigan, should be ranked among the great American metropolises. One of the boomtowns of the gilded age of US urbanism, its centre is stuffed with glorious monumental skyscrapers, and it gave the world Ford and General Motors, Motown and Eminem. Sadly, though, when you hear the name Detroit, it's entirely possible you don't associate it with skyscrapers or soul or even, necessarily, Eminem. Just as likely, if you have any associations with the name at all, you hear it as a byword for poor government, decline and urban decay.

This is not entirely unfair. In the century to 1950, the population of the city proper increased by a frankly ludicrous 8,800 per cent, from just 21,000 to around 1.85 million. But then, in a way the populations of cities in rich countries are not really supposed to do, it began to slide, by an average of over 10 per cent a decade, until by the year 2000, it was little more than half what it had been. Over the next ten years, it lost a quarter more, leaving it with a population of under 714,000 – well below the 750,000 the city government said was required to give it a viable tax base.

Today, vast chunks of Detroit are all but empty, with as few as one in ten homes occupied; many lots are entirely vacant. In 2011, the *Atlantic* breathlessly noted that 'the city possesses enough vacant land to hold the entire city of San Francisco'; that its main events stadium, the Pontiac Silverdome, had recently sold for 'the price of a modest one-bedroom apartment in Manhattan'; that there were '50,000 stray dogs roaming the streets'. Two years later, the city filed for bankruptcy.

Many factors were involved in the decline of what had once been the US's fourth largest city. One is the contraction of the American motor industry, on which the city's boom had been founded and which had given the city's music scene its name (*mo*-tor town). Another is – there's no way of sugarcoating this – racism. In 1940, the city was less than 10 per cent black. Half a century later, that number was 75 per cent and the city had become a textbook case of 'white flight' as affluent white people headed for the suburbs, taking their tax dollars with them.

But there's another contributor to the fate of Detroit. You can probably make an educated guess.

Detroit began life in 1701 as a trading post somewhere in the middle of 'New France', a sprawling French territory stretching from Louisiana to Hudson Bay. Its name – French for 'strait' – refers to the narrow waterway that links Lake Erie to Lake St Clair, a small inland lake which connects via a river onto the vast expanse of Lake Huron. The city, such as it was – home to a few hundred people, no more – was captured from the French by the British in 1760, then ceded by the British to the US in 1796. For most of the nineteenth century it was a backwater, but this was a time when the US was surging west in a 'It's not like any Native Americans are *using* this land' sort of way, and cities could boom fast. A child born in Chicago in 1840 would, in the course of a fairly reasonable human lifespan, see it grow from a town of less than 5,000 to a metropolis of 3 million by the mid-1920s. Detroit's boom came later but it still more than tripled in size during the first two decades of the twentieth century.

The reason was the arrival of the car – or, more specifically, the man who figured out how to mass-produce them. Henry Ford test-drove his first car on the streets of Detroit in 1896; the first moving production line, of the sort that would revolutionise manufacturing, was installed in the Ford factory in the suburb of Highland Park in 1913. By then, the area was stuffed with motor companies. More factories meant more jobs, which meant more people, which meant more houses.

The result was one of the biggest speculative real estate booms any city had ever seen – in the words of Paul Sewick, of the Detroit Urbanism blog, 'an abnormal amount of building activity, surpassed only by New York and Chicago'. Both those cities, remember, were much, much bigger.

Detroit's boom was also unusually suburban for the age: developers would buy stretches of land on the urban fringe, give them bucolic names like Oak Park or Pleasant Ridge, then chop them into individual plots. Some they'd build homes on; others they'd sell to families who wanted to build themselves. To help sales along, they'd take out newspaper ads with headlines like, 'Profit! Absolute certainty that your property will increase rapidly in value.' This, in retrospect, feels like something of a red flag.

The thing that had generally prevented developers from getting into the suburban sprawl game was the difficulty of guaranteeing access to things that were coming to seem like basic necessities. It was one thing to build a house, quite another to provide it with the electricity, plumbing and streetcar services that its occupants had come to expect. What's more, while cities were mandated to provide a certain level of service to residents inside their limits, much of the development in Detroit was initially outside them.

The only reason this suburbanisation was possible was that Detroit had lost control of its boundaries. In 1909, the Michigan state government passed the Home Rule City Act to streamline the process by which cities would absorb the land around them. If the locals followed the correct procedure – a petition, an election – then no government official could prevent annexation. It was 'an attempt', Sewick notes, 'to put the power over city boundaries into the hands of local citizens, rather than politicians'. What it actually did was to hand it to the real estate industry, who campaigned aggressively for the land-value boosting annexation of whatever they happened to own.

And so, between 1905 and 1917, the physical size of Detroit tripled. That meant vast new areas in which the city government was required to provide services, and that meant spending a lot of money. To make matters worse, where the council was forced to swallow previously unincorporated communities, it was forced to take on their debts, too. The city's leader talked a big game about providing Detroit with concert venues or subway networks, all the things a modern American boomtown deserved. But increasingly, what the council *actually* spent money on was paved streets and sewers for speculative property developments, or bond repayments for unincorporated communities that had built schools for families who'd never shown up.

For a while, all this could be funded by Detroit's issue of hundreds of millions of dollars of municipal bonds of its own. Indeed, the bigger the city got, the more it could borrow, and those newspaper ads assured everyone that it would last forever. It came as a shock, then, when the city's head beancounter, Comptroller William J. Nagel, announced in 1923 that Detroit had maxed out the value of bonds it could issue – was, in effect, broke. He recommended that the city think very, very carefully before annexing any more land.

There was just one problem with this suggestion: thanks to the Home Rule City Act, the city had no power to prevent it. City officials argued that Detroit and its infrastructure were already extensive enough to accommodate twice the population it currently held – 'Detroit does not need more area any more than the average home needs to annex a dozen extra bedrooms,' said one – but the public kept voting for annexation all the same. On a single day, 6 October 1925, the voters chose to add thirty-four square miles to the city – more land than the whole of Detroit just twenty years earlier. In a manner for which it's tempting to find parallels throughout human history, the people of a polity just kind of liked the idea of that polity being *bigger*.

The expansion finally ground to a halt with the rejection of yet another round of annexations in November 1926. But by then it was too late: Detroit was too big for the population it contained and was struggling to provide it with services. Worse, the economy was about to turn. Believing the market was saturated, Henry Ford paused production at his factory in 1927. Two years later, the stock market crashed and the Great Depression began.

The city's overall population would continue growing for another two decades but large chunks of the inner city had already gone into decline. 'Unsurprisingly,' writes Sewick, 'people moved out of disinvested parts of Detroit. And it started long before the city's actual population peak in 1955.' To make matters worse, the federal government's economic recovery policies promoted slum clearance but funding for actual development was restricted to suburban areas; the city could get money to knock things down but not to replace them. That meant more urban decline and more flight to those more fiscally viable suburbs which lay outside the city limits. And as Detroit proper declined, the appeal of moving to those suburbs only grew.

But not for everyone. Many of those new suburbs came with race occupancy restrictions, a legally enforceable form of segregation which barred African-Americans from moving in. This, indeed, was a key part of the sales pitch to the white families arriving from the increasingly depressed inner city: move here and everyone will look like you. Black families who tried to move to the new neighbourhoods anyway would sometimes be greeted by furious white mobs, making it abundantly clear they weren't welcome.

The decline of the US motor industry in the late twentieth century worsened all these problems, of course. After the oil shock of 1973, Americans began to worry for the first time about quaint concepts like 'fuel consumption', and gas-guzzling vehicles of the sort Detroit specialised in began to lose ground to more efficient foreign cars. But both the inability of the city to pay its own way and the pattern of white flight that would see its richest residents move out had begun long before that. And its problems resulted in part from the way the city had been forced to draw its boundaries.

If the wrong city limits are partly to blame for Detroit's problems, the right ones could help solve them. Dave Bing, mayor during the 2013 bankruptcy, advocated for a smaller Detroit, switching off street lights in areas which are only 10–15 per cent occupied to encourage the last remaining residents to leave. (He stood down before he could implement this plan.) Others have argued for a bigger Detroit, so that taxes from the richer, whiter suburbs can subsidise the poorer inner city once again. Either way, there seems to be a consensus that the city has set its boundaries in precisely the wrong place.

In 1805, when the city was still little more than a village, it burned down. The Great Fire, as it's known, destroyed almost everything. This was depressing, of course, but it does explain the city's mildly pointed Latin motto, *Speramus meliora; resurget cineribus*: 'We hope for better things; it will rise from the ashes'. Perhaps, more than two centuries on, it will prove true again.

Washington, DC, and the Square Between the States

Or: why is it that ridiculous shape?

There are a number of weird things about Washington, DC. One is that the street names repeat, with lettered ones running both north and south from the centre, and numbered ones running both east and west. This means that, if someone tells you something is at, say, 3rd and D, or 7th and G, there will be four separate points they could mean and you might want to make sure you get a geographic pointer, like 'NE', too. (This scheme begins at the Capitol. Does that lie at the exact centre of the city? Don't be stupid, that'd be too easy. It's actually a bit to the east.)

Then there's the city's bizarre and shadowy political status. It's an awkward fact that, despite the US's self-image as the greatest democracy in the world, residents of its capital don't actually get to vote for its Congress, even though their city literally *contains* Congress. It's only relatively recently that they've been able to vote for the president.

If you're neither living in nor visiting Washington, though, merely looking at it on a map, then the oddest thing about it is its shape. The District of Columbia – the territory which once contained the city of Washington and is now, a couple of centuries of urban sprawl later, effectively a subset of it – is bordered, on three sides, by the sort of entirely straight lines you only find in ex-colonial territories. To the southwest, though, its borders look much more organic, because they follow the path of the Potomac River. The impression you get is that DC was intended to be a

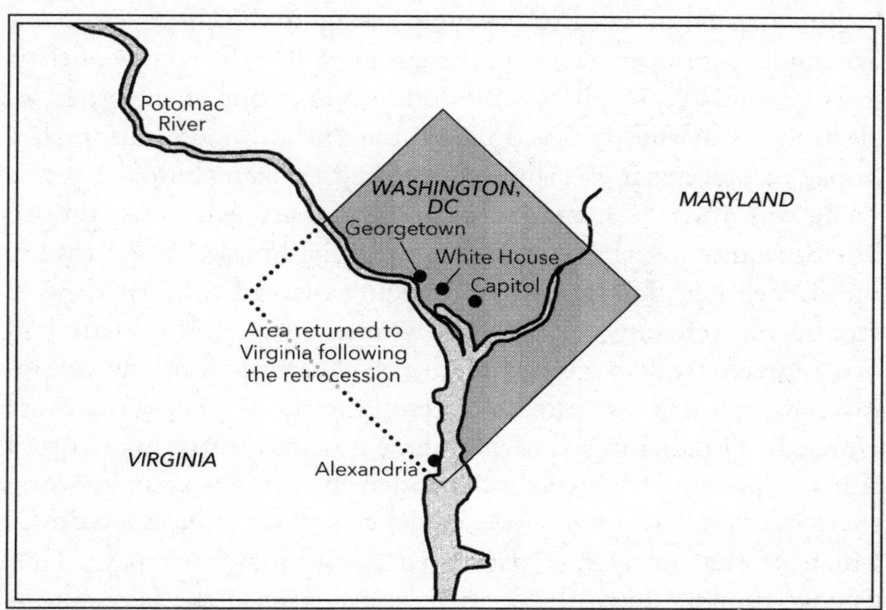

The District of Columbia, then and now. Alexandria County, west of the river, was returned to Virginia in 1847; Washington County, on the Maryland bank, constitutes the US capital today.

massive square, ten miles or so on each side, but that someone took a giant bite out of it.

As it turns out, someone did: specifically, the Commonwealth of Virginia. One reason for that lies in a phenomenon that comes up an unnerving amount in the early history of the United States: the enthusiasm among some of its citizens for the institution of slavery. But another – the reason why it's possible, however unlikely, that this story could repeat; the reason it's still relevant today – is that democratic deficit we just talked about.

To understand all this, it helps to know why the District of Columbia exists at all. Even before the revolution, New York and Boston were on their way to becoming great cities; so was Philadelphia, where much of the country's early political history took place, not least the drafting of its constitution. But the newly independent country decided not to base its capital in any of those and instead to build a new city from scratch. The story of why begins with a mob of furious people besieging the US government, leaving its legislators fearing for their lives. But the source of their grievance wasn't, to pluck a random example out of the ether, an election result they believed illegitimate or an inauguration they hoped to prevent: it was the fact they hadn't been paid.

It was June 1783 and the Revolutionary War was almost, but not quite, over. The actual fighting had ended some twenty months earlier, but talks were dragging on and the British were stubbornly refusing to vacate New York until peace terms had been agreed. And so, even though the government of the emerging new country was already meeting at the Pennsylvania State House in Philadelphia to debate how a new country made up of thirteen previously fiercely independent bits might actually work, the army that had won its independence had yet to be stood down. Much of that army was also owed substantial back pay.* This, as governments down the centuries have learned the hard way, is generally not a good situation to be in when they're the ones with all the guns.

On 17 June, Congress – not yet the body we all know and love but another, technically known as 'the United States in Congress Assembled' but let's not get picky – received a message from a group of soldiers demanding payment for their service and threatening action if their complaints went unaddressed. Congress ignored it, which helped, and two days later, around eighty troops from the nearby town of Lancaster stumbled into town and joined forces with a couple of hundred local militia, before proceeding to besiege the government.

A bunch of delegates led by Alexander Hamilton – who was exactly as trustworthy as that musical makes him appear – talked the mob into freeing Congress so that it could meet and address their concerns. Hamilton *did* hold a meeting that evening but topping its agenda was not back pay for hungry soldiers; it was

---

* The trigger was actually Congress's promise to disband the army so that former soldiers could earn a living while it sorted out their back pay, a job it claimed would take years. Many soldiers feared this was just a clever way of getting out of paying them altogether.

writing a furious letter to the Pennsylvania state government demanding it mobilise its own troops to protect them from ruffians. If it didn't, Congress threatened to move itself somewhere safer and to take the honour of hosting a national capital with it.

Whether because its governor was sympathetic to the soldiers' cause or whether he simply didn't trust his own troops not to join the mutiny, the state declined to help – and so the fledgling US government took its ball away. Congress spent the next couple of years bouncing around, from Princeton to Annapolis to Trenton. When national politicians did return to the city in 1787 to draw up the constitution, Congress remained in New York. One of the items on its agenda was ensuring that the Pennsylvania Mutiny could never happen again. Not, you understand, by making sure people got paid (don't be ridiculous) but by creating a federal district where the government wouldn't be reliant on the goodwill of a state for its security.

By 1789, two sites were under consideration for the new district. One was Germantown, an area so close to Philadelphia it's since been swallowed by it; the other was, ironically, Lancaster, the place the mutiny started. But both the newly elected first president George Washington and the Virginian delegation that dominated Congress favoured a different site, a hundred miles further south. Placing the new capital on the banks of the Potomac, which divided Maryland from Virginia, would allow access to both the Atlantic Ocean and the interior. It would also – incredible coincidence, this – make life easier for any government official who happened to own slave plantations in Virginia.

It was that man Alexander Hamilton who broke the deadlock, through what became known as the Compromise of 1790. Southern senators had blocked his proposal to nationalise the states' war debts, on the grounds that this was largely a northern problem. (If you want to pay down your debts quickly, it turns out, it helps to have an economy based largely on keeping other human beings imprisoned and forcing them to work for free.) But in a closed-door meeting with two Virginians, Thomas Jefferson and James Madison, Hamilton agreed to throw his support behind their proposed site for the new capital, just so long as they backed his plan for the new federal government to take on the debt.*

So the site of the new capital was agreed: a square, ten miles on each side, sited on the Potomac on land donated by two southern states. Roughly sixty-eight square miles of the new federal district would be taken from Maryland, another thirty-one square miles from Virginia.† In honour of the man generally, if wrongly, credited with discovering the Americas, the new district was to be named 'Columbia'; in honour of the president and hero of the Revolutionary War, the new seat of government was to be named 'Washington'. The Virginians – representatives of the union's most powerful and populous state – had won.

But perhaps not *all* Virginians. Those who found themselves living inside the new District of Columbia soon came to regret it because it rapidly became clear that their part of the territory was doomed to be an afterthought. It wasn't simply that the federal government, with all the business opportunities that came with it, was on the other side of the Potomac: in 1791, that government had amended the Residence Act which created Washington, DC, to ensure new public buildings couldn't be constructed *except* on the Maryland bank. Congress literally passed a law to make sure its members never had to go south of the river.

And so, while Georgetown, the pre-existing Maryland town in the district, boomed from its proximity to the new capital, Alexandria, the pre-existing Virginian town, had been cut out. Worse: much of the business it did have was dependent on the slave trade. As the US began the long slide towards civil war, the residents of Alexandria began to panic that the federal government might ban slavery in the district altogether, thus destroying their livelihoods. And because DC wasn't a state, merely a district, and thus not entitled to representation in Congress, they couldn't even vote to oppose it.

---

* This, *Hamilton* fans, is the event commemorated in the musical as 'The Room Where It Happens'.

† Why do these not add up to 100? Because the Potomac is a fairly wide river.

The result was a decade of furious campaigning until, in 1847, all parties agreed that the third of DC that lay on the southern side of the Potomac should be returned to Virginia, in an event referred to by the whizzy name of 'the retrocession'. To put it another way, the big reason that the District of Columbia is today such a stupid shape – why the NW quadrant is so big and the SW so small; why a bunch of things you associate with Washington, DC, (Arlington Cemetery, the Iwo Jima Memorial, the Pentagon) aren't in Washington at all – is because a bunch of local worthies on the Virginian side of the river really, really liked being able to keep other human beings as slaves.* Cheery thing, history, isn't it?

One result of all this is that those in what had been the Virginian side of DC got their democratic rights back. (This would have been a great comfort to their slaves, I'm sure.) Those on the Maryland side did not – and still haven't, to this day. Over the decades since, they've gained an elected mayor and their own council. Since the passage of the Twenty-third Amendment to the Constitution in 1961, they've had the ability to vote for the electoral college that elects the president, too (though not the right, it's worth noting, to have greater representation in that college than the least populous state, no matter how big the city's population grows). Even today, though, the residents of Washington, DC, still can't vote for Congress. Given that there are over 700,000 of them, there are those who think this isn't great.

A couple of solutions have been proposed. One is for there to be another retrocession, reintegrating the northern bank into Maryland just as the southern was handed back to Virginia: the

---

* It's not the only place you can still spot this legacy on the map of the modern United States. The entire reason West Virginia exists is that, when enthusiasm for slavery caused Virginia to secede from the union in 1861, it rapidly became clear that most of those in its northwestern corner wanted to do no such thing. So just as Virginia had left the United States, so West Virginia left Virginia. The new state was admitted to the union, on whose side it fought in the civil war, in 1863. By the 2010s, of course, Virginia – thanks to the sprawling DC suburbs – was an increasingly liberal and Democratic-leaning state. Meanwhile, folks in parts of rural, Republican West Virginia liked to display the flag of a Confederacy their entire state was literally created to repudiate. But I digress.

'District of Columbia' would remain but would be restricted to the land occupied by the actual federal government. Another is simply turning DC into the fifty-first state.

Both plans, however, smack straight into the barriers presented by party politics. Once, full DC voting rights would have clashed with northern states' fear of handing more votes to the pro-slavery south. Now, the block is Republicans worrying about handing the Democrats two extra senators and a congressman or two, or turning Democrat-leaning but occasionally marginal Maryland into a state so reliably Democrat that they might as well go home.

So, at time of writing, at least, there seems little prospect the largely African-American population of the capital of one of the world's proudest democracies will actually get a chance to vote for their own national lawmakers. God bless America.

Borders from a Land Down Under

The oddly straight lines on the map of Australia

If you ever want to look at a map from a parallel universe, you could do worse than David R. Horton's map of Indigenous Australia. We are used to viewing that country – the sixth largest by area, a continent in its own right – as a single slab of land, undivided into individual nations. But the map produced by the Australian Institute of Aboriginal and Torres Strait Islander Studies (AIATSIS) in 1996 shows the land divided up into hundreds of First Nations. It's a reminder that there was nothing inevitable about any of this.*

The boundaries between both the peoples and territories the map shows are inherently uncertain (something reflected in the design by the blurring of the lines between them). But even at a glance, you can tell that some areas of the continent – generally those of desert or mountain – are divided into relatively few pieces. The lusher, more hospitable landscapes of the east and the north coasts, by contrast, are divided into dozens upon dozens of roughly county-sized chunks. Sydney straddles the boundary between the Eora and the Kuning-gai peoples; Melbourne, the Woiworung and Boonwurrung. Even little Tasmania, the smallest of Australia's states, a landmass slightly smaller than Ireland, contains no fewer than eight different peoples.

The administrative map of today's Australia is rather simpler. The mainland is divided into six vast slabs – five states and the

---

* The Torres Strait Islanders are the Melanesian people of the islands to the north of Queensland and are ethnically distinct from the Aboriginal peoples who occupy the mainland. The umbrella term for both groups is 'Indigenous Australians'.

Northern Territory – plus a couple of other, smaller internal territories. The average size of these is around 1.3 million km^2 (500,000mi^2). To put it in context, this is roughly twice the size of Texas or two and a half times the size of France. At over 2.6 million km^2 (1 million mi^2), the largest state, Western Australia, would be big enough to be the eighth largest country in the world in its own right. The states' boundaries, what's more, are overwhelmingly the long, straight lines suggesting not careful surveys but colonial imposition.

So, how did the states come to be? And why, compared to, say, the continental United States (average state size 168,000km^2, or 65,000mi^2; slightly smaller than Uruguay), are they so huge?

Australia's modern borders have essentially nothing to do with the territorial claims of what AIATSIS describes as 'the world's oldest surviving culture'. Instead, their history begins with the arrival of (this'll shock you) the British. When Captain Cook first showed up in 1770, he claimed – or 'took possession of', though the possession at this point was fairly theoretical – the entire eastern seaboard of Australia on behalf of King George III. At first, he named it New Wales but that name was then in its brief period of attachment to a freezing chunk of northern Ontario, so he soon amended it to 'New South Wales'. Whether he meant this in the sense of *New* South Wales (i.e. a newfound land that reminded someone, presumably someone quite near-sighted, of Cardiff Bay) or 'New, *south* Wales' (i.e. a new, more southern Wales), no one seems to know.

Cook's claim stretched south from Cape York, the continent's northern tip, and included adjacent islands, too, but he didn't define either its western or southern limits. Since the Dutch had claimed the western half of the continent and an unidentified chunk of Tasmania ('Van Diemen's Land') as 'New Holland', this meant that nobody was quite sure where the line between the two claims should be. This wasn't an immediate problem – the continent was over 2,000 miles across – but when the British showed up with 778 convicts and a plan to turn New South Wales into a penal colony, demarcation of the two claims began to seem a little more important.

In the Old World, borders were generally defined by physical features such as mountains and rivers, but the people charged with defining the limits of British influence in this new one had not the faintest idea where the rivers or mountains were. They turned instead to a combination of earlier European claims and largely notional lines upon the earth. The royal commission giving Captain Arthur Phillip the power to found the new colony defined its western limit as the 135th meridian east, approximately a third of the way across the continent. Researchers like Dr Gerard Carney, of the University of Queensland, credit this to the Treaty of Tordesillas (see page 66): 135 east was the antimeridian of 45 west, the two lines which had marked the limit of the Spanish hemisphere; seventeenth-century Dutch colonial efforts had generally tried to stick to the Portuguese sphere of influence so as not to open yet another front in their decades-long war with Spain. The British of the eighteenth century weren't that fussed about the Treaty of Tordesillas but they *were* fussed about the Dutch, whom they wanted to keep as an ally.

Within a few decades, though, the facts on the ground rendered much of this irrelevant, and in 1825, the British pushed the border of New South Wales west, to the 129th meridian. It's possible that this was because this was the line specified by the more helpful Portuguese interpretation of Tordesillas and its various offshoots, but just as plausible is that the British no longer cared about any of this, since in 1829 they began settling the Swan River colony on the far side of the continent in what definitely had been New Holland.

That settlement – it's now Perth – would form the nucleus of Western Australia, the only state that was never simply an offshoot of New South Wales. Tasmania spun off the original British colony in 1825; South Australia followed in 1829, giving it its own proud boast that it's the only one of the six Australian states that was never a penal colony.

Two weird things about the boundaries of the latter are worth noting. Firstly, its western border was originally set at 132 degrees east, creating a strange, uninhabited no man's land between it and Western Australia, which was still technically classed as New South Wales. (One possibility is that this was a deliberate attempt to leave a space between the new colony and the convicts of Western Australia; more likely, considering the distances involved, it was because it was basically uninhabitable.)

The other odd thing about South Australia is that, for nearly half a century, it stretched right across the continent to its northern coast, forming what is sometimes referred to as 'the Great Central State'. Developing and defending such a vast, empty area proved expensive, though, so in 1911, the state government handed back its own northern half to what was by then the Commonwealth of Australia. That became the Northern Territory, which was not a self-governing entity but instead run directly by the national government. All this had the helpful side effect that the name 'South Australia' no longer seemed so bloody stupid.

By then, Australia was beginning to take on its modern form. Victoria had been carved out of New South Wales as a separate colony in 1851, beginning life as the 'District of Port Phillip'. Queensland had had a false start in 1846 when it briefly became 'North Australia' (this too would have included the Northern Territory). But so long did word take to travel in those days that it was literally months before inhabitants of the new penal colony at Gladstone learned that, thanks to a combination of grumbling in Sydney and a change of government in London, their permission to break away from New South Wales at all had been revoked. The colony began again, on different boundaries but this time for good, in 1859.

That made, if you're counting or frankly even if you're not, six colonies. In 1901, they federated to form the Commonwealth of Australia. There were a couple of relatively minor changes still to come but, broadly, the administrative map of the new country had already been set.

Relatively few of its boundaries had been determined by natural features. Stretches between New South Wales and both Victoria (to its south) and Queensland (north) follow rivers, with the inevitable debates about whether the line runs down one bank or the other or the middle, how to deal with islands, whether the nearest source of a particular river is actually the source of one of its tributaries and so on. One chunk of the NSW/QLD border, unusually, is demarcated by the watershed: in other words, which state you're in is defined by which way any nearby rivers happen to follow on their journey to the sea. Mostly, though, Australia depends on what one commentator* has described as 'celestially described boundaries': longitude and latitude.

There are a few problems with relying on such boundaries, though. Running a border along a parallel or a meridian is very easy to do from a nice cosy office in London or Sydney. On the ground, in a pre-GPS age when people could not be expected to have the faintest idea of their longitude and latitude, it was very hard to know where the borders were without extensive surveys.

Even those were fallible. The border between Queensland and the Northern Territory, for example, was surveyed in the mid-1880s and is meant to follow the 138th meridian. It doesn't, quite; by the time it reaches the sea, it's 600 metres (2,000ft) too far west. Great news for Queensland.

These were not just theoretical problems. In the early days of British settlement, it was not always clear which colony people were actually in. In 1846, the South Australian land commissioner wrote to the colonial secretary to complain that, 'There are at least twelve or fourteen settlers whose runs lie so near the boundary that I considered my jurisdiction over them uncertain . . . and therefore refrained from interfering with them.' That uncertainty meant taxes going uncollected and laws unenforced.

Eventually, a temporary boundary was laid down but this, predictably, turned out to be wrong, by about two miles, so the South Australian government tried to get the boundary moved. The result was a lengthy legal process in which some judges

---

* Gerard Carney again: his 2013 lecture, 'The Story behind the Land Borders of the Australian States – A Legal and Historical Overview', was invaluable in writing this chapter.

argued that governors on the ground shouldn't be allowed to overrule the naturally occurring meridians, while others replied that this would logically mean moving a boundary every time surveying technology improved, and that this would be stupid. After several years of this sort of thing, pragmatism broke out: today, the country's courts generally accept the fact that imperfections in the work of nineteenth-century surveyors is not reason enough to keep shoving boundaries around the place willy-nilly and disrupting the rights of actual people.

Or, at least, the rights of actual *white* people. At no point in this process, you will notice, has anyone mentioned those 500 or so Aboriginal groups.

A couple of other oddities are worth noting before we dive into something else entirely. First, those 'other, smaller internal territories' I mentioned. The major one of these is the Australian Capital Territory (ACT), a roughly Luxembourg-sized chunk of land that houses the capital at Canberra. This was carved out of New South Wales in 1911 for roughly the same reasons that the District of Columbia was carved from Maryland and Virginia: to ensure that no state could gain advantage from housing the new, planned capital, and that it would be governed directly by the Commonwealth. In 2022, the ACT began talks with the surrounding state about the acquisition of roughly 1.3 square miles of farmland known as Parkwood, which had remained part of New South Wales despite the path of a river meaning it was only accessible from within the ACT. The smaller territory planned to build a housing estate on it. This would be the first change in Australia's internal borders since 1915, when another, even smaller territory was carved out of NSW.

That was the Jervis Bay Territory, frequently, but wrongly, assumed to be a part of the ACT as it grew out of the same process. Just as the new Commonwealth was thought to need control of its own capital, so it was decided it would need its own port. This was a problem, however, because all the sites considered for the new capital were a bloody long way from the sea and the state of New South Wales didn't want to give up that much land. In the end, the state ceded both the territory for the ACT, around ninety-three miles inland, and a chunk of southeast Australian coastline, roughly a hundred miles south of Sydney and home to a couple of hundred people. Although ACT laws apply in Jervis Bay, it remains a separate territory and since the ACT became self-governing in 1989, Jervis Bay has been governed directly by assorted departments of the federal government.

Last but not least there's the matter of a vast chunk of territory that isn't in Australia at all, although it could have been. In the earliest days of British settlement, the country's eastern neighbour New Zealand was informally governed as part of New South Wales, despite being an implausibly great distance from it. That's because the original colony, as set out in 1788, included the entire eastern seaboard of the continent and 'all the islands adjacent in the Pacific Ocean'. The problem with this system, though, was that it turned New Zealand into a sort of lawless wild east, where European mercenaries could do what they wanted while missionaries wailed and the authorities in distant Sydney were helpless to stop it. (In one high-profile case, the crew of the brig *Elizabeth*, under Captain John Stewart, helped one lot of Māori slaughter another lot of Māori, in exchange for some flax. They weren't tried for murder because no one could work out who had jurisdiction.) Eventually, the British government decided to formally establish New Zealand as its own colony, which, for some reason, meant bringing it into the legal system as an official part of New South Wales in 1840, then spinning it off the following year.

Six decades later, when the Australian colonies decided to federate they invited New Zealand to join them, but there were multiple factors against union. New Zealand's leaders preferred the idea of having their own country. Its people, thanks to the islands' lack of history as a penal colony, saw themselves as superior. Most of all, there was the fact that approximately 1,200 miles of open sea lay between the two countries. This is approximately the distance that separates London from Albania.

Nonetheless, the unusual clause six of the Australian constitution specifically gives New Zealand the right to join the Commonwealth. It is unlikely the two countries will become one but, legally speaking, the door remains open.

Some Accidental Invasions

Or: why do the Swiss keep bombing Liechtenstein?

In our tour of Europe's microstates (see page 217), I rather skipped over the Principality of Liechtenstein, which is a shame because it's one of Europe's most fascinatingly bizarre nations. A tax haven and winter sports destination, it's home to just 40,000 people and occupies a landmass of around just over 160km^2 (62mi^2). (To put that in context, it's slightly bigger than the New York City borough of Staten Island but slightly smaller than Brooklyn.) It was a part of the Holy Roman Empire, then of the German Confederation and was then tied to the Austrian Empire. By the mid-twentieth century, though, it had somehow ended up attached to neither Germany nor Austria, but stubbornly independent.

Like most microstates, what's more, it's among the few countries on the planet not to maintain its own military. It did have one, once – its last engagement was the 1866 Austro-Prussian War, to which the principality sent eighty men; eighty-one returned, which is a mark of the terror the Liechtenstein war machine could rain down on its enemies* – but not long after that, its parliament decided it no longer wished to fund such things and disbanded the army. Since then, the defence of Liechtenstein's sovereignty has been largely a matter of working closely with bigger countries. The country's four railway stations are part of the Austrian Federal Rail Network; its buses, customs union, currency and patent system are all joined with Switzerland. A key goal of

* The eighty-first man appears to have been an Austrian liaison officer, which in some ways is a shame because the version of this story in which they just made a friend is far funnier.

Liechtensteiner foreign policy down the decades, then, has been maintaining harmonious relations with its neighbours.

This is from some perspectives a problem because one of them keeps invading or bombing it.

To be fair to Switzerland – for it is that terrifying military junta of which I am speaking – this seems to be an accident, albeit an accident happening with the sort of frequency that might well have Liechtenstein's friends staging an intervention and asking if everything is definitely all right at home. The first such incident – or, at least, the first to have made the English-language media, which may not be the same thing – seems to have been in October 1968, when Swiss soldiers practising their firing techniques accidentally lobbed five mortar bombs across the border two miles away. They landed on the picturesque ski resort of Malbun: nobody was hurt but some chairs in a restaurant garden had had better weeks.

For nearly eight years after that, all was quiet on the Alpine front, until one night in August 1976, shortly before midnight, the Swiss arrived in force, with seventy-five soldiers in steel helmets marching into the hamlet of Iradug with no fewer than fifty horses. The cause this time seems to have been a wrong turn at a junction, around a quarter of a mile back. The Liechtensteiners offered the invaders drinks but the troops, presumably fearing what their senior officers and the Swiss Defence Ministry might say, executed a rapid retreat.

And so it's continued. In December 1985, the Swiss army decided to go ahead with another missile-based training exercise despite a howling winter storm. Nobody was hurt then either, but, following a short bombardment, a patch of Liechtenstein forest caught light, resulting in significant damage to the local wildlife, a lengthy diplomatic dispute and, after some grumbling about the possibility it was the fault of dodgy missiles rather than Swiss incompetence, a compensation payment. Then, in October 1992, officers ordered some cadets to set up an observation post in an area called Triesenberg. They'd apparently forgotten that Triesenberg was on sovereign foreign soil and therefore not the sort of place you're meant to build observation posts on.

The biggest invasion though, by troop numbers if not by diplomatic fallout, was the most recent. In March 2007, a commander conducting a (yes, another) training exercise in bad weather led 171 troops more than 2km (1.2mi) into Liechtenstein before realising his mistake and leading them out again. The Liechtensteiners, who only found out when their invader apologised, seemed remarkably unperturbed. 'It's not like they invaded with attack helicopters,' said one. That is, by my count, two aerial bombardments and three land invasions.

Why does this keep happening? One reason is surely hinted at by the number of these incidents involving training exercises. The Swiss army operates conscription, which means a regular flow of teenagers blundering about the Alps without really knowing what they're doing. They're thus liable to accidentally stumble straight over the second reason: the entirely open border which runs for over 40km (25mi) between the two countries. For most of that length, to be fair, the fact you'd left Switzerland would be pretty obvious from the fact you'd ceased to be on a mountain or had fallen in the Rhine. But between the existence of bridges and the fact that several kilometres of border are free of all such obvious features, there is still ample opportunity for the go-getting Swiss army cadet to do some accidental invading.

My natural literary instinct is to begin this paragraph with something along the lines of 'You'd think this would be an isolated incident . . .' But having read this far into the book, you are of course thinking no such thing. You're thinking that there are probably loads more examples of this sort of cock-up in international relations, and you would be right.

Some of these are similar to the Swiss army strife detailed above: one basically friendly nation mistakenly putting a foot on the wrong side of a border, some awkward apologies, no harm done. In 2002, for example, Britain accidentally invaded a close European ally, when a troop of thirty Royal Marines on (yes) a training exercise stormed the beach in the Spanish town of La Linea. They'd mistaken it for the mildly contested but nonetheless British territory of Gibraltar. This caused at least some raising of eyebrows among the locals, who observed to the *Guardian* that the real Gibraltar was 'easily recognisable because it had a 1,398ft high rock sticking out of it'. Nonetheless, despite the fact that Spain has been trying to get the British to give said rock back for three centuries now, Britain and Spain are basically friends and the incident didn't go any further.

Other such incidents have been greeted with rather less good humour. An internal review which found that the Australian navy had a nasty habit of accidentally breaching Indonesian territorial waters was greeted in Indonesia like, well, exactly like you'd expect a report announcing that a foreign military kept invading you would be greeted. (Noting that literally knowing where they are is one of the things modern naval vessels have got pretty good at by now, an Indonesian government spokesperson sniffed, 'It was baseless for them to say that what happened was unintentional or a form of ignorance.')

Then there was the time in 2017 when heavy rains caused a South American river to slightly change its course, which meant that Venezuelan troops engaged on routine patrols inadvertently wandered across an established international boundary and set up camp on a sovereign Colombian banana plantation. This led to a war of words about 'falsehoods' and 'conspiracies', a bit of a row about whether the border was defined by the river (which could move) or its historic course (which could not) and, one imagines, a lot of worry on the part of the banana farmer.

And then there was the time a couple of officers from the Police Service of Northern Ireland – an arm of the British state – wandered a few dozen metres over the border into the Republic of Ireland, set up a checkpoint and started stopping cars on someone else's soil. This was in 2010, over a decade after the Good Friday Agreement had settled relations on that most fractious of borders – in part by decreeing that it shouldn't have things like checkpoints any more – so it didn't cause the chaos one might have feared in days gone by. It did, though, give Sinn Féin politicians on both sides of the border an excuse to complain about the overbearing British state.

As it happens, popping over to your neighbour's country and starting to build is something else that seems to happen with alarming frequency. Remember the issue on the Quebec–Vermont border, when it turned out that the forty-fifth parallel wasn't where everyone believed it to be? Well, in 1816, with the War of 1812 and the burning of the White House still fresh in the memory, the American military started building a massive defensive fort on what turned out to be British-Canadian soil. They stopped again once they realised their mistake. 'Fort Blunder' was finally completed after all parties agreed to move the border in 1842, even though by then the terrifying threat of Anglo-Canadian invasion had receded somewhat.

China tried a similar trick in 2017, sending its military to start building a road on land that the rulers of the tiny Himalayan kingdom of Bhutan were pretty sure was theirs. The fact it took a confrontation with not only Bhutan but Indian troops to resolve that one suggests it's at least possible this was not an accidental invasion at all.

Incidentally, the resulting confrontation between Chinese and Indian troops involved 'jostling': literally banging chests together in an attempt to force each other backwards. The idea soldiers from the world's two largest countries are facing off in the low-tech manner more familiar from nature documentaries than modern warfare seems amusing until you realise that

a) the decision not to arm either set of border guards was an entirely deliberate choice, because
b) border incidents involving guns have a nasty habit of escalating, and
c) escalating is something you really want to avoid when the powers involved are both
    i) massive and
    ii) nuclear-armed.

At which point, the whole 'jostling' thing doesn't seem quite so funny. The Liechtensteiners must be grateful that the Swiss do not, thus far, have the bomb.

Costa Rica, Nicaragua and the 'Google Maps War'

One invasion that probably wasn't an accident but also might not have been an invasion

Oddly enough, the most infamous accidental invasion of all time might not have been an accident at all. The incident, in which Nicaragua invaded a remote corner of Costa Rica, leaving the two Central American minnows on the brink of war, was referred to by much of the world's press as 'the Google Maps war'. This was terribly unfair because it's entirely possible that Google Maps had remarkably little to do with it.

In October 2010, the Nicaraguan government sent fifty soldiers to a remote corner of its country hard by the Costa Rican border and the Atlantic coast, to dredge a 33km (20.5mi) stretch of the Rio San Juan. This would not, in the normal course of events, have been very invasion-y, had it not been for the fact that there was some debate over whether this actually *was* a remote corner of Nicaragua. The Costa Ricans maintained that it was theirs and that the Nicaraguans were invading. The Nicaraguans, you'll be shocked to learn, disagreed, and replied that actually it was the Costa Ricans who had been invading *their* territory. 'We cannot invade our own territory,' its vice president, Jaime Morales Carazo, said, which was true but also kind of missed the point.

Costa Rica was having none of this and sent seventy police officers – the country has no military, apparently because that way you can avoid having military coups – and appealed to the Organisation of American States for a resolution. 'This is not a border problem,' said the Costa Rican president, Laura Chinchilla. 'It is the invasion of one nation to another.'

A majority of the thirty-five members of OAS voted in favour of a resolution calling on the two neighbours to meet before the end of November and to refrain from deploying armed forces. With the distancing effects of both geography and time, this sounds reasonable enough – accidents do happen, as should be obvious by now, and throwing armed troops into the mix is rarely a recipe for happiness. The OAS seemed to be doing a sterling job as a local mediator.

Alas, one person who didn't think this sounded reasonable was the Nicaraguan president Daniel Ortega, who accused the organisation of having 'completely killed the possibility of dialogue'. This is strange, given that all it had done was, er, call for dialogue. Ortega refused to withdraw his troops, ignored the OAS resolution on the grounds that he didn't believe the OAS had jurisdiction and also, in a 'my dad's bigger than your dad' sort of a way, announced his intention to file a claim with the International Court of Justice.*

The row went on for several more years and, frankly, has as many twists and turns as the ever-shifting river the Nicaraguans wanted the right to navigate, but the ultimate end was that very little actually changed. There was no war, thankfully; but eventually the ICJ ruled that the disputed territory which Costa Rica had effectively been managing was, in fact, Costa Rican. By way of compensation, Nicaragua was ordered to pay a fine of $378,890.59. That curiously specific fine is also surprisingly small, which highlights the fact this story is not really very important.

The only reason it got as much attention as it did was because of the explanation that Edén Pastora, the Nicaraguan commander on the ground, gave for his actions. He said he had decided

---

* Ortega went on to accuse five of his neighbours, including Mexico, Colombia and Honduras, of having been influenced by their stance on the region's drugs trade. That December, the Spanish newspaper *El País* went on to report on cables leaked by Wikileaks, which showed that Ortega and his party had received campaign contributions from drugs traffickers in exchange for freeing prisoners. This does rather suggest that their stance on the drugs trade was certainly influencing *someone* in this story.

where to tell his men to dredge based on the international border shown on a certain popular online mapping application. That was all everyone needed. 'Google Nicaraguan map error threatens to escalate into regional dispute,' thundered the *Guardian*. 'An embarrassing error on Google Maps has been blamed for Nicaragua's accidental invasion of Costa Rica,' reported *Wired*.

It's not that those headlines were untrue; those things had happened, Google itself admitted the error, and said, in not so many words, that it was completely insane that any sovereign state would rely on its data to determine their own borders. But it wasn't the whole story. It wasn't even the whole of Pastora's quote. He also mentioned an 1858 border treaty, a process of arbitration by US president Grover Cleveland that came thirty years later and another clarification that followed nine years after that. What had actually happened, argued Frank Jacobs in his 'Borderlines' column in the *New York Times*, was that 'Google Maps' imprecision' had 'reignited a long-standing border dispute that, with a few miscalculations, could have led to a real war'.

That dispute dates back to the early nineteenth century, long before Google, long, even, before the very large number from which it took its name.* After the region achieved independence – from Spain in 1821 and then again, in 1823, from the short-lived First Mexican Empire – Nicaragua and Costa Rica alike became provinces of the Federal Republic of Central America. A certain amount of shuffling of deckchairs often accompanies the creation of new nations and, true to form, in the mid-1820s, a trio of Nicaragua's border towns voted to jump ship to its southern neighbour, taking 11,000 square miles of territory with them.

The problem was that there was no formal legal definition of where those towns ended. And two decades later, Costa Rica and Nicaragua were no longer neighbouring provinces of a single state but sovereign entities. Suddenly it rather mattered where one ended and the other began. Treaties were repeatedly drawn up to

* The googol, the number written as 1 followed by 100 zeroes, or 10^{100}, was invented by a nine-year-old in 1920 and first appeared in a book in 1940.

solve the problem, but none were ratified by both parties and it took decades for a border to finally be agreed. Even when it was, in the Cañas-Jerez Treaty of 1858, tensions remained and repeated international arbitration was required.

One complicating factor was that, although part of the border officially runs along the right bank of the Rio San Juan, effectively handing it to Nicaragua, Costa Rica has the right to navigate it. This feels like one of those messy compromises designed to leave everyone only a bit unhappy. Another is that that river has an annoying habit of changing its path, and moving, gradually, northwards.

So which is the 'correct' border? The river as it is today – which the Costa Ricans favour, not unnaturally, since it means that a chunk of Nicaraguan territory has since become Costa Rica? Or the river as it was in the nineteenth century – which the Nicaraguans, equally understandably, preferred? Google, relying on US State Department data, went with the latter. That was enough to give President Ortega's government an excuse to send Pastora's party out to start dredging a silted-up channel in the hope of fixing the reality on the ground, which is where we came in.*

In other words, the problem was not that Google had misrepresented a universally recognised border; the problem was that the border was not universally recognised at all. Google had messed up, sure, but it hadn't done anything as simple as showing the wrong border when the right one was just over there. There *was* no right answer. Google's mistake had been to suggest certainty where none existed.

---

* In 1982, in the case of Hazlett v Presnell, the High Court of Australia came up with a useful rule for what to do with a river boundary when the course of that river changes. Where the change occurs as part of a gentle process of change ('gradual and imperceptible erosion and accretion'), then the boundary will continue to follow the river's new course. Where it occurs suddenly as an 'avulsion' – a word meaning 'fracture', mostly found in reference to bones – then it probably doesn't. This strikes me as an excellent rule that could benefit political authorities the world over, so it's a shame the High Court of Australia has no jurisdiction over the rest of the planet.

Why, then, did the tech giant get the blame? One reason is simply that its maps were, as it admitted, on this occasion, wrong. But another must be that 'Google Maps sparks border dispute' is an interesting, clickable story for the internet age, in a way that 'Two small nations you're probably not fussed about continue centuries-old row about some sand' is not.

And then there's the fact that Google Maps and its competitors really are on the frontline when it comes to border disputes these days.

The Mapmaker's Dilemma

Some notes on the challenges facing online cartographers

In late February 2014, Russia invaded the Ukrainian oblast of Crimea. A few weeks later, it announced that the area was now an 'autonomous republic of the Russian Federation'. At time of writing, the sequel to that incursion, the full-scale invasion of Ukraine that began in early 2022, is still going on and much of the smaller country is still being euphemistically described as 'contested territory', so I don't want to make too many assumptions about how its borders, or indeed anything else, may look by the time this book comes out.* Let us turn instead to the problems such contested territories pose to the world's online cartographers.

In the wake of that first invasion, back in 2014, the *Guardian* technology writer Alex Hern noted that Google had begun presenting a very different view of the region and its boundaries to people looking at its maps from different territories. Those viewing the Ukrainian version of the company's website would see a gentle dotted line between the Crimean Peninsula and Ukraine's Kherson oblast immediately to its north, representing the fact this was an administrative border within a single country. Those who used the Russian version of the same site to look at the area would instead see the same border represented by a solid line – an international border, not an internal one, and thus suggesting Crimea was not part of Ukraine. And the rest of us? We got something in between, a broken line rather than a dotted one. To the inhabitants of the world's roughly 192 other countries, if not to

* Partial exception: the assumption inherent in writing any book that the world will not have dissolved in nuclear fire by the time it's due to be published.

the combatants, Google was happy to admit that this border was disputed.

What was happening here? An understandable, if weaselly, desire to suck up to local users? Corporate cowardice in the face of Russian aggression? Well, capitalism being what it is, both those things, probably. But there may be something else going on, too. In 2014, Google had offices in both Russia and Ukraine (the latter seems since to have closed), which meant local staff, who are likely to have their own views regarding the 'correct' border, and who could, more to the point, face legal or political consequences that the company's bosses, safe in Silicon Valley, would not. Given that duty of care, what else was a multinational to do? Reflecting a state's views about its own border was not merely a matter of reflecting local niceties: not doing so risked breaking local laws, threatening its operations, even endangering its staff.

This situation is not unique: Russia is hardly the only country to take its borders and view of the world extremely seriously. In 2016, the government of India drafted a law that would have meant fines of up to 1 billion rupees ($12.2 million) for anyone found to be publishing 'wrong or false topographic information' about the country's disputed borders with Pakistan and China. The law was never passed but the Indian version of Google Maps obligingly shows Indian users the government-approved version of the country's borders all the same. This is perhaps not surprising. Two years earlier, the tech giant's top geographer Ed Parsons had told the *Independent*: 'They could lock up our staff in India.'

If this problem is not unique to one region, though, it is unique to one time: the first moment in history in which everyone is looking at the same maps and expecting them to reflect their own worldview. Once upon a time, maps were a relatively local sort of affair, produced in particular places for particular markets. So important were they to state formation and colonialism, and so costly and resource-intensive was the research required, that cartography tended to be the preserve of governments. The oldest national mapping agency in the world, Britain's Ordnance

Survey, started out in 1747 as an arm of the military, mapping the Scottish Highlands to prepare for possible uprisings. Even in the twentieth century, as the role of the private sector grew, you were still most likely to encounter a map produced in and aimed at a particular market; you would know, when you looked at an atlas, whether you were looking at an American view of the world, or a German one.

Since the 2000s, though, everything has changed. Now the world relies overwhelmingly on online maps, produced by the tech giants. A slight adjustment to the code can direct traffic down one road instead of another, or promote favoured shops or bars or cafes while starving their rivals. Like so much else about the modern age, their dominance of mapping gives those companies – or, at least, Google, which dominates the market, and Apple, which has a corner – a previously unimaginable degree of power.

But it also presents them with a problem – because there is no consensus about how the map of the world actually looks. Those on one side of the sea separating Iran from Saudi Arabia look out across the water and see the Persian Gulf; those on the other side see the Arabian Gulf. The people of Morocco look at territory generally known as 'Western Sahara' and see another, sparsely populated part of Morocco; many of those who actually live there see the Sahrawi Arab Democratic Republic. In these and a hundred other cases, there is no consensus, merely conflicting views. But there are still governments willing to exert legal or financial pressure on any company that picks the wrong one. 'Naively perhaps,' Parsons told the *Independent* in 2014, Google had 'hoped we could have one global map of the world that everyone used, but in some countries we are legally obliged to represent borders in particular ways.' The same interview also suggested the Google Maps team responsible for disputes has a hotline to the UN.

There's another way in which the rise of online mapping has changed our expectations of maps, as well as creating problems for those who make them. There used to be something ever so slightly dusty about cartography. Atlases came in heavy, leather-bound volumes that would be updated, at most, once a year; there was time before publication for confusion to give way to consensus, and those looking at a map were anyway aware that they were looking at a view of the world that came from the past.

Today, though, the code for Google or Apple maps is updated constantly and changes can be rolled out all the time.* They're still official and definitive – but now we expect them to show the world as it is today, not as it was two or three years ago. The date of publication is always now. That means yet more pressure on digital mapmakers to get things right, in situations where it may not yet be clear what right actually is. When a border suddenly moves, as seemed to happen in Crimea in 2014, Google and co. face an unappetising choice. They can reflect reality on the ground and thus appear to legitimise geopolitical developments that do not, in moral terms, deserve it; or they can leave maps unchanged and risk being misleading, if not outright wrong. At least printed maps came accompanied by a key and an index, and thus had an obvious space for explanatory notes to outline live disputes. Despite theoretically containing space for all the information in the world, their minimalist design means their online descendants do not. There may be no good answers.†

In 2022, with the wars to expand Russia's borders raging, the Moscow-headquartered tech company Yandex took the unlikely step of removing national borders from its mapping app altogether. This, spokespeople claimed, was not a political decision. But nobody quite believed them. After all, if borders can move, and showing the wrong ones could land you in prison, would you want to keep them on your mapping app either?

---

* The same is probably true of Microsoft's Bing Maps, too, although I'm not sure anyone has ever bothered to find out.

† Or perhaps democracy provides one. As of late 2022, the open, collaborative, Wikipedia-style OpenStreetMap showed national borders between Crimea and both Ukraine and Russia. Some addresses in the region are listed as Republic of Crimea or Autonomous Crimea, both in Ukraine, others as part of the Southern Federal District of Russia. This is presumably the result of editing wars but it does have the advantage of showing that the territory is disputed.

PART THREE

EXTERNALITIES

Boundaries between times – boundaries at sea – boundaries in the air

A Brief History of the Prime Meridian

The beginning of time

In 2021, pollster YouGov conducted a survey to find out how famous the forty-four men who had preceded Joe Biden as president of the United States currently were. Chester Arthur came forty-fourth. America's twenty-first president had taken on the job following the shocking assassination of James Garfield in September 1881 and held it for nearly four years until March 1885. Yet in 2021, he was less well-known than such Victorian obscurities as Zachary Taylor, Benjamin Harrison and Millard Fillmore. The only president *less* famous was Franklin Pierce. Who? Precisely.

This is a shame, really, as President Arthur shaped the modern world far more – and far more literally – than any of those other forgotten men in tailcoats. In the autumn of 1884, his government invited representatives of all nations with diplomatic ties to the United States to Washington, 'for the purpose of fixing upon a meridian proper to be employed as a common zero of longitude and standard of time-reckoning throughout the globe'. In other words, Chester Arthur helped invent the prime meridian and everything that flows from it. Did Millard Fillmore do that? No, he did not.

Although *the* prime meridian was not agreed upon until 1884, the concept of *a* prime meridian has been around for rather longer. The story begins in Egypt in the third century BCE with one of those infuriatingly impressive polymaths that the ancient world seemed to specialise in. In his eight and a bit decades on the planet, Eratosthenes of Cyrene managed to: become one of the greatest poets of his age; get a job running the library at

Alexandria; found the scientific discipline of chronology, making it possible to date events in the ancient past; create a system for finding prime numbers; calculate the diameter of the sun; *and* examine the mathematical basis of music. It's like Kendrick Lamar became vice chancellor of Oxford University then turned into Brian Cox – possibly, given the scale of his achievements, *both* Brian Coxes, the actor and the physicist. At some point, you're surely just showing off.

The thing about Eratosthenes that's relevant to our purposes, though, is that he also essentially invented the scientific discipline of geography by devising the system of grid lines we know as longitude and latitude. That allowed for more accurate mapping, making it possible to determine where distant places were in reference to each other. It also meant that, by comparing noon shadows cast in two places on the same longitude and doing some clever things with trigonometry, he could get agonisingly close to calculating the size of the Earth – a feat that seems all the more impressive when you look at his maps of the known world and realise how little of it he actually knew. (Honestly, Africa is *not* that shape.)

The reason this was so clever, in a 'Well done, Eratosthenes, you've changed the world *again*' kind of a way,* is because the shape of the Earth means the two halves of the system actually had to work in subtly different ways. For one thing, while lines of latitude run parallel, those of longitude only appear to – follow them far enough and they all converge at the poles. As a result, we refer to lines of latitude as 'parallels'; lines of longitude, though, are 'meridians', from the Latin word for noon, on the grounds that the sun will be highest over everywhere at a given longitude at the exact same moment.

---

* I am oversimplifying wildly here. For one thing, Eratosthenes's meridians and parallels seem to have wobbled about an unnerving amount, so as to run through defined places that were roughly, but *only* roughly, east/west or north/south of each other. For another, much of his work *Geography*, which ran to three volumes, is lost and what we have is pieced together from the bits quoted by later writers. But to the extent any individual was responsible for this stuff, it was him.

More than that, latitude has a clear starting point in the equator, the midpoint of the planet where the Earth is widest. All the other parallels can be defined in reference to it: a point is at 30 degrees north because it's where an angle 30 degrees north of the equator bisects the surface of the planet. Measures of longitude, though, have no such objective reality. There's no naturally existing line that divides the Earth into eastern and western hemispheres, and thus no objective way of measuring an east-west position upon it.

Eratosthenes got around this in the same way everyone who came after him would: by simply picking somewhere convenient to him and decreeing that the prime meridian, the point from which all other east-west positions would be measured, was there. He chose the line through Alexandria, partly because it was one of the world's largest and most important cities, but, also, let's be honest, because it was where he happened to live. A few centuries later, another Alexandrian, Claudius Ptolemy, would decide *his* prime meridian would be a line running through the 'Fortunate Isles', the westernmost land then known, probably what we call the Canaries. This was apparently in order to minimise the need for any tricky mucking about with negative numbers. Generally speaking, though, most geographers - Arabs, Indians, Chinese, Japanese - would select prime meridians on essentially the same basis on which Eratosthenes had chosen his, opting for lines through Arabia, India, China or Japan respectively. There were loads of prime meridians. The globe was littered with them.

For a long time, this lack of an international standard didn't matter because relatively few ships voyaged into regions mapped by other peoples based on other meridians. Even when they did, it didn't matter that much. Latitude could be measured using nothing but the noon sun, some complex but nonetheless doable maths and an astrolabe (a sort of mechanical star chart). Calculating your longitude, though, required accurate timekeeping - and most people, for most of human history, had access to no such thing. The lack of consensus over where to put a prime meridian was quite a long way down the list of problems.

By the late nineteenth century, though, the timekeeping problem had been solved and the world was entering its first great period of globalisation. More and more mariners were crossing oceans and, as they did so, hoping not to get lost, bang into some rocks and drown. At the same time, new technologies like the railways and the telegram were bringing distant places closer together and increasing the need for a global standard time (we'll be coming back to that). Both problems required a universally understood way of communicating how far east or west somewhere was. So if the planet didn't come equipped with a natural equivalent of the equator, helpfully dividing it into east and west, then mankind would have to invent one.

And so, starting in the 1870s, the international geographic community held a string of meetings intended to, in not so many words, sort this mess out. The process culminated in October 1884, with forty-one delegates from twenty-six countries 'renowned in diplomacy and science' gathering in Washington, DC, at the invitation of President Chester Arthur. Their goal, in the words of their chair, an American rear admiral by the name of C. R. P. Rodgers, was 'to create a new accord among the nations by agreeing upon a meridian proper to be employed as a common zero of longitude and standard of time reckoning throughout the world. Happy shall we be,' he continued, with the air of a man who fully expects his words to be remembered by posterity and popping up in books nearly a century and a half later, 'if, throwing aside national preferences and inclinations, we seek only the common good of mankind, and gain for science and for commerce a prime meridian acceptable to all countries, and secured with the least possible inconvenience.'

Looked at from this distance, that seems like a pretty big ask. In 1884, the European empires were poised to carve up the last chunk of the globe left untouched by imperial hands in the Scramble for Africa. It was only a few years since a German army had marched into Paris and the tensions that would lead to the First World War were already starting to build. Getting representatives of every major European power, the United States, Japan and half a dozen Latin American states to agree about *anything* seemed staggeringly unlikely. Getting them to agree on something which spoke to national pride as much as designating an entirely arbitrary centre for the world? That would surely be impossible.

Yet not only did they manage it, they picked a line that ran through the capital city of just one of their number. And not even through the centre but through a suburb: Greenwich, five miles to the southeast of central London. Indeed, a French resolution that 'the initial meridian should have a character of absolute neutrality [and] should cut no great continent' – a fairly reasonable proposal to place the meridian in the Atlantic Ocean, dividing Old World from New – won support from just two other nations, Brazil and San Domingo (today's Dominican Republic). Support for Greenwich was overwhelming.

Why did nations from Venezuela to the Ottoman Empire all line up to support a line through what one American newspaper had recently dubbed a 'dingy London suburb'? The reason was that, in the 1880s, geolocation was still largely a subset of astronomy: to ensure the accuracy of the required measurements, the international scientific community had already agreed that the new meridian should 'pass through an astronomical observatory of the first order'.

That effectively limited the options to four: Paris, Berlin, Washington and Greenwich. The dingy London suburb won out over its competitors in large part because it was already in widespread use as an international reference point – in the system of time zones, recently established in the United States (more on which in the next chapter), and in the charts used by nearly three-quarters of the world's commerce. And it was already in widespread use because, home as Britain was to the largest navy the world had ever seen,

a) its leading observatory was chucking out astronomical data like nobody's business, and

b) Greenwich already featured as the meridian on vast numbers of extant maps.

In other words, it was path dependency. It's not quite true to say that Greenwich got the meridian because in 1884 the British Empire was then the biggest and scariest superpower the world had ever seen. But it's not quite *untrue* to say it either.

Not everyone was happy about this. Paris had its own dingy suburb of growing importance to international science: Saint-Cloud, which since 1875 had been home to the International Bureau of Weights and Measures. The French delegation was thus so upset by the snub to their own Paris meridian that they refused to recognise Greenwich Mean Time as the starting point for the universal day until 1911. Even when they did, they insisted on referring to it as 'Paris Mean Time, retarded by 9 minutes and 21 seconds' right up until 1978. (Since then, it's been 'Coordinated Universal Time'.) But for most of the world, since 1884, the Greenwich observatory has been the source both of longitude's man-made answer to the equator and of universal time.*

Greenwich's days as a dingy London suburb are a long way behind it. Nowadays it's a rather *nice* London suburb, where million-pound houses abound. Thanks to assorted museums and markets, it's on the tourist trail, too, and one of the stops on that trail is the observatory, which stands on a hill in Greenwich Park looking north across the river. To mark the meridian which it gave to the world, you'll find a brass strip set into the ground; the museum's website and social media encourage visitors to take a selfie with one foot either side and post it with the hashtag #PrimeMeridian. By night, a green laser fires out towards the Thames to mark the path of the famous line.

---

* Perhaps Chester Arthur doesn't get the credit for any of this because the conference would have happened whoever was president. Perhaps it's because the consensus that Greenwich was the correct meridian was already well underway. Or perhaps it's because the line ultimately chosen was British in origin, and that's not the sort of thing US presidents are supposed to do. But Chester Arthur fans, if such people exist, can perhaps take some comfort from the fact the twenty-first president is today at least as famous as Eratosthenes. And, let's be honest, the maths genius musician and poet who invented geography definitely deserves it more.

These are all complete and total lies. The prime meridian isn't there at all and providing you have a smartphone you can prove it. Check your maps app while standing atop the brass strip immediately outside the observatory and you'll find yourself at 0.0015 degrees west – not on the prime meridian at all but approximately 102 metres (335ft) into the western hemisphere. To find the *actual* prime meridian, 0 degrees longitude, you need to move slightly to the east. There are no brass strips or nocturnal lighting effects to tell you when you have reached it. The closest thing you'll find is a bin, suggesting itself as a repository for any dog faeces you happen to have about your person.

If you're wondering how the observatory, which originated the prime meridian in the first place, managed to commemorate it in slightly the wrong place, then the good news is: it didn't. The bad news is, it's moved.

The meridian was placed in Greenwich in the first place, after all, because the measurement of time and the creation of maps depended on having the knowledge of the stars that a top-class observatory allowed for. By measuring the distance travelled by certain 'clock' stars, which served as reference points, you could tell exactly how much time had passed. Perfectly accurate measurements, however, require a perfectly accurate idea of which way is up, and this is harder to achieve than one might immediately assume.

The way the astronomers at Greenwich calculated it was by first using a basin of mercury to create a perfect horizontal plane; from that, they could find a perfect *vertical* plane and calibrate their instruments accordingly. The problem was that the Earth is not a perfect sphere: it bulges around the middle, and the presence of things like mountains and hills means that the planet's mass is not completely evenly distributed. A truly vertical line should pass through the centre of the Earth: the vertical line calculated from the basin of mercury did not. Result: the measurements were off, which is a problem when the measurements are the reference point for the entire world's system of timekeeping and geography.

All this has been clear since the 1970s, when systems such as the satellite-based global positioning system (GPS) first began to produce measurements that couldn't be messed up by some minor oddity in the local gravity. Faced with the choice between redoing the entire global longitude system, and thus rendering a century's worth of measurements obsolete, or just redefining the meridian, the global scientific community opted to do the latter. The Greenwich meridian still exists as a historic artefact and a brass strip in the ground, but longitude is measured instead from the IERS Reference Meridian, a notional line calculated using measurements taken from a network of hundreds of ground stations and satellites and maintained by the pithily named International Earth Rotation and Reference Systems Service.

Why has the observatory not marked the new line? Partly, one suspects, because it would be a bit embarrassing – and potentially, if they want to attract tourists, counterproductive – to install a new line that very obviously doesn't pass through the observatory buildings. A better excuse, though, may be that, thanks to plate tectonics, the ground beneath our feet literally moves – Greenwich, like most of Eurasia, is moving west–southwest at a rate of a couple of centimetres a year – and any physical marker would be clearly out of date within a scant couple of decades.*

Incidentally, the coordinates used by satellite navigation systems rely on 'geocentric reference frames', introduced by the International Time Bureau (BIH) in 1984. The reason the acronym for the BIH isn't ITB is because its official name is the Bureau International de l'Heure, and the reason its name is in French is that it's based at the Paris observatory.

Those French astronomers who spent decades rejecting the Greenwich meridian out of little more than patriotic spite had the last laugh after all.

---

* Dr Megan Barford, the curator of cartography at the Royal Museums Greenwich, who was kind enough to meet me for a chat while I was writing this book, told me that their proposals that the observatory sell a 'make your own meridian' kit had been turned down. 'There's a reason they don't let me decide what to sell in the gift shop,' they said.

Some Notes on Time Zones

Crossing the timelines

There are many ways to rebel against a repressive state. You can criticise a government. You can break its laws. You can attack its property.

Or, if you're one of the Muslim Uyghurs of western China, you can rebel against the government by setting your watch to the unofficial local time zone, rather than the time officially approved by Beijing.

China, you see, stretches over 2,000 miles from east to west, enough in theory to need as many as five time zones. But in 1949, in an attempt to advance national unity, Chairman Mao decreed that everyone in the country should set their clocks to Beijing time (UTC+8). One result of the entire country using the time zone most appropriate to the historic heartlands of its far east is that, in midwinter in the far west, the sun doesn't rise until nearly 10am. Another is that, while Beijing time is observed by the Han Chinese population of Xinjiang – a region, incidentally, that is three times the size of France – many Uyghurs, and people from the region's other minorities, instead follow the unofficial Xinjiang, or Ürümqi, time, which is two hours behind (UTC+6).

This can obviously create confusion when scheduling cross-community meetings but it can cause more serious problems, too. A 2018 report from Human Rights Watch found many reasons why people from Xinjiang have been sent to 'vocational education and employment training centres', the 're-education camps' – internment camps – which are believed to hold over a million Uyghurs. For some, it was wearing the wrong clothing or having the wrong beard; for others, it was running 'Islamic' restaurants that don't allow smoking or drinking. And for one man, an interviewee said, it was 'for having set his watch to Ürümqi time – they say that's what makes him suspicious for terrorism . . . They think many things show you have incorrect thoughts.'

Almost all of the lines discussed in this book are in some sense political. Perhaps it was naive to expect time zones to be any different.

Whether travelling for business or pleasure, most of us have at some point crossed the invisible line between time zones. Some countries (Afghanistan, Nepal, the Marquesas Islands of French Polynesia) are so geographically or temporally isolated that going anywhere else at all necessitates changing your watch. Others (the US, Canada, Australia, Russia) are so huge that even internal trips may involve multiple time zones. The weird thing about China is its refusal to bow to this pattern: both the sun and logic may suggest a change in clock; the authorities, though, have other ideas.

All this is a modern sort of phenomenon. Until relatively recently, communication between places far enough apart to require different time zones took so long that the fact they had different views on what time it was didn't seem to bother anyone. More than that, time was, for most of human history, a pretty imprecise sort of affair. There were sundials, which could tell you how far the sun had made it through its daily rounds across the heavens; there were water clocks, which released or collected water at a known rate, allowing you to tell how long it had been since a certain point. But such wonders were not universally available and, anyway, their limitations meant that the ancients had a very different sense of time to our own. The Romans, for example, divided each day into twelve equal hours, regardless of its length. Hours could thus stretch from as little as forty-five minutes in winter to as long as seventy-five in summer. Or would have done, had the average Roman had any concept of 'minutes'.*

---

* Please don't ask me what they did at night; every time I look into it my nose begins to bleed.

A few centuries ago, though, all that started to change. The seventeenth century brought pendulum clocks, the eighteenth increasingly accurate chronometers, and the time became something you could check. Even then, there were as many time zones as there were human communities, as every town or village would maintain its own local time based on when the sun was directly overhead. But the nineteenth century brought a pair of inventions that made the world much, much smaller.

One was the electric telegraph, which allowed people to send messages to distant places far faster than anyone could travel. The other was the railways, timetabling of which, in a world with no standard time, proved to be something of a nightmare. If you were hoping to take a train from New York City to Buffalo, nearly 400 miles and perhaps twenty minutes' time difference away, then whether the times on the timetable reflected New York time or Buffalo time or the time at each individual stop was the sort of thing you probably needed to know. In a United States which used hundreds of different local time zones, though, this was not the sort of thing the people running your train could necessarily tell you. Another problem was that it was very difficult to work out how long a train journey would take when, measured by local time, it seemed to take longer travelling west to east than it did from east to west. Worst of all, confusion about exactly when an express train was due to pass through was the sort of thing that could, and occasionally did, lead to disaster.

Perhaps unsurprisingly, then, it was railway companies that led the charge towards temporal unification. In 1840, Britain's Great Western Railway, which linked London with the port of Bristol, a hundred miles and eleven minutes to its west, introduced 'railway time' – a unified system of timekeeping across its network based on the time set by the Royal Observatory in Greenwich. Other railway companies gradually adopted it over the next dozen years or so but, even then (this part may be familiar) provincial towns remained reluctant to accept a standard time set by a city in the far east of the country. For decades to come, many towns displayed two times on their public clocks, one local and one national.* It was 1880 before the British government legislated to officially make Greenwich time national.

Other countries gradually followed. France adopted a standard national time in 1891, Germany in 1893. Italy was ahead of the game, with many cities falling in line with Rome as early as the 1860s. The US and Canada were far too big for a single time zone, of course, but in October 1883, the nations' railroads agreed the 'General Time Convention' that divided North America into five time zones, which generally share the names, if not the boundaries, of their modern successors.†

Much of the credit for that lay with a Scottish-born immigrant by the name of Sandford Fleming, who by 1883 had worked his way up the ranks to become Canada's foremost railway engineer. Fleming had spent much of the 1870s as chief engineer of the proposed Canadian Pacific Railway, which today stretches right across the continent from Vancouver to Montreal. That would, you'd think, be quite an achievement in itself, but he's remembered for something else entirely: inventing the modern clock. One day, the story goes, he missed a train in Ireland because a timetable wrongly listed times as pm rather than am. So annoyed about this was Sandford that he spent the next few years inventing first the twenty-four-hour clock, then the concept of 'universal'/'cosmopolitan'/'cosmic' time, about whose name he kept changing his mind.

I have my doubts about this story, which has been much reproduced in a manner that suggests a lot of versions are simply copying what other people have written. Most accounts offer little if any detail of where this train was or what time Fleming expected

---

* The Exchange, an eighteenth-century Bristol building housing offices and markets, still has a nineteenth-century clock with two minute hands – one for local time, the other for London/railway time.

† There's one exception. Atlantic Time, the zone covering eastern Canada, which is four hours behind Greenwich, was then named Intercolonial Time, after the region's railway operator.

it to leave; several refer to its subject as *Stamford* Fleming.* He certainly wasn't the first person to propose dividing the world into twenty-four time zones, each fifteen degrees of longitude wide: a Bolognese mathematician calling himself Quirico Filopanti outlined precisely such a plan in the marvellously named book *Miranda* in 1858 (not that anyone seemed to notice at the time). What is clear, however, is that Fleming outlined his own proposals in his 1876 page-turner *Terrestrial Time* and then proceeded to bore on about it to anyone who'd listen.†

In this, he was only partly successful. He did persuade the delegates at the International Meridian Conference of the value of 'the adoption of a universal day for all purposes for which it may be found convenient'. And he won himself the title of 'the father of standard time' and a Google doodle on his 190th birthday. But the other delegates stubbornly refused to accept his cartographically neat but politically implausible time zone scheme, which would have seen places allocated to time zones on strictly geographic grounds, in a manner reminiscent of Abbé Sieyès carving up France. The world would adopt Greenwich Mean Time as the standard time, against which all other clocks are measured, and would later give it the less geographically contentious name of Coordinated Universal Time, or UTC.‡ But how the nations of the world set their watches would remain an entirely local affair.

This is why the modern world is not divided neatly into twenty-four time zones. Thanks to those territories which opted for time zones separated from UTC by a period not measured in

---

* I, of course, would never do such a thing, and every sentence of this book is based upon original first-hand research. Ahem.

† These proposals, incidentally, involved allocating each time zone a letter between A and Y (J was dropped, to prevent confusion with I). A fossil of this scheme survives in the widespread military use of the phonetic alphabet to refer to time zones, with Zulu time meaning UTC, Alpha to Mike meaning UTC+1 to UTC+12, and November to Yankee meaning UTC-1 to UTC-12. Mike time and Yankee time are thus the same time but a day apart.

‡ The acronym is a compromise between English CUT and French TUC.

whole hours – Iran (+3½), India (+5½), Nepal (+5¾) and so on – the actual number is more like thirty-seven. Different approaches to daylight saving complicates things further: Australia, for example, has five time zones in summer but only three in winter, because the southern states observe daylight savings time but the northern ones do not.

Matters of time may rarely be quite as politically charged as in Xinjiang but they inevitably remain contentious, nonetheless. Numerous countries, in recent years, have debated scrapping daylight savings time altogether as an unnecessary complication that just messes with everyone's heads twice a year. But such ideas have generally foundered on the fact that this change would create losers as well as winners, and the former – often farmers – tend to shout more. Then there are those countries which have changed time zone just to make a point. In 2007, Hugo Chávez moved Venezuelan clocks back by half an hour: officially, this was so children could wake up for school in daylight but the move was widely perceived as a statement that the country would henceforth be doing its own thing. In 2015, the ever-delightful North Korean government followed suit, ensuring that the good people of that happy kingdom would no longer suffer the indignity of sharing a time zone with the capitalist republic to their south. Both changes were later reversed; the latter lasted less than three years.

In 2019, Steve Hanke and Dick Henry, a pair of academics at Johns Hopkins University in Baltimore, came up with a proposal to simplify things and de-politicise the clock: scrap time zones altogether. If it's 15.00hrs in London, it'd be 15.00hrs in New York and Hong Kong, too. This plan wouldn't just bring an end to the confusion about what time to make that call to the Chicago office, it'd mean that people and institutions would naturally orientate themselves around the best time for their locale, ensuring they sleep and rise when the sun tells them to rather than when some distant authority dictates. It would, in other words, allow more flexibility based on local needs than the current system.

Against that, though, it would require everyone who didn't live on a similar longitude to London to fundamentally rethink what concepts like '5pm' mean, which doesn't seem very likely. It also wouldn't make it easier to travel. You'd still switch time zones but instead of outsourcing keeping track of the fact to watches and phones and public clocks, you'd have to keep it in your brain at all times, constantly doing maths to remind yourself that 11am in this time zone is what you think of as 7pm. And since UTC already exists for those who need it (airlines, traders and so forth), it's not clear what the advantage of forcing it on everyone would be. As the delegates at the International Meridian Conference understood, and the Chinese authorities may be grappling with today, time will always have a local component.

Something the delegates to the IMC did do, though, was establish some sense of where in the world one day should end and another begin. Which brings us to our next line.

A Brief History of the International Date Line

Between today and tomorrow

It had been a long and tiring journey. The fleet of five ships and around 270 men had left Andalucía in September 1519. Under the command of the Portuguese explorer Ferdinand Magellan, the mostly Spanish crew was in search of a western route to the Moluccas, a chain of Indonesian islands famed for their exotic spices and thus known, creatively, as 'the Spice Islands'. The fleet had sailed across the Atlantic and down the east coast of South America. It had discovered a sheltered passage between the mainland of that continent and the archipelago of Tierra del Fuego to its south, which Magellan had modestly named Estrecho de Todos los Santos ('Strait of All Saints') but which would, in time, be renamed the Strait of Magellan in his honour. From there, it had crossed the Pacific and reached the Philippines, where Magellan had preached his Christian faith and baptised local chiefs. When one tribe resisted, he'd launched an attack, only to lose both the resulting battle and his life.

So it was a depleted and demoralised fleet which finally reached the Moluccas in November 1521. Even then, the survivors faced yet more long months of bad weather and worse food before the last surviving ship in the fleet had limped back to something that resembled Europe.

On Sunday 9 July 1522, though, the *Victoria* finally arrived in the Portuguese colony of Cape Verde. By now things were desperate – around twenty men had starved to death the last two months alone – but at long last, they were in a place where the authorities were Christian, where they spoke a recognisable language, where they would be understood.

It must have felt pretty strange, then, when those same authorities continued to insist that the date was in fact Monday *10* July. The survivors had dealt with nearly three years of sabotage, starvation and storms; not only had they come through, they had kept a daily record of everything they had experienced for three whole years. And now these Portuguese randoms were insisting that they'd lost a day? Half mad with hunger as they were, it must have been both unnerving and infuriating, like coming back from a trip to discover all your friends now think the sky is green.

But no, they hadn't somehow collectively lost a day and yes, their records were correct. Travel west around the world and for every fifteen degrees of longitude you travel, you effectively lose an hour. Circumnavigate the globe and you will lose an entire day. Do so over a period of, say, three years, and these effects will be unnoticeable, experienced simply as days imperceptibly shorter than they should be, but the result is that you will return to your starting place to find that your calendar is wrong. You have experienced one less day than those you left behind.

We no more need a supernatural explanation for this disparity than we do the existence of Thor to explain thunder; we, unlike the crew of the Magellan expedition, have grown up in a world in which the relationship between geography and time is well understood. The mind-blowing yet entirely explicable phenomenon has featured in everything from bad Victorian poetry, to not so bad short stories, to the final plot twist of a classic novel I'm not going to spoil.*

Even by the time Magellan and co. set out, the 'circumnavigator's paradox', as it's known, had been understood for centuries. As far back as 1321, the Arab geographer Abu al-Fida

* The story is Edgar Allan Poe's descriptively titled 'Three Sundays in a Week' (1850); the poem is Francis Bret Harte's 'The Lost Galleon' (1867) and it truly is a stinker. I'm not going to spoil the novel, even down here. While you're here, though, it's worth stressing that this is a quirk of the clock and not of physics itself: it doesn't matter how fast you fly west around the world, you still can't travel backwards in time. That 1980s *Superman* film lied to you.

had produced his masterwork *Taqwim al-buldan* (literally, 'a calendar of the countries' but generally translated as 'A Sketch of the Countries' or 'Locating the Lands'). In it, he had noted that a traveller who circumnavigated the globe westwards would, because he moved in the same direction as the sun, count one day less than someone who stayed still; in the same way, a traveller who went eastwards would count one more.* For most of human history, though, this was a theoretical problem, an intellectual curiosity. It was only in the sixteenth century, with the arrival of regular transoceanic journeys and intercontinental empires, that people began to frequently grapple with it for real.

Even after that, humanity managed without a system for determining where exactly you should adjust your calendar for several more centuries – manages, indeed, without any *official* system to this day. Most of us are not in the habit of taking journeys that involve a change of date – I realised as I wrote that sentence that I have literally never done so – and those who do can probably cope. Even the confusion about the date in Cape Verde wasn't the main concern among the survivors of the Magellan expedition: that was the fact they'd lost 90 per cent of their crew and now the Portuguese wanted to arrest them for the gall of rocking up with some spices.† Nevertheless, as travel became faster and easier, and technology made it possible to speak and trade with those on entirely different continents, it began to seem like it might be a good idea to impose some order on all this.

The result is a line familiar to anybody who has ever looked at a map of the world's time zones: in the words of Robert van Gent, an astronomer and historian of science at Utrecht University, the

---

* The common idea that, until Columbus crossed the Atlantic, everyone assumed the Earth was flat is wrong. The fact it's a globe has been known since several centuries BCE.

† A short-term problem. Around eighteen of the crew returned to Spain on 6 September 1522, just two weeks shy of the third anniversary of their departure; another dozen were detained in Cape Verde but found their way back over the next year or so.

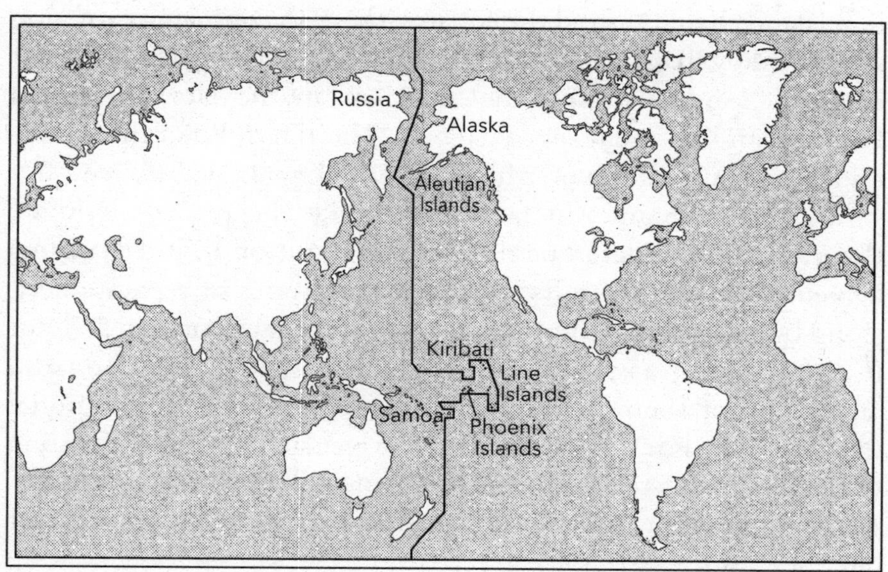

The crooked path of the largely notional international date line.

international date line (IDL) 'indicates the boundary line between "today" and "tomorrow"'.*

The odd thing is, though, no formal agreement has ever been reached about where that line should go. Delegates at the International Meridian Conference did conclude that it made sense to place the 'discontinuity of date' (the place where two dates meet) in the same place as the 'discontinuity in the reckoning of longitude' (the point where 180 west becomes 180 east); indeed, one reason for the enthusiasm for siting the prime meridian in Greenwich was that its antimeridian, on the far side of the globe, passed almost entirely over the Pacific Ocean. All this, though, had the force of a suggestion and nothing more.

It's also very obviously not the line we actually got. Look at a map and you'll see that the international date line doesn't run neatly down the 180 line of longitude. It zags east to avoid eastern Russia, then west to avoid the outermost edges of Alaska's Aleu-

---

* This entry owes a substantial debt to van Gent's history of the international date line.

tian Island chain. Around the equator, there's a confusing extrusion shaped oddly like a hammer, or a T-Rex on a shelf, where it lurches over 3,000km (1,864mi) to the east to ensure the date on assorted Pacific islands is today, not yesterday. The IDL follows the antimeridian for only a little over half its 20,000km (12,427mi) length.

Despite its name, in fact, and unlike the prime meridian, the international date line did not come out of an international agreement at all; it results instead from a series of separate decisions by individual countries and commercial concerns. To put it another way, as American geographer George Davidson did at the end of the nineteenth century, 'There *is* no international date line. The line actually used is the result of agreement among the commercial steamships of the principal maritime countries.' Those countries which border the line are free to pick whichever day they choose.

Several have. Until 1994, Kiribati, a Pacific republic composed of thirty-two atolls and the remote coral island of Banaba, was split down the middle by the IDL, with its easternmost islands consistently a whole day ahead of the rest. This was of course inconvenient – just imagine how annoying it would become if it was only the weekend in half your country. And so, the government decided to put the clocks forward on some of its islands by an entire day. The Phoenix Islands switched from their previous time zone of UTC-11 to UTC+13; the Line Islands from UTC-10 to UTC+14. Neither archipelago experienced New Year's Day 1995; instead, they jumped straight from 31 December to 2 January. This, if you were wondering, explains the bit that looks like a dinosaur.

Samoa and the New Zealand island territory of Tokalau did much the same in December 2011, when they shifted forward a day (UTC-11 to UTC+13) to make it easier to trade with Australia and New Zealand. In Samoa's case, this was a reverse of the temporal journey it had made in 1892, the year it showcased the importance of its US links by celebrating 4 July, twice.

Then there's Alaska, which the US bought from Russia in 1867 for a cool $7.2 million, and which thus managed to cross the international date line before anyone had even thought to define where that line was. This did not, however, mean it moved back a day and repeated a date as one might expect. Because nineteenth-century Russia still used the Julian calendar, rather than the Gregorian one, it was thirteen days behind the West: Alaska simply switched its time zone and its calendars at the same time, so that 6 October 1867 was followed, confusingly, by 18 October. The latter date is still celebrated as Alaska Day.

Last but not least, there are the Philippines, which spent much of the early modern period not only as part of the Spanish Empire but part of 'New Spain': the territory we met on page 104, focused on Mexico, Central America and other bits of land that were very obviously on the other side of the Pacific. By the mid-nineteenth century, though, with most of New Spain having achieved independence, trade with Asia was coming to seem more important than trade with Mexico, and the insistence that the Philippines set their calendar to match territories thousands of miles away, rather than those just across the South China Sea, was starting to seem ridiculous. To fix this anomaly, the governor general Narciso Clavería announced that 30 December 1844 would be followed by 1 January 1845. But because the international date line had yet to become a thing, and because no one was paying much attention to the Philippines anyway, it took Europeans literally decades to notice. Well into the 1890s, maps would still show the line between today and tomorrow taking a weird swerve west across the Pacific to place the islands on the American side of the line.

One odd result of all this, and of the line's zigzagging path, is that each day on planet Earth it is briefly three different dates at once: 10.30hrs on 1 May in Greenwich (UTC) will be 23.30hrs on 30 April in American Samoa (UTC-11) and 00.30hrs on 2 May on Kiritimati, the part of the Republic of Kiribati known as Christmas Island (UTC+14). Travellers may no longer be surprised to find that they've lost a day but that doesn't make the reality of our system of time zones any less baffling.

Of Maritime Boundaries and the Law of the Sea

Clear blue water

A thousand miles south of Osaka, a thousand miles east of Taiwan, in an empty stretch of the western Pacific known as the Philippine Sea, there lies an atoll. It looks pretty in the aerial photographs – waves breaking into white foam against a coral reef enclosing a roughly pear-shaped lagoon, aquamarine amid the dark blue ocean – but I wouldn't bother visiting because there's almost literally nothing there. Although the reef is nearly three miles long, big enough to accommodate a fair-sized international airport, the only solid ground consists of three tiny islands, between them just a few metres square, as well as a research station housed on a platform on stilts.

Despite the fact that nobody lives here – nobody could live here – this is, officially, a suburb of Tokyo, in the village of Ogasawara. It is named Okinotorishima – 'remote bird island'. And it is the basis for a dubious Japanese claim over a vast area of the western Pacific.

We've encountered maritime boundaries, the idea that a state's sovereign territory could include sea as well as land, already in this story, not least in China's attempts to control its neighbourhood (see page 185), so it's probably about time I explained the rules. They are, it turns out, surprisingly new.

States have always sought control of the seas. The Romans unselfconsciously used the phrase '*Mare Nostrum*' (our sea) to refer first to the waters surrounding Italy and later, once the empire had grown sufficiently vast, to the entire Mediterranean; the British Empire was founded on its navy; and so on. These forms of control, though, were built on might rather than right, naval strength rather than a system of rules. It's probably not a coincidence that the earliest attempts to codify the notion of territorial waters, dating from around 1700, was the three-mile limit: ships were understood to be in another country's seas when they were literally in cannon-fire range of the coast.

By the mid-twentieth century, though, two things had changed. One was that offshore drilling technology had reached the point at which control of the neighbouring seabed could have a real impact on a country's economic fortunes (oil being rather more lucrative than fish). The other was that everyone felt they had to at least *pretend* that national sovereignty was a thing and you shouldn't simply bully smaller countries into doing whatever you wanted them to. And so, under the auspices of the UN, everyone decided it was time to work out who owned what.

As always with these things, though, standardising the rules turned out to be a bit more complicated than simply making a decision and getting everyone to agree. The UN held its first Convention on the Law of the Sea in 1958. (Hilariously, it held it in Geneva, next to some mountains and the better part of 200 miles inland.) UNCLOS I succeeded in defining what sovereignty countries did and did not have over their territorial seas. It did not, however, define how wide those seas were. At that point, different states made radically different claims, ranging from the standard three miles to well over twelve, and the idea of getting them all to agree was dumped into the 'too difficult' pile. That took until UNCLOS III,* which began in 1973, was not completed until 1982 and couldn't come into force until 1994, one year after the sixtieth state, Guyana, had ratified it. The world has really only had a system for defining maritime boundaries for a single generation.

So, if you do find yourself in possession of a small coastal state, how do you work out how much sea you get with it? The first thing you need to do is establish your baseline, a sort of line around the coast that marks exactly where your country ends.

* UNCLOS II didn't go great – so often the way with trilogies.

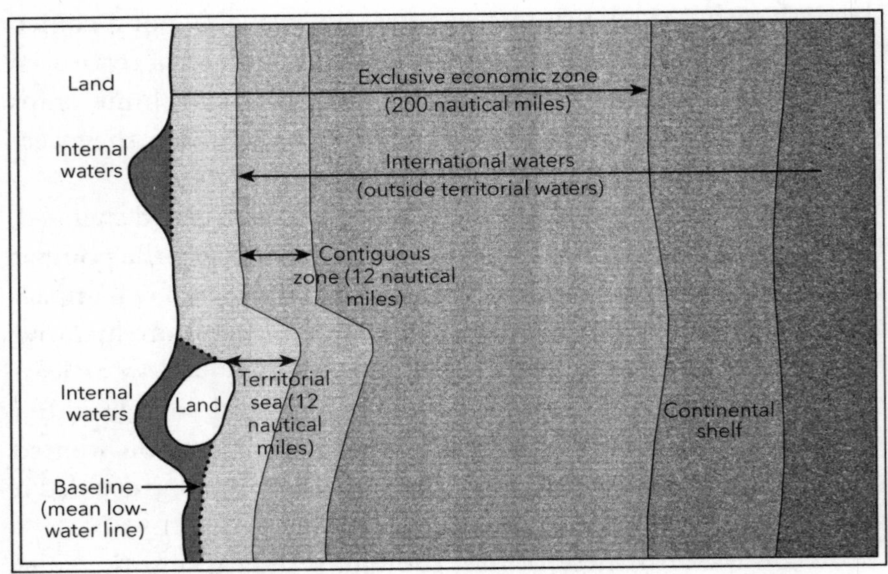

An illustrative map of the different categories of territorial waters defined in international law.

Generally, that's the low-water line, the farthest the tide goes out;* in places, it'll be a straight line through open water dividing things like bays and estuaries from the open sea. (There are plenty more rules on this, which UNCLOS I goes into at frankly fascinating length, but that should be enough for our purposes.) Inside the baseline are your inland waters. You have exactly as much sovereignty there as you do on dry land, only damper.

Beyond that come a series of concentric zones, over which your sovereign nation has gradually receding degrees of control. The first twelve miles are your territorial seas: here, you have full sovereignty over the waters, the airspace above them and the seabed below. That said, the right to innocent passage applies; that means, basically, that other people can sail boats through

* This can have a substantial effect: the Isle of Wight, off England's south coast, has the distinction of being its smallest county but only at high tide. When the tide goes out, the extra beaches exposed make it bigger than landlocked Rutland. (*Proper* counties, anyway. Technically, Bristol is a county too. So is the City of London. But let's not get into that here.)

them just so long as they're not doing anything dodgy (spying on you, firing at you, stealing your fish and so on).*

The twelve miles beyond that are your contiguous zone. This is not actually your sovereign territory and, unlike the territorial waters, is not something you get automatically, you have to assert it. But in here, you can do whatever is necessary to prevent anyone breaking your customs or laws. It's there, so far as one can tell, to make sure seaborne criminals can't just float twelve and a half miles offshore, smuggling and polluting and otherwise taunting you.

Last but very much not least, there is another set of rights which you may want to claim because they can reach as much as 200 miles from your country's shore: those of your exclusive economic zone, an arrangement in the 1982 treaty that grew out of fishing rights. In this area, you have full sovereign rights to extract any oil, gas or other useful minerals; install windfarms or oil rigs; plus, of course, fish.

The EEZ is the last form of sovereignty available to your state. You may, if geology has been kind, have an extended continental shelf, which means you can use the seabed physically attached to your land (once your claim has been recognised, of course). But the water above it is part of the high seas, the common heritage of mankind, where international law holds and which you have no greater claim over than anybody else.†

Unless, that is, you have a conveniently placed island from which you can start making these claims all over again. The usefulness of well-positioned islands in providing not just strategic bases but also national sovereignty explains much about modern geopolitics. It explains, for example, why the Chinese are building

---

* A point I'm mentioning here because it's as good a place as any: international law also recognises the right of maritime traffic to pass through straits, even when they're well inside a state's territorial waters. Britain or France could, theoretically, plug the Channel but they'd be breaking the law of the sea.

† The bit of the high seas that excludes the sea above your continental shelf and so on is sometimes also referred to, with that sinister talent US government agencies have for naming things, as 'the Area'.

new islands in the South China Sea. It explains, too, why Argentina is so determined to win control of the Falklands/Malvinas, a small, windswept archipelago in the South Atlantic, even though their inhabitants are overwhelmingly keen to stay British.

It's also why Japan is so keen to claim those tiny rocks of Okinotorishima – so keen that since the late 1980s, the *Guardian* reported in 2016, it had spent roughly $600 million on steel breakwaters, concrete flood defences and titanium netting to make sure the atoll isn't simply washed away. The reason it has spent so much on a place you can barely stand on is because it wants the vast EEZ it brings with it.

This may not, in the strictest of legal terms, be enough. UNCLOS states that 'rocks which cannot sustain human habitation or economic life of their own shall have no exclusive economic zone'. (Some Japanese politicians have responded, with a measure of optimism, that the treaty doesn't technically define 'rock'.) China, Taiwan and South Korea have all challenged the Japanese claim; Jon van Dyke, a law professor at the University of Hawaii, compared the situation to Britain's doomed attempt to claim an EEZ around Rockall, a desolate bit of Atlantic granite nearly 200 miles west of Scotland. Okinotorishima, he said, 'consists of two eroding protrusions no larger than king-size beds . . . It is not, therefore, entitled to generate a 200-mile exclusive economic zone.'

It's at least possible, though, that the lure of a juicy EEZ is not the only factor behind Japanese determination to claim the sea around its rocks. That's because Okinotorishima lies in a strategic position, roughly midway between Taiwan and Guam, a US territory equipped with a naval base. Obviously, then, the Chinese would like to be able to patrol the seas around the atoll. Just as obviously, US-aligned powers would rather not let them.

A couple of other points before we move on. Firstly, what do you do if your state is *all* islands, meaning that much of the space between your population centres is, well, sea? The UN convention also has a provision for 'archipelagic waters', in which the baseline around your 'internal' waters is effectively drawn around your entire archipelago. There are some limits on the water/land ratio, to keep this sane – Britain could not claim the water between itself and the Falklands – but nonetheless, some twenty-two states have so far adopted this status.

The other is what you do when, as inevitably happens in much of the world, two claims clash. Parts of the sea around Europe will be within a dozen miles of multiple countries and almost all of it within 200 miles of several. Where do the boundaries go then?

In theory, two principles cover most situations. One is that, where two states meet at the coast, their maritime border extends in a manner perpendicular from that coast. The other is the 'equidistance principle': where two countries face each other across an expanse of sea, the boundary should be halfway between them.

All this, though, is easier said than done. If a coast isn't straight, which direction counts as 'perpendicular' can be a matter of some dispute. The results may also not seem fair: a literal interpretation of these rules gave what was then West Germany only a tiny patch of the North Sea, even though that cold expanse had once literally been known as 'the German Ocean'. When oil was discovered beneath the seabed, these boundaries, which resulted from nothing more than an unhelpfully shaped coastline, became a source of more than merely academic irritation. The result was a case at the International Court of Justice and a frantic redrawing of the line.

Settling boundaries via adjudication or treaty is always an option – there's absolutely nothing to stop you trading away your EEZ for something your state might find more useful – but treaties can bring their own problems. One still-running dispute concerns the maritime boundary between the US and Canada in the Beaufort Sea, north of Alaska and the Yukon Territory. This was settled by the 1825 Treaty of Saint Petersburg, between Britain and Russia, as following the 141st meridian 'as far as the Frozen Ocean'.* But debates about whether the Frozen Ocean means the entire sea or merely the point where it starts to freeze

* Actually, just to complicate things yet further, it says it in French.

have been keeping diplomats busy for two centuries, with no sign of agreement yet. What happens when the Arctic stops freezing completely is best not to consider.

Arbitration, what's more, requires states that are happy to recognise the authority of the arbitrator. Turkey claims a portion of Cyprus's EEZ, on the novel grounds that islands aren't entitled to anything more than the basic territorial waters. This is not an interpretation that's widely shared – I don't imagine it's gone down well with Britain or Japan – but Turkey hasn't signed UNCLOS, and while other states have tutted and threatened sanctions, no one is going to war against a NATO member for doing some unauthorised offshore drilling. International law is all very well but there comes a point at which actually changing behaviour depends on a willingness to use force.

Lastly, throughout this entry, I've said miles when I actually meant *nautical* miles. How, you may wonder, do they differ from the regular, landlubber miles we're all used to?* The nautical mile, at around 1,852 metres (6,076ft), is actually roughly 15 per cent longer than its land-based namesake. The reason for the difference is because it's one minute of latitude: travel sixty nautical miles north or south and you've travelled precisely one degree. The reason people piloting ships – and aircraft and rockets, come to that – prefer nautical miles over regular ones is because it makes their calculations easier.

This has very little to do with boundaries. I just thought you might like to know.

---

* Or possibly, if you live in a country less weird about its measurements than the US or UK, that we're aware of from the olden days.

Some Notes on Landlocked Countries

The adventures of the Bolivian navy

One of the odder facts concerning the countries of the world is that there are two landlocked countries on the continent of South America, and that both maintain navies.

A landlocked country, as you almost certainly know, is one which doesn't have a coastline. The locals are thus required to cross someone else's sovereign territory if they wish to either launch a naval flotilla or go to the beach. Some, like Lesotho or San Marino, are enclaves surrounded by one other country, which is a bit of a nightmare from a geopolitical point of view. Most, though, have more than one neighbour and just happen to be sited some distance inland.

The number of landlocked countries in the world has grown rather rapidly these last few years. In 1990, there were thirty; now, thanks to the breakups of Yugoslavia, Czechoslovakia and the USSR, plus the creation of Eritrea and South Sudan, there are forty-four. Some of these – European microstates like San Marino, Andorra or the Vatican – are diddy. Some, like Kazakhstan, which is nearly two-thirds the size of the entire European Union, are huge. Two of them – Uzbekistan and Liechtenstein – are double landlocked, which means a resident would need to cross two international boundaries if they fancied a paddle. As things stand, there are no triple landlocked countries, though there's no theoretical bar to the possibility, if those in Vaduz, say, fancied declaring independence from Liechtenstein and thus creating a sillier country still.

Actually, though, like all the most fun facts, the statement 'there are forty-four landlocked countries in the world' is contested on several fronts. Firstly, it's surprisingly hard to pin down what counts as a state: 194 are universally recognised but, depending on how you define your terms, there are perhaps another dozen that have pretty strong claims to de facto independence. Four of these – Kosovo, South Ossetia, Transnistria and Artsakh, the territory 1990s fans may remember as Nagorno-Karabakh – do not have coastlines. Secondly, what counts as access to the sea? Another partially recognised state, Palestine, has a coastline in Gaza but not in the West Bank, where the majority of its population actually live. Since there is not at present free movement between the two, should that count as landlocked?

Then there's the fact that at least some of these landlocked countries seem to have – this may come as a shock – coastlines. Kazakhstan actually borders the Caspian Sea. So do Turkmenistan and Azerbaijan. But that, despite its name, is not really a sea, merely an endorheic basin: the water which drains into it does not continue to the oceans but evaporates into the atmosphere. Despite its name, the Caspian Sea is really just a lake – albeit a lake so big it contains upwards of 40 per cent of all the water in all the lakes in all the world.* At any rate, the only way from the Caspian to the world's proper oceans is via the Volga–Don Canal to the Black Sea, which is too small for ocean-going ships. And since the whole point of not being landlocked is 'in the event of emergencies, you can still get people/things in/out using massive, massive boats', this doesn't actually help.

None of this has stopped various landlocked countries from maintaining their own navies, however. Some of them play defensive functions, some merely logistical ones; some of them are just units of the army, some a fully-fledged arm of the military in their own right. Switzerland has a 'lakes flotilla', which patrols and performs search and rescue functions within its various inland

* Some countries, notably Iran and Turkmenistan, have claimed that the Caspian should count as a real sea because under UNCLOS they could then make a claim on its oil and gas fields. Which, fair play, you probably would, wouldn't you?

waters, as well as a full merchant marine which takes exports to and imports from the world via the Rhine. Ethiopia scrapped its navy after it lost its coastline to Eritrean independence in 1991; its government recently relaunched it to defend its maritime interests, all the same. (Sadly, I have not been able to verify the widely reproduced zombie fact that it still maintains a single boat on Lake Tana.) Then there's Hungary, which, according to a Wikipedia page I suspect of having been edited by the Hungarian authorities, 'has one of the heaviest and most qualified warship battalions in East-Central Europe'.

Over in the Americas, Paraguay has a surprisingly large navy which patrols the Paraguay and Paraná rivers, and which could, if required, use them to break out into the Atlantic via Argentina. Unless it's Argentina it's fighting a naval war with, in which case things presumably start to get tricky.

The fun one, though, is Bolivia, which, unlike Paraguay, actually did start out with a coastline. The country which won its independence from the Spanish Empire in 1825 after a sixteen-year war was substantially bigger than the one that exists today. But it spent the next century or more having fights with its bigger, richer and scarier neighbours, ceding outlying territories to Brazil, Argentina and Paraguay in the process.

For our purposes, though, the key loss was that of the Department of the Litoral, a contested stretch of Atacama desert which gave Bolivia access to the Pacific. Despite having recognised it as Bolivia's in 1866, Chile invaded in 1879, beginning the conflict known variously as the War of the Pacific (after where much of it was fought), the Saltpetre War (after the mineral resource it was mostly fought for) or the Ten Cents War (after the tax regime which kicked it off). When the dust had settled, both Bolivia and Peru had lost territory, and the former found itself landlocked. This seems something of an injustice – the main thing Chile has is coastline, unless you count mountains – but no one ever said that war was fair.

Over a century later, the postmodernist short story writer Jorge Luis Borges is said to have proposed a novel solution to the war between Britain and his native Argentina concerning the sovereignty of the Falkland Islands: give them to Bolivia to make up for its lack of a coast. Perhaps that is why the country still maintains a navy to this day. Its 5,000 or so troops patrol the waters of Lake Titicaca, in the heights of the Andes, and every 23 March take part in the parades to mark Día del Mar – the 'day of the sea'. The landlocked country's navy remains as a symbol of Bolivian national pride, of its foreign policy goals – and the lingering hope that, one day, it may again reach the open ocean.

How the World Froze Territorial Claims in Antarctica

A slice of the pie

Antarctica has a population, give or take, of 40 million – providing, of course, that you're a penguin. From the perspective of a human, it's rather lower – up to 5,000 in summer, when the coast can bask in a relatively balmy zero degrees centigrade, but just 1,000 in winter, when the average temperature at the South Pole falls to −49°C (−56.2°F). This is, quite literally, unimaginably cold. I have no idea what it feels like. I hope never to find out.

These few thousand are mainly scientists who inhabit a few dozen isolated research bases scattered across an area a third bigger than Canada. But the fact there is, to the first approximation, nobody here has not stopped countries on the other side of the globe from staking their claims and attempting to carve up the continent. It's a story worth telling, partly because it shows just how far humanity is prepared to go in its hunger to draw lines on maps, but also because it hints that there might, just might, be a limit to it.

Antarctica is vast – bigger than Australia, or Europe, or any country in the world except Russia, and it is five-sixths the size of that. Its existence has been long suspected – its name was coined in the second century CE by the Greek geographer Marinus of Tyre to refer to the region on the opposite side of the globe from the Arctic. For centuries, European thinkers assumed there must be unknown landmasses on the far side of the world, if only to balance those in the north. (Their conclusions were sort of right, even if their logic was entirely wrong.)

And yet, until as late as the 1840s, it's not clear that anyone so much as set eyes on the place. Sitting as it does atop the South Pole, the continent is as inhospitable to human life as anywhere on this planet, so cold that 'freezing' would be an improvement and dark for long months of the year. The vast majority of the landmass is covered by an ice shelf that averages a mile thick, too. Little wonder that the first people who visited were almost certainly seal hunters. (We can't be sure because seal hunting was a competitive business and those engaged in it weren't in the habit of announcing where they'd been.) Most of those who see it today are scientists, researching everything from geophysics to astrophysics (the high altitude and stable atmosphere helps), to the aforementioned penguins.

Between those two groups, though, came the 'Heroic Age' of Antarctic exploration: the years between roughly 1897 and 1922 when a succession of explorers competed to explore previously unseen areas of the frozen continent, or be the first to cross from one side to the other, or achieve other magnificent physical feats. There was no real motive to conduct such expeditions except a desire for glory, and not everyone made it back: Robert Falcon Scott's attempt to be the first to reach the South Pole famously ended in failure after his team arrived to find that a rival expedition led by Roald Amundsen had got there thirty-three days before; all five men died on the return journey. Ernest Shackleton's equally famous, if probably apocryphal, newspaper ad, intended to recruit crew members for the *Endurance* as part of the Imperial Trans-Antarctic Expedition, conveys some sense of the era's tone: 'Men wanted for hazardous journey. Low wages, bitter cold, long hours of complete darkness. Safe return doubtful. Honour and recognition in event of success.'*

* Although these words have been much repeated over many decades, it's not clear whether any such ad was ever actually placed: the offer of a $100 prize to anyone who could identify the original source of the ad, made by the website Antarctic Circle back in the year 2000, seems to have gone unclaimed. If it was real, though, it was prophetic: the *Endurance* became trapped in the pack ice and then sank. By some miracle, the entire crew survived.

Not everyone's motives for visiting the Antarctic were concerned with personal glory alone. As far back as 1840, a French explorer by the name of Jules-Sébastien-César Dumont d'Urville had discovered a slab of frozen territory, claimed it for France and named it after his wife, Adélie. The following January, a British naval captain by the name of James Clark Ross discovered another bit of snow and ice, claimed it for Britain and named it after Queen Victoria. These claims were at first fairly theoretical, so nobody much cared, but when the Heroic Age kicked in, and the imperial powers began taking a more industrial approach to their Antarctic exploration, they started to look a bit more plausible.

Until, in 1924, US secretary of state Charles Evans Hughes felt moved to assert his country's doctrine 'that the discovery of lands unknown to civilization, even when coupled with a formal taking of possession, does not support a valid claim of sovereignty, unless the discovery is followed by an actual settlement of the discovered country' – in other words, the Americans were having none of it. This, though, was one of those statements made precisely because the assertion it conveyed was looking increasingly shaky. By 1924, the claims were piling up.

For one thing, the British had claimed yet more land, on the grounds that its antipodean territories were the closest inhabited places to it. The Ross Dependency, named after its discoverer, had passed to New Zealand in 1923; two other massive chunks surrounding it, and making up nearly half the continent, would pass to Australia a decade later. At least those claims had some basis in geography. The 1930s saw the Norwegians get into the game, too, and while it had admittedly been a Norwegian team that was first to the Pole, you'd be hard pressed to think of a country with less geographic basis to make claims in Antarctica.

Last but not least there were the Argentine (1932) and Chilean (1940) claims. These were arrived at partly through geography and partly through exploration, but also, at least in Chile's case, through reference to the Treaty of Tordesillas, which – as you'll remember – had claimed almost the entire western hemisphere for the Spanish Empire all the way back in 1494. This seems silly

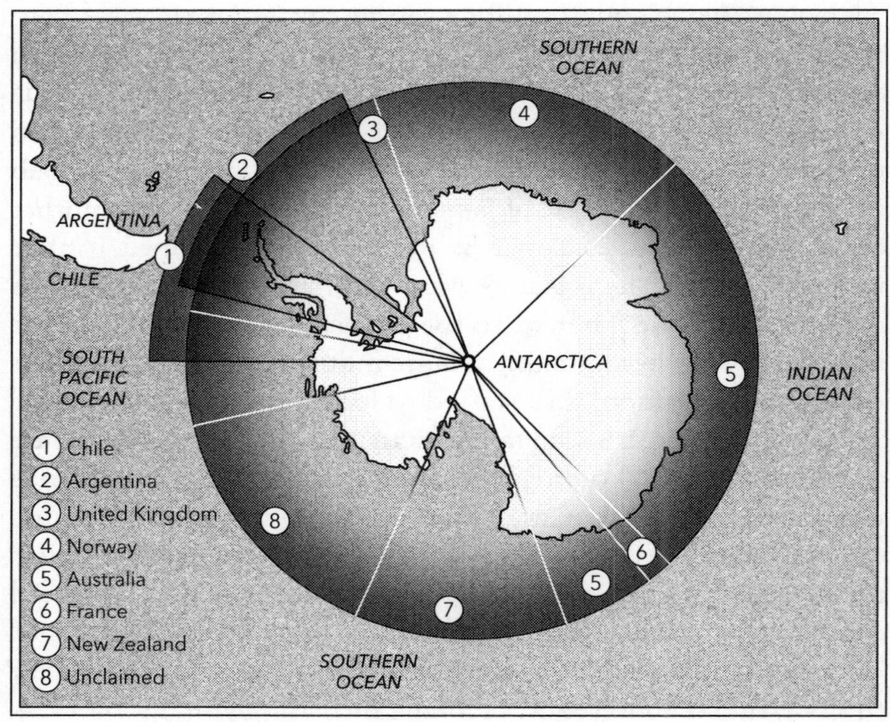

The overlapping territorial claims that slice Antarctica up like a pie. Only Marie Byrd Land, in the bottom left, remains unclaimed.

but I guess in these situations you use what you've got. The two helpfully recognised each other's claims in 1948.

All of which means that seven countries have now made formal claims. Their boundaries follow lines of longitude and divide the frozen continent up like a pie, albeit a pie in which some of the slices overlap, which is not something you can do with an actual pie. These do not include the abandoned claims, like Nazi Germany's brief attempt to claim part of Queen Maud Land as 'New Swabia', and to mark the fact by sprinkling it with metal swastikas. Neither does it include the claims never made official, like the 1929 attempt by US naval pilot Richard Byrd, the first man to fly over the South Pole, to claim a large block of land for the United States simply by dropping a flag on it. (This didn't work – it's in contravention of his own government's policy – but it did at least result in the largest block of unclaimed land on the planet being named in honour of his wife, Marie.)

One fact, and one story, should suffice to give a sense of the potential chaos of this time. The *fact* is that the slender peninsula that reaches out from western Antarctica,* as if it's pointing to South America, has no fewer than five different names. To the Argentinians, who claim it as part of their southernmost province of Tierra del Fuego, Antarctica and South Atlantic Islands, it's San Martin Land; to the Chileans, who claim it as part of *their* southernmost province of Antártica Chilena, it's O'Higgins Land. (Bernardo O'Higgins turns out, in a manner calculated to cause surprise followed immediately by guilt about poorly grounded assumptions, to have been a leader of the Chilean independence movement who was descended from Irish nobility.) Meanwhile, to the British – who, yes, claim it too – it was Graham Land; to the Americans, Palmer Land. Today, it's generally known as the Antarctic Peninsula, apparently to simplify matters.

The *story* concerns British–Argentine rivalry in the South Atlantic and a war, though possibly not the one you're expecting. Around the time the Luftwaffe were dropping those teeny swastikas on Queen Maud Land, the British decided that there might be good military and security reasons for stepping up their activities in the deep south. One taskforce visiting the marvellously named Deception Island in 1943 came across a brass cylinder announcing an Argentine claim. Appalled by this, the British destroyed

---

* There is no north and south Antarctica – or rather, towards the Pole is south, towards the coasts is north, which is not much use in terms of geographic identifiers (inner and outer are more easily grasped). East and west, though, are divided by hemisphere: broadly, East Antarctica is the bit that faces the Indian Ocean, while West Antarctica is the bit that faces South America and includes the peninsula. In fact, it is almost all peninsula: the apparent roundness of the continent stems from the fact the massive Ronne and Ross ice shelves fill two of the gaps between hunks of land.

Of the two regions, East Antarctica is several times bigger but West Antarctica contains the only growing land, at the very tip of the peninsula where, at the height of summer, you can find moss and lichen on the rocks. The boundary between the two is at the Transantarctic Mountain Range. So, now you know.

all signs of Argentine presence, hoisted the Union Jack, posted their own claim of ownership, and – nicely pass-agg touch, this – returned the cylinder to Argentina.

All this raised the possibility of ostensibly neutral Argentina growing friendly with Nazi Germany and being able to control traffic between Atlantic and Pacific oceans, which caused some disquiet back in London. And so the British government began making plans for a more permanent base on the island. When the team tasked with setting it up arrived, though, they found the notice of British claim gone, the Union Jack torn down and an Argentine flag in its place. Hmm.

The real war ended but the one of claim and counterclaim continued. In 1952, indeed, it led to actual shooting, when the Argentinian navy fired on a British meteorological party that had landed on contested territory at Hope Bay. (The Argentinians later apologised.) There was no shortage of other incidents, either. To back up their own claim to Queen Maud Land, the Norwegians mounted a joint expedition with the British and Swedes. Australia and France established bases; the South Africans raised their flag over some offshore islands. The US continued to refuse to recognise anyone's claims, despite having a base of their own, while the Soviets pretended not to care, then made plain they'd be recognising nobody's claims unless everyone asked their permission. By the early 1950s, it was obvious there was a need for some kind of treaty.

In the end, though, it wasn't politics that cleared up this mess but science. With sunspot activity due to peak in 1957–8, the scientific community designated it the 'International Geophysical Year' and began making plans for expeditions to an empty continent whose high altitude and lack of light pollution made it ideal for sunspot observations. To enable these expeditions, political leaders magnanimously agreed to a moratorium on territorial claims. With teams from across the world engaged in research that could benefit all mankind, and governments stepping back to let them do it, everyone suddenly seemed to be playing rather well together.

So, in the autumn of 1957, the US state department began sounding out the other eleven governments by that point active on the continent about making the moratorium permanent. In the end, after months of negotiation and multiple conferences, they went even further: the Antarctic Treaty, signed on 1 December 1959, reserved the entire continent for peaceful and scientific use, and agreed that nations could inspect each other's bases at will to ensure their compliance. It came into force in 1961. Later attempts to adjust the treaty, to create room for exploitation of any mineral wealth found on Antarctica, have so far failed: the continent is officially 'a natural reserve, devoted to peace and science'.

All that said, the competing claims are still there – article IV of the treaty explicitly states that signing the treaty does not amount to a renunciation of one. More than that, occasional attempts are made to strengthen them. In 1977, the Argentinians flew a pregnant woman out to give birth at Esperanza Base, on the grounds that an Argentinian birth on the station would bolster their claim: Emilio Palma became the first human being known to have been born on the frozen continent on 7 January 1978. In 1996, the British attempted to assert their soft power by turning one of their own bases in the region into the 'Penguin Post Office' – the most southerly post office in the world, a genuine Royal Mail sorting office, with four permanent staff. There's even a gift shop.

I wouldn't feel too warm and fuzzy about the chance of the scientific community managing to defer further disputes, either. Since the early 1980s, around two dozen countries have signed up to the Commission for the Conservation of Antarctic Marine Living Resources, which aims to do for the seas around Antarctica what the treaty has done for the continent itself. But while a small area off the South Orkneys, and a much larger one in the Ross Sea, have received protection, other schemes have been blocked by the difficulty of obtaining unanimity. In 2016, the commission proposed to turn an area of the Antarctic coastline five times the size of Germany into a giant nature reserve, where fishing and hunting would be banned and penguins, seals and whales protected. But in 2018, the plans hit the skids when Russia, Norway and China – not, as it happens, one of the nations that originally agreed the Antarctic Treaty – refused to back them. Science is all very well but national interest still has an annoying habit of outvoting it.

The Antarctic Treaty has been in place for over sixty years – but in the long sweep of history, that's nothing. And in 2048, it's up for review. Millions upon millions of years ago, the frozen continent was covered in tropical forest: beneath the ice there may be oil or other mineral riches. If human ingenuity allows us to get hold of the stuff, how confident can we really be the detente will hold?

The Other, Bigger, More Musical Europe

The European Broadcasting Area, and why Israel and Morocco can enter the Eurovision Song Contest

In 1974, Abba faced their Waterloo and won the contest for Sweden. Thirty-two years later, a heavy metal band named Lordi dressed up as monsters and the crown went to Finland. Twice now, in 2003 and 2021, the UK recorded a final score of *nul points*. Between the music, and the politics, and the countries shamelessly voting for their neighbours, and the countries using their songs to make political statements about something appalling another country did to them at some point in the twentieth century and thus triggering a diplomatic incident – using, let's not forget, a dance routine – the Eurovision Song Contest can be a lot of fun.

But it can also be pretty baffling, even if you ignore the bits involving people trying to dance to upbeat pop music under floodlights while dressed in heavy traditional costume or, in one case, as a giant hand.* That's because, despite literally being called *Euro*vision, some of the countries involved are not obviously in Europe. There are the three countries of the Caucasus region and while, sure, two of these, Georgia and Azerbaijan, have small patches of land on the European side of the mountains, the third, Armenia, is definitively on the Asian side. Then there's Israel,

* Germany's 2021 entry 'I Don't Feel Hate' by singer Jendrik Sigwart. The hand costume was meant to be a middle finger, as mentioned in the song's lyrics. Eurovision rules prevented such an outrageous thing from being worn on stage but were apparently happy with a costume showing *two* fingers raised aloft because it counted as a peace sign – even though the dancer, one Sophia Euskirchen, could revert it to a middle finger simply by lowering an arm.

which has entered most years since 1973 and won, four times, despite very clearly being in the Middle East. Morocco entered in 1980; Lebanon and Tunisia both promised to but then withdrew. Most bafflingly of all, since 2015, there's Australia.

That makes at least four countries that have entered the Eurovision Song Contest, and another two that came close, despite not being in Europe. The reason this is allowed is that a country's eligibility for participation in Eurovision has remarkably little to do with actually being in the geographical region known as Europe.

Eurovision's creation in the 1950s stemmed from the same impulse that gave rise to the European Coal and Steel Community (ECSC): a belief that cross-border cooperation between the nations of Europe would be the best way to prevent another crippling continental war. Where the process that led to the Treaty of Rome, and ultimately the EU, would do it through politics, the European Broadcasting Union, an alliance of public service broadcasters from across western Europe, would do through entertainment. To that end, it established both Eurovision (its TV arm) and Euroradio (you can probably guess) to distribute live broadcasts to its members across the continent. Events featured in its early years included the coronation of Queen Elizabeth II, the Narcissus Festival in Montreux and a tour of the Vatican, complete with apostolic blessing from Pope Pius XII.

By 1955, though, the EBU was keen to find new initiatives, ideally with some of the tension and competitive edge you'd get from live sport. (However the coronation went, there was very little doubt who'd be crowned at the end of it.) So, in January that year, its newly formed 'Programme Committee' met in Monte Carlo and approved two plans. One was a contest of amateur entertainers, a sort of primordial 'Europe's Got Talent', which was swiftly abandoned (the language barrier, one suspects, was a problem). The other, though, had more promise. Sergio Pugliese from the Italian broadcaster RAI proposed a song contest, an idea shamelessly lifted from the Italian-only one that had been held a few miles up the coast from Monte Carlo in Sanremo every year since 1951.

The first Grand-Prix Eurovision de la Chanson Européenne was held in May 1956, in Lugano, Switzerland. Only seven countries entered (oddly enough, the six members of the ECSC, plus the hosts); each, for the first and only time, offered two songs. And, after a broadcast lasting just one hour and forty minutes, Switzerland won.

The reason every future contest would restrict entrants to a single song is because the number of countries involved soon expanded. A lot. It had doubled by 1961 and hit twenty by 1978. By the twenty-first century, with the number of entries frequently topping forty and nobody wanting to sit through six to eight hours of Europop and geopolitics, Eurovision introduced semi-finals for everyone except the host nation and the 'Big Five' contributors to the EBU budget (France, Germany, Italy, Spain and the UK).

A total of fifty-two countries have participated in Eurovision to date, fifty-one of them still extant.* The number of sovereign states in the region has increased markedly since the 1990s, thanks to the dissolution of both the USSR and Yugoslavia, but, even so, there aren't fifty-one countries in Europe. On the most expansive definitions, which include every accepted sovereign state that occupies even the tiniest corner of the continent, you can only get to fifty.

The reason for the disparity, of course, is the assorted definitely non-European countries who've participated. And the reason for *that* is that the European Broadcasting Union has its own definition of Europe. A country can join the EBU, and thus participate in Eurovision, if it's in an area defined by the International Telecommunication Union, a UN agency, as follows:

> The 'European Broadcasting Area' is bounded on the west by the western boundary of Region 1, on the east by the meridian 40° East of Greenwich and on the south by the parallel

* Yugoslavia: the Soviet world didn't join the contest until after the dissolution of the USSR.

> 30° North, so as to include the northern part of Saudi Arabia and that part of those countries bordering the Mediterranean within these limits. In addition, Armenia, Azerbaijan, Georgia and those parts of the territories of Iraq, Jordan, Syrian Arab Republic, Turkey and Ukraine lying outside the above limits are included in the European Broadcasting Area.

Got that? Good.*

What that means in practice is that the EBA is everything between the Atlantic, a line running slightly to the east of Moscow and Sochi, and another running slightly to the south of Cairo (which was, you may recall, the boundary between Upper and Lower Egypt all those millennia ago). It was then extended a bit to make sure certain countries in eastern Europe and the Middle East are included in their entirety, and then, in 2007, extended further to include three in the Caucasus,† which fall outside that zone entirely. That means the EBA includes sixty globally recognised sovereign states: forty-nine to varying extents in Europe and eleven (Morocco, Algeria, Tunisia, Libya, Egypt, Israel, Jordan, Saudi Arabia, Iraq, Syria, Lebanon) outside it.‡

So could we one day see a sixty-nation Eurovision? Well, probably not. A number of countries – Syria, Saudi Arabia, Iraq – are not in the EBU, even if they are theoretically eligible. Even those that are may not want to get involved. Morocco, after all, entered

---

* Actually, I'm oversimplifying to keep the book readable; the full text is even worse. How is the western boundary of Region 1 defined? By 'Line B': 'a line running from the North Pole along meridian 10° West of Greenwich to its intersection with parallel 72° North; thence by great circle arc to the intersection of meridian 50° West and parallel 40° North; thence by great circle arc to the intersection of meridian 20° West and parallel 10° South; thence along meridian 20° West to the South Pole'. Another way of putting that might be 'the Atlantic Ocean' but if we've learned anything from this book it's surely that it's precisely that sort of vagueness that causes all the trouble.

† Although the westernmost point of Georgia is within 500m (1,640ft) of the meridian.

‡ You're wondering why there are fifty states with territory in Europe but only forty-nine of them in the EBA, aren't you? Knew you were. Don't worry, we'll get to that soon enough.

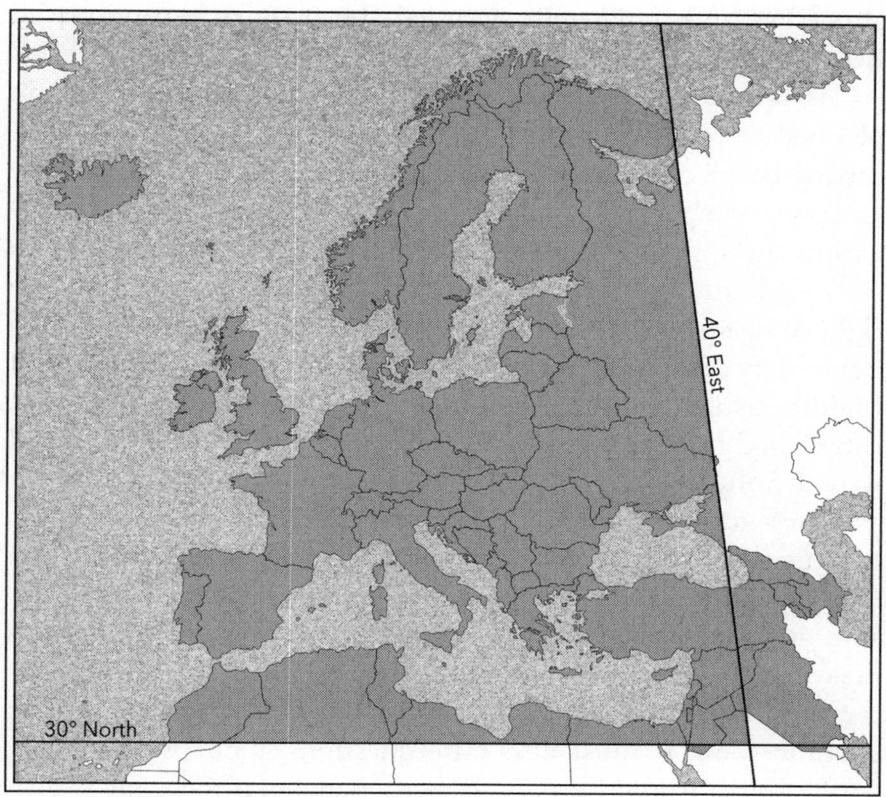

The European Broadcasting Area, shaded in grey. Note the extensions to include the Caucasus countries, plus outlying areas of Ukraine, Turkey, Syria, Jordan and Iraq.

in 1980, with Samira Bensaïd's 'Bitaqat Hub', both the only entry ever to come from a North African country and the only one sung in Arabic. It placed second to last and the Moroccan authorities were so incensed they vowed never to return.

Then there's the issue of Israel. Tunisia intended to enter the contest in 1977 but withdrew at the last minute. The reason has never been specified but it's widely believed to be because its government didn't want to compete with the Jewish state. The following year, the authorities in Jordan declined to show the Israeli entry, opting for some pictures of flowers instead. When it became clear that Israel was going to win, they cut the broadcast altogether and unilaterally awarded the prize to second-placed Belgium.

As late as 2005, Lebanon's national broadcaster Télé Liban planned to repeat this trick, getting around laws against broadcasting Israeli content by simply cutting away during Israel's entry and pretending it didn't exist. This, Eurovision said, was not really within the spirit of the exercise, and so Lebanon withdrew from the competition. After Israel won the 2018 contest, and thus the right to host the 2019 one, its minister of communications Julien Bahloul tweeted that he would personally invite a number of Middle Eastern countries to compete next year. But since some of those cited fell well outside the European Broadcasting Area and were definitely not eligible, nothing more was heard of it.

These days, if anything, the contest is getting smaller. In 2021, Belarus was expelled from the EBU over concerns about media freedom; Russia followed the following year because of the invasion of Ukraine. The union's commitment to basic liberal values makes it seem extremely unlikely that Kazakhstan – which has a corner in Europe, if not in the EBA – will be invited to join anytime soon. It must also raise questions about whether, say, Saudi Arabia would be allowed to participate, if for some reason it expressed an interest.

It's worth noting that there are some countries in Europe, too, which have never participated. On the only occasion Liechtenstein considered entering, back in the 1970s, it was pre-emptively disqualified on the grounds that it is not a member of the EBU. The Vatican has never taken part either, which is, with that talent for costuming, a shame. So the dream of a sixty-country Eurovision – possibly one that goes on for weeks – seems likely to remain just that.

That said, Australia – which is very clearly neither north of Cairo nor west of Moscow – gets to take part simply because the contest has a lot of fans down there. So who knows how the organisers of Eurovision will be defining the borders of Europe in the decades to come?

Boundaries in the Air

How the aviation sector carves up the world

At around 10.35 one Thursday morning in December 1903, Orville Wright became the first man ever to successfully pilot a plane. This is, it must be said, a fairly generous definition of the word 'successfully' – that first flight in Kitty Hawk, North Carolina, lasted all of twelve seconds and travelled only thirty-six metres (118ft). The event nonetheless marks the beginning of a new phase in human history – one in which it was possible to slip the bounds of earth in machines heavier than air.

By 2017, data from FlightAware suggests, there were around a million people in the air at any given moment. At the time the first pharaohs were unifying Egypt, a mere 5,000 years before the Wright Flyer left the ground, there were probably substantially fewer than 50 million people on the entire planet: the idea that a million of us might be up in the sky at any given time, and that this is not any kind of special achievement but merely the way things are, should never cease to blow our minds.

The air above us, of course, is free of the sort of seas and mountains and resource constraints that led humanity to divide the ground below into pieces. Yet even there, we've found reasons to carve it up using man-made lines.

No government in its right mind would entirely surrender control of its own airspace, of course. Yet a system in which every country jealously guarded its skies without reference to its neighbours would risk failure, in the most dramatic and visible way. Attempts to find a compromise, so that everyone could feel confident they weren't in danger of bombs or bits of burning aircraft raining down on them at random, are thus almost as old as aviation itself. As far back as 1919, attendees to the Paris peace conferences were agreeing that, given all the aerial warfare the world had just witnessed, this might be a good time to try regulating this whole air travel thing.

So alongside the various other treaties that popped out of that process came the 'Convention Relating to the Regulation of Aerial Navigation'. That established both the principle of sovereign control of airspace and the first agency, the International Commission for Air Navigation, charged with regulating the whole sector. Both the theory of airspace sovereignty and the recognition of the need for an international agency to make it work in practice survive to this day, although the details have changed. Today, the job falls to the International Civil Aviation Organization (ICAO), a part of the UN, established by the Chicago Convention of 1944.

One of its key jobs has been to carve the sky up into pieces more rational in shape or size than the lands below. First came the continent-sized ICAO regions, an attempt to sort the planet into sections in which it made sense for air traffic controllers to be in constant contact and to coordinate quite closely – Australia or the US may be able to exist in glorious isolation, but if you're running air traffic control (ATC) for Belgium, you probably also want to know what's happening in the Netherlands and France. Initially, there were ten of these but, following some periodic shuffling, there are currently only nine, and they bear only a loose relationship to the continents on the ground below. The European Region, like the Roman Empire and the Eurovision Song Contest alike, includes North Africa and the Levant; the Caribbean one includes Mexico and northern South America; the North Atlantic and Pacific are their own regions; and so on.

Beneath those come the 'flight information regions' (FIRs), which define who is responsible for managing passing planes (normally a government agency: the UK's Civil Aviation Authority, say, or the USA's Federal Aviation Administration). In his *Financial Times* newspaper column, pilot Mark Vanhoenacker has described FIRs as 'the countries of the sky'. But these don't quite map onto the map of the world we're all used to either.

For one thing, they need to cover sea as well as land, as nobody wants planes colliding there either. Coastal waters are generally included in the same FIR as a neighbouring country; more distant international ones are sorted by 'oceanic' sectors, generally delegated to the closest authority. A large stretch of northeastern Atlantic, for example, is designated as 'Shanwick Oceanic', after a place that doesn't exist: it's a portmanteau of Shannon and Prestwick, home to the Irish and UK ATCs responsible.

Then there's the fact that the countries on the ground are (you may have noticed this) radically different sizes. To make sense of that, many are divided into multiple FIRs (France has five; the USA twenty), each with their own ATC centre. At the other end of the scale, some tiny states simply bunk up with a neighbour – Luxembourg, say, is covered from Brussels, on the grounds that it'd be stupid to do anything else.

Lastly, there are groups of countries which have delegated ATC to shared international agencies. These include ASECNA, which has covered a large chunk of West Africa and also, confusingly, Madagascar, a couple of thousand miles to the southeast, ever since 1959; and COCESNA, which has covered six different Central American countries since 1960. Since some of the countries involved have occasionally been at war, this feels like an impressive feat of building trust.*

As the continent with, on average, the smallest countries, Europe has been lumbered with the most complex set of air boundaries and has been attempting to simplify matters in a similar way. The European Commission, the executive arm of the

---

* There are other wrinkles. In some areas, airspace is also split into lower and upper layers, referred to as FIRs and UIRs respectively, and with slightly different borders. There are differences between 'controlled airspace', which comes in several grades requiring different levels of engagement with ATC, and where pilots have to follow instructions, and 'uncontrolled airspace', where they don't – a sort of aviation equivalent of driving off-road. There are also 'sectors', which FIRs themselves can create or merge at will depending on traffic flows, a sort of equivalent of air traffic local government. But even putting all this in a footnote, I fear, is burdening the reader with an unwelcome level of detail, so let's leave things there.

non-sovereign European Union, has been hoping to introduce a 'single European sky initiative'. This would divide the continent into a series of 'functional airspace blocks', which make more sense than the current jumble of national boundaries. It could also improve efficiency, cut CO_2 emissions and reduce the number of expensive air traffic controllers the continent needs. Great deal, right?

Alas, cutting well-paid jobs, it turns out, is not something national governments are that enthusiastic about. Nor is handing control of the skies over to a supranational body (EU countries still largely manage their own defence policies). So far, then, the single European sky remains carved into a couple of dozen bits.

An even trickier problem arose on the continent in 2014 when, as part of its invasion of the Crimea, Russia seized control of the local ATC frequencies. In the opinion of ICAO, though, this was actually still Ukrainian airspace. All this raised the unnerving prospect of two different national aviation authorities offering conflicting advice to the same planes through the same region – such an obvious recipe for disaster that European governments simply advised everyone to stop flying through it. Western airlines generally did, cancelling some flights and diverting many more, and thus, perversely, leaving the Russian national carrier Aeroflot to dominate the now empty Crimean aviation market. Oh dear.

If some regions have at times ended up claimed by more than one ATC, there are a couple which have been deliberately not assigned to any. One is a stretch of Pacific, south of Mexico and west of Peru – an attempt, it seems, to limit human activity in the Galapagos Islands. By international agreement, to protect their wealth of wildlife, all journeys there must begin in nearby Ecuador.

The other region left off the air traffic control map is a tiny stretch of land north of the Barents Sea, which fell through the cracks thanks to a decades-long border dispute between Norway and Russia. (That was actually resolved through a statesmanlike but not very interesting compromise back in 2010, but the air traffic control community has been slow to adapt.) The forgotten region is only a few miles wide and doesn't take long to cross. But, Vanhoenacker wrote in his aforementioned column in December 2021, 'It's not hard to imagine how, on the most special night of the year, every Christmas-loving child could guess at the mystery it shelters.'

Perhaps it's not. But any flying sleighs in the area should watch out for planes, nonetheless. Nobody else is.

The Final Frontier

Where does space begin, and who does it belong to?

In the summer of 2021, the planet entered a new space race. The first such race, which obsessed the world of the 1950s and 60s, had been part of an existential struggle between the USA and USSR, the West and the East, capitalism and communism, freedom and totalitarianism. This one, by contrast, had rather the quality of a dick-waving competition between two middle-aged men who were far too rich for their own good.

In the red corner was Britain's Richard Branson, the billionaire founder of the Virgin Group – Virgin Mobile, Virgin Money, Virgin Active (gyms), Virgin Atlantic (airlines) and so on – whose Virgin Galactic had been launching stuff into the sky with varying degrees of success since 2003. In the blue corner was Jeff Bezos, founder of Amazon and then the richest man the world had ever seen, whose Blue Origin had been doing much the same since 2005. Both were hoping that their company would be the first to offer passengers the chance to buy a ticket into space at a price that merely resembled a mortgage, rather than a small nation's GDP. Both – though they'd never admit it – must have been worried that the other would get there first.*

In the end, the gold went to Virgin, which won through the sneaky tactic of 'moving their launch date up a bit'. On 11 July

* Also involved in the private space race, if not in this particular skirmish, was Elon Musk's SpaceX. It is, at the least, striking that all these men have looked at their fortunes and immediately turned to space travel. Imagine what they could have done if they instead were interested in healthcare? Or buildings schools or roads in the developing world? Or, hey, just giving their staff a pay rise?

2021, Branson tweeted a video of himself, weightless in the cabin of the VSS *Unity*, 86km (53.4mi) above the Earth. Very few people on the planet below paid the slightest attention, alas, because Virgin had scheduled the flight to clash with the final of the UEFA European Football Championship. (England lost 3–2 to Italy on penalties, after a 1–1 draw in extra time.)

Blue Origin, though, did not seem disheartened. Two days earlier, the company had tweeted a graphic comparing its performance – the number of flights it had conducted, the existence of an 'escape system', the fact it offered the 'largest windows in space' – to that of Virgin. It led on the claim that, for '96 per cent of the world's population, space begins 100km (62.1mi) up at the internationally recognized Kármán line'. Its own spaceship, *New Shepard*, 'was designed to fly above the Kármán line so none of our astronauts have an asterisk next to their name'. Branson's spaceflight, Bezos's company was suggesting, did not count. Neither, more to the point, would that of any passenger who decided to waste their money on a trip with Virgin Galactic.

Oh, and by the way, they wouldn't be able to see much out of the windows, either.

Who had truly won this new phase of the space race would, in other words, come down to a question about a boundary: where does Earth's atmosphere end and outer space begin?

The best-known answer to this question came in 1957 from a man who may not have been trying to answer it at all: a Hungarian physicist and aerospace engineer by the name of (you may have seen this coming) Kármán. Theodore von Kármán, to give him his full name, was active in both aeronautics, which concerned the science of flight within the atmosphere, and astronautics, which concerned the science of flight beyond it. At some point, he theorised, the one must give way to the other. He put the boundary at the point in the atmosphere where the air becomes too thin to contribute aerodynamic lift. The Fédération Aéronautique Internationale (FAI), the world governing body for air sports, would later place the altitude where this happens at a frankly suspiciously round 100km (62.1mi) up. By that definition, the Blue

Origin social media team was quite correct: Richard Branson has never actually been to space.

The thing is, though, Kármán was not trying to come up with a definitive answer to the question of where space begins, merely that of where aircraft would no longer be able to fly. More to the point, his calculations actually came out at around 84km (52.2mi); at some point, somebody had started to round up. VSS *Unity* breached that limit – just.

Why this vagueness about the number? After all, the Kármán line has been widely discussed and debated among scientists. It came out of discussions at conferences among the very cleverest people who think about this kind of thing, and Kármán discussed it in his posthumously published autobiography *The Wind and Beyond*. But it never formally appeared in a peer-reviewed journal. That, according to the astrophysicist and space historian Jonathan McDowell, makes it not settled science but what's known as a 'folk theorem'. So: Virgin might have exceeded the Kármán line, which might not be that meaningful anyway.

Blue Origin's attempt to dismiss its rival's achievement is already looking pretty shaky. But, as it happens, its claim that the definition of the edge of space is 'internationally recognized' is pretty questionable, too. The UN accepts it, sure, but, well, a lot of other bodies rather closer to the space race have recognised rather a lot of other lines, too. A 2014 paper with the title 'Where is Space? And Why Does That Matter?' written by a pair of researchers at the Institute for Defense Analyses think tank found no fewer than five altitudes then in common use. They ranged from 80km (49.7mi) ('roughly the point at which aerodynamic control surfaces are no longer useful') to 129–150km (80.2–93.2mi, a curiously roomy figure, cited by a US army training reference text as the lowest point at which you could orbit). Within both the US military and NASA, different definitions have been used at different times and for different reasons. NASA used to follow the FAI definition but switched to the lower US military one (50 miles; just over 80km) in 2005, apparently to avoid the possibility of some pilots getting to count themselves proper astronauts while others did not, even though they'd flown on literally the same trip.

In other words, despite what the Blue Origin social media team may want us to think, there is no consensus whatsoever. Spreading a little doubt, though, may be good enough for Jeff Bezos. For potential passengers, the point of going to space is bragging rights. Is the risk that your friends might say you didn't *really* go to space a risk worth taking? Better choose Blue Origin over Virgin, just in case.

This debate hasn't really mattered thus far. 'Over the past sixty years of space travel, most things have not hung out in this liminal region for long periods of time,' McDowell told the *Atlantic* in 2021. That, though, might change. The point where space begins, after all, is also the point at which national airspace ends. 'Below this line, space belongs to each country,' Kármán wrote in his autobiography. 'Above this level there would be free space.'

To understand why this is important, imagine a satellite placed in orbit around the Earth at the plausible, if uncomfortable, height of 90km (55.9mi). If space begins at 80km (49.7mi) then this is just another of the several thousand satellites currently in orbit above our heads: no harm, no foul. If space doesn't begin until 100km (62.1mi), however, then our satellite is passing through national airspace. And a hostile power would be within its rights to shoot it down.

In other words, the beginning of space isn't just about rich boys and their toys. It is, as with so many of the other borders we've discussed, a matter of national security.

This may, indeed, be why the US has been so reluctant to formally define an altitude at which space begins. Were it to state, definitively, that the line is at 80km (49.7mi), then it would be inviting Chinese or Russian satellites at 81km (50.3mi), while simultaneously making it impossible to place its own satellites at 79km (49.1mi) above other states. Why tie your hands when you don't have to? Even if the border is never formalised, though, low Earth orbit could still become a flashpoint. The geography writer Tim Marshall has noted that it's the point at which spacecraft may one day be able to refuel for longer-distance journeys. That makes it a 'rough equivalent of the geopolitical choke points on Earth, such as the Strait of Hormuz or the Suez Canal'.*

Nor will arguments about sovereignty necessarily stop at the water's edge, as it were. The 1967 Outer Space Treaty, signed by a sizable majority of the world's nations, defined space exploration as 'in the interests of all countries and . . . the province of all mankind'. Space itself, it said, was 'not subject to national appropriation by claim of sovereignty, by means of use or occupation, or by any other means'; while the Moon and other celestial bodies 'shall be used exclusively for peaceful purposes'. All this sounds lovely. Alas, the treaty did not offer any definition of peaceful purposes, which seems to limit its value. (Does mining of resources that could, theoretically, be used in war count? Do purely defensive weapons?) A follow-up, the 1979 Moon Treaty, attempted to answer some of the outstanding questions. That, though, has been agreed by just eighteen countries. China, Russia and the USA are not among them.

Indeed, there are signs of what looks unnervingly like a turf war breaking out. In 2020, the US and seven of its allies agreed a new framework for space exploration. The Artemis Accords reaffirm the Outer Space Treaty's assertion that space should be reserved for peaceful purposes and, in a move reminiscent of the Antarctic Treaty, commit their signatories to inform each other of their activities on the Moon or other celestial bodies. They also provide for the creation of 'safety zones', a form of lunar spheres of influence, which other signatories are expected to respect and avoid. But the recent chill in relations means that both Russia and China were excluded, despite being two of the nations most likely to set up resource extraction projects or other forms of presence on the Moon. This has gone down about as well as you might expect. As one Chinese military commentator, Song Zhongping,

* This quote is from an article in *Prospect* but in the name of crediting one's sources, Marshall's 2021 book *The Power of Geography* was a substantial influence on this entry from this point on.

told the *Global Times*: 'The US is developing a new space version of an "Enclosure Movement", in pursuit of colonisation and claiming sovereignty over the Moon.' And what happens if a power that never signed the accords breaches them by landing their own spacecraft within a safety zone? Allowing a potentially hostile power to get too close to lunar operations hardly seems an option. But the wrong reaction could serve to prove Song's point.

In 1980, a recently divorced American businessman named Dennis Hope found what he believed to be a loophole in the Outer Space Treaty. As you'll recall, the 1967 agreement had claimed that celestial bodies are 'not subject to national appropriation by claim of sovereignty'. Dennis, though, was not a nation but a person. So, he says, he wrote to the UN, claiming that he now owned the Moon and promising to subdivide and sell it. When nobody replied, he took that as permission and began selling small plots of land for around $20 per acre. There are a lot of acres on the Moon. Hope has made millions.

This is obviously nonsense: Hope's loophole doesn't exist; his certificates of ownership are unenforceable, a novelty gift not a true title, and those who own them no doubt know that.

But it isn't nonsense because lunar or celestial sovereignty are theoretically impossible – they are, indeed, all too plausible. 'Without an up-to-date legal framework governing these strategic points in space,' Marshall adds, 'we may end up competing for them as we did for control of those on Earth.' Even as humanity reaches for the stars, our flaws and our vanities will be with us on the ride.

Conclusion: The End of the Line

The myriad border crises of 2023 and beyond

On 12 July 2021, Russia's president, Vladimir Putin, published an essay with the ominous title of 'On the Historical Unity of Russians and Ukraine'. In it, he argued at length – great length: 7,000 words, more than twice the length of any of the entries in this book – that the peoples of Russia, Belarus and Ukraine were one, a concept known as the all-, pan- or triune-Russian nation. All three, he said, could date their origins to the state known as Kievan Rus' in the ninth century; all three shared a language, a religion, a cultural heritage.

The reason *Velikorossiya*, Great Russia, had become divided from *Malorossiya*, Little Russia – Ukraine – was the machinations of, variously, early modern Lithuanians and Poles, the Catholic church and the modern West. But he did not entirely spare his countrymen from criticism: the Lenin-era Communist Party had erred by redrawing Ukraine's borders, handing it territory that by all rights belonged to Russia. So had their successors, who had allowed Ukraine to secede.

All this, Putin argued, was his people's 'great common tragedy' – one it was clear that he, at least, had no intention of allowing to continue. So on 21 February of the following year, he made a speech in which he argued that Ukraine had 'actually never had stable traditions of real statehood' and recognised the 'independence' of two breakaway provinces in the east of the country. Three days later, his army invaded Ukraine.

The reason I mention all this is not because, on almost the last page of the book, I have decided it's time to evaluate the truth of Putin's claims. There are, as it happens, plenty of historic and cultural links between Ukraine and Russia, but one could say the same about Austria and Germany, or Ireland and the UK, and to my mind, such links matter a lot less than the question of whether the people of the other country actually want to be united with your own. (This, I suppose, is why I'm a soggy liberal writer and not a genocidal dictator of some kind.) No, the reason I mention it is because the war in Ukraine remains one of the biggest news stories happening in the world as I write, affecting geopolitics, the energy markets and the economy, too. It's the biggest war Europe has seen in decades. And it is, fundamentally, a story about where the line between two peoples should go, and whether there should be a line between them at all.

The very name *Ukraina*, indeed, comes from a Slavonic word meaning 'borderland', a term roughly equivalent to 'march': one of the reasons its government would really prefer you didn't refer to its country as *the* Ukraine is because to do so would inadvertently pose a question about what exactly it is the borderlands *of*.

The war in Ukraine is a war about a border.

This may be the biggest and most dangerous, but it is far from the only story about borders dominating the headlines as I write. Turning to the domestic news pages in the spring of 2023, I can read about the British government's promise to 'stop the Channel boats', an ongoing 'crisis' in which a few thousand desperate people attempt the crossing from France in dinghies each month in order to claim asylum. This is a story about a border in the obvious sense that that of the US–Mexican border wall discussed on page 103 was. But it's a story about a border in another, less talked about sense, too. Until a few years ago, relatively few migrants would attempt the dangerous crossing because European law meant they would be returned to the first EU country that they entered: it was therefore just not worth the risk. Since Brexit, though, European law no longer applies in Britain. One side effect of the decision that Britain should leave the EU is that a refugee crisis in the Mediterranean has become one in the English Channel.

Elsewhere, I can see that the Northern Ireland protocol, a bafflingly complicated set of issues relating to the exact status of the one part of the UK with a land border with the EU, is in the headlines again. Meanwhile, the Scottish National Party government, which runs the devolved administration in Edinburgh, is demanding a referendum over whether Scotland should leave the UK altogether (this has been true for quite a few years now). Oh, and the Argentine defence minister has claimed that the Malvinas – the Falklands – are to be 'returned' to a country that has never really held them.

The borders of the United Kingdom have been remarkably stable, considering the effect the country has wrought upon those in the rest of the world: despite the best efforts of the SNP, they have been unchanged since 1922.* If ever there were a country that should be immune to banging on about its own borders then surely it's this one.

And yet, my compatriots clearly aren't: questions of where one thing ends and another begins, of exactly where to draw the line, remain a remarkably potent force in our politics. Even the UK's current economic weakness – resulting in part from the new barriers to trade between us and our neighbours, and the lack of investment that followed – can be blamed at least partly on a referendum expressing the idea that *we* are not the same as *them*.

It may be hard, in the light of everything covered in this book, to convince yourself that borders are a good thing. I hope the stories contained within have entertained, even made you laugh, but surely none of them has left you thinking, *Wow, what a brilliant, life-affirming border.* Yet it is also not clear they are something we can do away with.

Throughout history, untold numbers of communities – urban, national, imperial – have established, expanded and defended their borders. They've done so for a variety of interrelated reasons: to highlight their power, mark their territory and assist

* It often feels to me like we pretend it's been longer even than that. We ignore the fact that the majority of Ireland broke away following a rather nasty war of independence through the clever trick of pretending to ourselves that Ireland was never *really* in the UK in the first place. That, though, is another story.

in its administration; to defend themselves from external security threats and make sure those threats are pushed ever farther from the centre of power; to mark the limits of their responsibility, delineate 'us' from 'them', and then 'keep' them on the far side of some notional line. The exact details of these motivations, and the lines that result, may be constantly shifting but their existence seems pretty much eternal. The idea of a world without borders, where people are as free to move as money, is an attractive one, but the last person who seemed to think he had a plan to create it was John Lennon, and look what happened to him.

In the opening pages of this book, I noted that if you searched for a map of the world, your search engine of choice would almost certainly provide you with one showing borders aplenty. If you were to do the same in a hundred years, the lines it shows will almost certainly have changed. But do you imagine for a moment they'll be gone, either abolished or seen now as unimportant? Do you imagine the headlines in that far-off year will be free of stories that relate, however indirectly, to a line that somebody, somewhere, once drew on a map?

Any specific border may be changeable and contingent, but the underlying *concept* of borders may be eternal, as potent a force as gluttony or greed. Humanity has been drawing lines between 'us' and 'them' since long before anyone invented maps to draw them on. We're surely not going to stop now.

Further Reading

In retrospect I was researching this book for many years before I ever knew I was going to write it. The idea of a book about borders specifically has its origins, sort of, in 'Boundary Issues', an occasional series about weird or amusing borders I wrote for *CityMetric*, the late lamented *New Statesman* website I launched in 2014 and ran until 2020. But a slightly obsessive interest in both world history in general and the development of national identity in particular has guided my reading and listening choices over many years.

Top of the list comes *How to Invent a Country*, the long-running BBC Radio 4 documentary series presented by Misha Glenny and produced by Miles Warde. Other things that have had a disproportionate impact on this book include Simon Winder's trilogy for Picador, *Germania* (2010), *Danubia* (2013) and *Lotharingia* (2019); Jonathan Holslag's *A Political History of the World,* Pelican, 2018; Zoran Nikolic's *Atlas of Unusual Borders*, Collins, 2019; Norman Davies' *Vanished Kingdoms: The History of Half-Forgotten Europe*, Penguin, 2012; and a number of instalments in the *Great Courses* lectures series, especially Peter N. Stearns' 'A Brief History of the World' (2007) and Vejas Gabriel Liulevicius' 'War, Peace and Power: Diplomatic History of Europe, 1500–2000' (2008). I should also credit *Encyclopaedia Britannica* and Wikipedia, two very different but equally invaluable resources, which the history sections, especially, leaned on extensively; Frank Jacobs' *New York Times* column 'Borderlands'; the BBC's *In Our Time* series; and the excellent *The Rest Is History* podcast.

Introduction: The history of the concept of borders was inspired by a conversation with Philip Steinberg, director of the IBRU Centre for Borders Research at the University of Durham. The quote from historian John Mears of Southern Methodist University is taken from 'Analyzing the Phenomenon of Borderlands from Comparative and Cross-cultural Perspectives', a conference paper presented to the American Historical Association in 2001.

PART ONE: HISTORIES

The Unification of Upper and Lower Egypt: Toby Wilkinson, *The Rise and Fall of Ancient Egypt*, Random House, 2011; Bob Brier, 'The History of Ancient Egypt', *The Great Courses*, 1999.

The Great Wall of China, and the Border as Unifier: Jared Diamond, *Guns, Germs & Steel*, W. W. Norton, 1997; *In Our Time: The Great Wall of China*, BBC Radio 4, 2010. The *National Geographic* quote was taken from a travel article entitled 'Discover China's History Along the Great Wall'; the list of early walls from *Encyclopaedia Britannica*.

Why Is Europe Not a Peninsula in Asia? Herodotus, *Histories* (specifically book IV); Martin W. Lewis and Kären E. Wigen, *The Myth of Continents: A Critique of Metageography*, University of California Press, 1997. The observation about the Istanbul rail network is my own, and I apologise profusely.

The Roman *Limes* and the Power of the Periphery: *The World History Encyclopaedia*'s entry on 'The Crisis of the Third Century' and the 2022 episode of the *Rest Is History* podcast entitled 'When Did the Roman Empire Fall?' (episode 156) were both invaluable in shaping this essay. Other sources included Terry Jones and Alan Ereira, *Barbarians: An Alternative Roman History*, BBC Books, 2007; and Jack Keilo's attempts to map the distribution of Roman legions on centrici.hypotheses.org.

The Legacies of Charlemagne: Simon Winder, *Germania*, Picador, 2010; Simon Winder, *Lotharingia*, Picador, 2019; *In Our Time: The Carolignian Renaissance*, BBC Radio 4, 2006; Charles West, 'Plenty of Puff', *London Review of Books*, 19 December 2019.

The Borders of Great Britain: Max Adams, *The First Kingdom*, Apollo, 2021; Marc Morris, *The Anglo-Saxons*, Hutchinson, 2021; Norman Davies, *Vanished Kingdoms*, Viking, 2012 (specifically the chapter on Alt Clud, the kingdom of Strathclyde). The Tacitus quote is taken from his biography of his father-in-law, Gnaeus Julius Agricola.

Of Feudalism, Marquises, Margraves and Marcher Lords: The broader arguments about early European state formation, and what it mean for border territories, is something I have absorbed from a variety of history books. Explanations of the problem with feudalism can be found in Elizabeth A. R. Brown, 'The Tyranny of a Construct: Feudalism and Historians of Medieval Europe', *The American Historical Review*, 1974; and Susan Reynolds, 'Still Fussing about Feudalism', from *Italy and Early Medieval Europe*, OUP, 2018. The delightful fact about the French verb 'se marquiser' comes from *Encyclopaedia Britannica*'s entry on the word 'Marquess'.

The Open Borders Policies of Genghis Khan: Peter N. Stearns, 'A Brief History of the World', *The Great Courses*, 2007; John Man, *Genghis Khan: Life, Death, and Resurrection*, Thomas Dunne, 2005; Mohammad Iqbal, 'The Impact of Mongol Invasion on the Muslim World and the Political, Economic and Social Ramifications', *Social Science Research Network*, 2021; 'One Steppe Back', *Economist*, 23 December 1999. The rather expansive claims about Khan's descendants come from Tatiana Zerjal et al., 'The Genetic Legacy of the Mongols', *American Journal of Human Genetics*, 2003; the riposte from Charmaine D. Royal et al., 'Inferring Genetic Ancestry: Opportunities, Challenges, and Implications', *American Journal of Human Genetics*, 2010.

Spain and Portugal Carve Up the World: *The Invention of Spain*, BBC Radio 4, 2012; Simon Winder, *Danubia*, Picador, 2013. The J. H. Parry quote comes from *The Age of Reconnaissance: Discovery, Exploration, and Settlement 1450–1650*, Cardinal, 1973.

Holy, Roman and an Empire: Simon Winder, *Germania*, Picador, 2010; *The Invention of Germany*, BBC Radio 4, 2011; James Hawes, *The Shortest History of Germany*, The Experiment, 2019. The Humboldt story is from Eric Dorn Brose, *German History 1789–1871*, Berghahn

Books, 2013; the inclusion of Gandersheim should be credited to Dr Matthew Symonds of University College London. The problem with treating Westphalia as the creation of the modern state system was outlined by Andreas Osiander in 'Sovereignty, International Relations, and the Westphalian Myth', *International Organization*, MIT Press, 2001.

Britain, Ireland and the Invention of Cartographic Colonialism: Both the decision to write about the Down Survey map, and to compare it to the Jefferson grid, were influenced by James Vincent's *Beyond Measure: The Hidden History of Measurement*, W. W. Norton, 2022; glorious aerial photographs of the latter can be found all over the internet, for example on the Jefferson Grid Instagram account or in Kaushik Patowary's 'The Jefferson Grid', *Amusing Planet*, 5 June 2018. My description of William Petty's life and works comes largely from his biography on the Institute for New Economic Thinking's History of Economic Thought website.

The Much Misunderstood Mason–Dixon line: Phil Mawson, 'The men who drew the Mason–Dixon Line', BBC News, 2 September 2017; William F. Swindler, 'Mason & Dixon: Their Line and its Legend', *American Heritage Magazine*, February 1964; Charles W. Mitchell, 'When Maryland Almost Got Philadelphia: The Remarkable Story of the Mason–Dixon Line', Maryland Center for History and Culture website.

The Local Government Reforms of Emperor Napoleon I: I have long been obsessed with the maps of the First French Empire, and its division of much of western Europe into départements, a period described in *The Invention of France*, BBC Radio 4, 2015. The history of local government in France is described on 'Les départements: la juste proximité depuis 230 ans', on the website of the Portail National Des Archives. The truth about Zhou Enlai's comment on the French Revolution was explained by Mark Pack, on his website in 2013.

The American Invasion of Mexico: Gary W. Gallagher et al., 'The History of the United States', *The Great Courses*, 2003; 'President Polk and the Taking of the West', Constitutional Rights Foundation; 'The Mexican–American war in a nutshell', National Constitution Center, 2023.

The Schleswig-Holstein Business: 'The Schleswig Holstein Question; Earl Russell's Dispatch to the Federal Diet', *New York Times*, 31 January 1864; *The Invention of Germany*, BBC Radio 4, 2011; James Hawes, 'History gave the world a German leader Putin reminds us of (and it's not Hitler)', *The Conversation*, 3 July 2014.

'. . . Where No White Man Ever Trod': Henry M. Stanley, *The Congo and the Founding of its Free State*, Cambridge University Press, 1885; *In Our Time: The Berlin Conference*, BBC Radio 4, 2013; Vittoria Traverso, 'The Tree that Changed the World Map', BBC Travel, 28 May 2020. The effects of poorly designed borders were described, with some excellent maps, by Elias Papaioannou and Stelios Michalopoulos in 'The Long-Run Effects of the Scramble for Africa', Vox EU/Centre for Economic Policy Research, 2012.

The Sudan–Uganda Border Commission: I first learned this story in *Tales from the Map Room*, a 1993 BBC TV documentary which my grandfather Walter Horsey videoed for me on the grounds he thought I'd like it: alas, he died in 2003 so didn't live to see quite what an impact this had had, but if he hadn't made that tape you wouldn't now be holding this book. More details of the story, including the extracts from Kelly's diary, can be found in *The Middle East and North Africa: World Boundaries Volume 2*, ed. Clive H. Schofield and Richard N. Schofield, Routledge, 1994.

European Nationalism and the United States of Greater Austria: Simon Winder, *Danubia*, Picador, 2013; Simon Winder, 'Who Was Franz Ferdinand?', *New Statesman*, 28 June 2014; *The Spectacular Rise and Fall of the Habsburgs*, BBC Radio 4, 2003; Ian Chapman-Curry, 'The United States of Greater Austria', Vaguely Interesting/Almost History.

Britain and France Carve Up the Middle East: Malise Ruthven, 'The Map ISIS Hates', *New York Review of Books*, 25 June 2014; 'A Century on: Why Arabs Resent Sykes–Picot', Al Jazeera, 18 May 2016; Robin Wright, 'How the Curse of Sykes–Picot Still Haunts the Middle East', *New Yorker*, 30 April 2016; Aaron W. Hughes, 'The Sykes–Picot Agreement and the Making of the Modern Middle East', *The Conversation*, 12 May 2016; James L. Gelvin, 'Obsession with Sykes–Picot Says More About What We Think of Arabs than History', *The Conversation*, 12 May 2016.

The Partition of Ulster: *The Rest Is History* podcast's four-part 2023 series on Ireland (episodes 336–9), featuring historians Dan Jackson and Paul Rouse, was invaluable in getting a sense of the sweep of British rule. Other helpful sources included the History Ireland website, and the BBC's late, lamented history website. Northern Ireland's changing demographics featured in reports of the 2021 UK census results, for example Amanda Ferguson and Padraic Halpin, 'Northern Ireland has more Catholics than Protestants for first time', Reuters, 22 September 2022.

The Partition of India: Two excellent documentaries guided this chapter: *India 1947: Partition in Colour*, Channel 4, 2022; and Andrew Whitehead's *India, a People Partitioned*, BBC World Service, 1997. The recency of these events was brought home to me by the fact that the latter features many eye-witness interviews with people who experienced the upheaval first-hand, interviewed in a year in which I was already approaching adulthood. Mountbatten's later uncertainty over whether he should simply have tried to outwait Jinnah was relayed by Larry Collins and Dominique Lapierre in *Mountbatten and the Partition of India*, Vikas, 1982. Other sources included Alex Von Tunzelmann, *Indian Summer: The Secret History of the End of an Empire*, Henry Holt, 2007; Narayani Basu's *V. P. Menon: The Unsung Architect of Modern India*, Simon & Schuster India, 2020; Saurabh Banerjee, 'When Jinnah Agreed to a United India', *Times of India*, 15 August 2022.

The Iron Curtain and the Division of Berlin: Both the weirdness of Berlin's divided metro maps, and the fact the city's division is visible from space, are things I discovered while editing *CityMetric*: the former are available via the excellent TransitMap.net, the latter via the European Space Agency website. Other valuable sources included Emily Wasik, 'Inside the Forgotten Ghost Stations of a Once-Divided Berlin', *Atlas Obscura*, 10 March 2014; 'The Berlin Crisis, 1958–1961', history.state.gov; and 'Deconstructing the Wall', *New York Times*, 6 November 2009.

PART TWO: LEGACIES

Königsberg/Kaliningrad, Eastern Germany/Western Russia: Marc Bennetts, 'Kaliningrad: the Russian exclave with a taste for Europe', *Guardian*, 31 May 2018; 'Operation Hannibal 1945: the Germany evacuation that dwarfed the "miracle of Dunkirk",' *BBC History Magazine*, 20 February 2020; Daniel S. Hamilton and Adrianna Pita, 'Why is Kaliningrad at the center of a new Russia-NATO faceoff?', Brookings, 23 June 2022; Andrius Sytas, 'Lithuania widens curbs on Kaliningrad trade despite Russian warning', Reuters, 11 July 2022; 'Kaliningrad row: Lithuania lifts rail restrictions for Russian exclave', BBC News, 23 July 2022.

The Strange Case of Bir Tawil: I first learned this story through Ned Donovan's occasional blog 'Terra Nullius' (a legal term, you'll recall, that is frequently, if unfairly, applied to the territory). Many of the groups claiming to rule it for a giggle can be found online: some of them, such as the Emirate headed by Sheikh Andrew S. Edwards of Louisville, Kentucky, have gone so far as to issue press releases. For a longer version of this story, written by someone who – unlike those supposed rulers or myself – has actually been to Bir Tawil, I recommend Jack Shenker's longread, 'Welcome to the land that no country wants', *Guardian*, 3 March 2016.

The Dangers of Gardening in the Korean DMZ: This essay owes a debt to Allan R. Millett's fascinating and detailed entry on the Korean War for *Encyclopaedia Britannica*, as well as other entries on Korea.net and History.com. Other cheery articles that contributed details include Eric Wagner, 'The DMZ's Thriving Resident: The

Crane', *Smithsonian Magazine*, April 2011, and – one of the all-time great headlines, this – 'Koreas switch off loudspeakers', BBC News, 15 June 2004. (It also happened in 2018.)

China's Nine-Dash Line, and Its Discontents: Robert Kaplan's *Asia's Cauldron* was published by Random House in 2014; a flavour can be gained from his special report for *Foreign Policy*, 'The South China Sea Is the Future of Conflict', 15 August 2011. The student quote about *Abominable* is taken from Khanh Vu and Phuong Nguyen, 'Vietnam pulls DreamWorks' "Abominable" film over South China Sea map', Reuters, 14 October 2019; the *Time* piece referenced is Hannah Beech, 'Just Where Exactly Did China Get the South China Sea Nine-Dash Line From?', 19 July 2016. Other details were taken from Bec Strating, 'China's nine-dash line proves stranger than fiction', The Lowy Institute's *Interpreter* blog, 12 April 2022; 'Vietnam–China Boundary Delimitation Agreement in the Gulf of Tonkin', Vietnam News Agency, 11 January 2021; and Tan Kee Yun, 'Fans angry after Chinese K-pop stars display patriotism', *The New Paper/Straits Times*, 15 July 2016.

The Uncertain Borders Between Israel and Palestine: The story of the Green Line also comes from the BBC's *Tales from the Map Room* (1993). The Zionism episodes of the *Origin Story* podcast provide an excellent potted history. The quotes from Meron Rapoport come from 'The Line Separating Israel from Palestine Has Been Erased – What Comes Next?', *The Nation*, 10 August 2022; those from Yousef Munayyer from 'Green-lined Vision Is Blurring Reality in Israel–Palestine', *Foreign Policy*, 12 May 2021. More about the peace plan can be found at alandforall.org. An English translation of the *Local Call* article concerning the role of the wall, and breaches in it, during the Covid pandemic can be read on the website of *972 Magazine* (Suha Arraf, 'In ironic twist, Palestinians count on Israel's separation barrier to keep out coronavirus', 16 April 2020). Other useful articles included Uri Dromi, 'Israel Wants Peace, but It Won't Go Back to 1967', *International Herald Tribune*, 27 June 2000; William Eichler, 'Theodor Herzl and the Trajectory of Zionism', Open Democracy, 1 December 2016; Shakked Auerbach, 'No One Actually Knows

Where Israel Ends and the Palestinian Territories Begin', *Haaretz*, 8 June 2017; Michael Sfard and Oren Yiftachel, 'Who's Afraid of the Green Line?', *Haaretz*, 6 September 2022; and Roleen Tafakji and Sinan Abu Mayzer, 'Two textbooks, two stories as Palestinian parents protest Israeli curriculum', Reuters, 3 October 2022.

The Siamese Twin Towns of Baarle-Hertog and Baarle-Nassau: Another entry that has its origins in an article I once wrote for *CityMetric*. Aside from the usual scouring of encyclopaedias, sources included Frank Jacobs, 'An Apology of Enclaves', *New York Times*, 14 November 2011; Bruno Waterfield, 'Dining for some, whining for others in border town Baarle', *The Times*, 5 June 2020; Andrew Eames, 'Europe's strange border anomaly', BBC Travel, 11 December 2017; and the website of the local history society Amalia van Solms.

The US–Canada border, and the Trouble with Straight Lines: I was familiar with the Northwest Angle story from my time running *CityMetric* (this is becoming a theme); other details came from Zoran Nikolic's *Atlas of Unusual Borders*, Collins, 2019.

Some Places That Aren't Switzerland: Sources on Campione d'Italia included 'A tiny Italian exclave unwillingly joins the EU's customs union', *Economist*, 2 January 2020; and Larry Bleiberg, 'Campione d'Italia: An Italian town surrounded by Switzerland', BBC Travel, 19 May 2020. Those on Büsingen am Hochrhein included Larry Bleiberg, 'Germany's tiny geographic oddity', BBC Travel, 23 September 2019; and Frank Jacobs, 'See Where Switzerland Has Germany Surrounded', *Big Think*, 23 July 2010. A Borderlines column by Jacobs, entitled 'Enclave-Hunting in Switzerland' (*New York Times*, 15 May 2012), provided background on both.

Some Notes on Microstates: Gideon Defoe's *An Atlas of Extinct Countries* (Europa Compass, 2020) was very useful for identifying some interesting and forgotten microstates. The relationship between Italian fascism and Vatican sovereignty was described by David Kertzer's award-winning book *The Pope and Mussolini: The Secret History of Pius XI and the Rise of Fascism in Europe* (Random House, 2014); that between the other states and the business community by numerous op-eds, including Massimo Passamonti, 'Small states in outer space: Monaco's ambitions for the new space age', *Space News*, 18 October 2021, and 'Europe's microstates aren't irrelevant – and they can teach us a lot about sovereignty', *Strategic Forecasting/Business Insider*, 27 April 2015.

City Limits: Another entry which I didn't so much research as 'write down everything I have thought on this subject since I edited *CityMetric*' – or, indeed, since I was an obnoxious child, to whom it was critically important that I lived *inside* the boundaries of Greater London. The story of the consolidation of New York City was told by Harry Macy Jr for the New York Genealogical & Biographical Society in 2021; I first learned about the Commissioner's Plan of 1811 in *The Map That Made Manhattan* (BBC Radio 4, 2014). For an example of the kind of hysterical western press articles that talk about Chinese 'cities' covering an area on a par with Great Britain, consider Tracy You, 'China builds a mega-city larger than Britain with over 100 million people', *Mail Online*, 28 March 2017.

The Curse of Suburbia and the Borders of Detroit: I first learned of the role borders played in the decline of Detroit in an address that Michigan Congressman Dan Kildee gave to a Lincoln Institute of Land Policy conference in Washington, DC, in 2016. Many of the details come from Paul Sewick's excellent Detroit Urbanism blog, specifically an entry named '7 Historical Facts About Detroit's Suburban Sprawl' (24 May 2021). Other sources included Mark Binella, 'Don't Shrink Detroit, Super-Size It', *The Atlantic*, 29 March 2021; Aaron Mondry, 'How Detroit's borders were drawn and why it matters', Detour Detroit, 19 January 2021; and Lauren Davis, 'Detroit plans to shrink by leaving half the city in the dark', Gizmodo, 26 May 2012.

Washington, DC, and the Square Between the States: The strange shape and constitutional status of the US capital is a thing I have been thinking about since the same 2016 trip on which I learned about Detroit. Sources included 'Chasing Congress Away', history.house.gov.us, 1 June 2015; 'How Philadelphia lost the nation's capital to Washington', National Constitution Center, 16 July 2021; and Chris Myers Asch and George Derek Musgrove, 'Don't Fall for the D.C. Retrocession "Okey-Doke"', *Atlantic*, 5 May 2021.

Borders from a Land Down Under: The main source for this chapter was Gerard Carney's 2013 lecture, 'The Story behind the Land Borders of the Australian States – A Legal and Historical Overview', available on the website of the High Court of Australia; David R. Horton's fascinating 1996 Map of Indigenous Australia is available online via AIATSIS. Other details are taken from Michael McGowan, 'NSW and ACT in talks over biggest border shake-up in living memory', *Guardian*, 16 September 2022; 'New Zealand becomes a separate colony', National Museum Australia; 'New Zealand turns down federation with Australia', NZhistory.govt.nz.

Some Accidental Invasions: 'Pocket war', *Canberra Times*, 16 October 1968; 'Swiss Soldiers Inadvertently Invade Liechtenstein', *Sarasota Herald-Tribune*, 1 September 1976; 'Swiss in Liechtenstein "invasion"', BBC News, 3 March 2007; Nick Miroff, 'Venezuelan troops invaded Colombia this week. But just a little bit', *Washington Post*, 24 March 2017; Latika Bourke, 'Navy breached Indonesian waters six times under Operation Sovereign Borders, review finds', abc.net.au, 18 February, 2014; Giles Tremlett, 'Tell it to the marines . . . we've invaded the wrong country', *Guardian*, 18 February 2002; 'PSNI set up checkpoint on wrong side of border', *Belfast Telegraph*, 1 April 2010; Ken Jennings, 'The Border Battle That Led to "Fort Blunder"', *Conde Nast Traveller*, 7 July 2014; Michael Safi, 'Chinese and Indian troops face off in Bhutan border dispute', *Guardian*, 5 July 2017.

Costa Rica, Nicaragua and the 'Google Maps War': The full story was laid out by Frank Jacobs in 'The First Google Maps War', *New York Times*, 28 February 2012. Other sources: Mark Brown, 'Nicaraguan Invasion? Blame Google Maps', *Wired*, 8 November 2010; Josh Halliday, 'Google Nicaraguan map error threatens to escalate into regional dispute', *Guardian*, 15 November 2010; 'Google Maps Blamed for Conflict Between Costa Rica and Nicaragua', *Tico Times*, 5 November 2010. The accusations against President Ortega were reported as 'Cable en el que jueces sandinistas ponen en libertad a "narcos" a cambio de dinero', *El Pais*, 6 December, 2010.

The Mapmaker's Dilemma: The *Independent* interview with Ed Parsons was 'The man who's making Google Maps smarter' by Simon Usborne, 17 June 2014. Other sources included Alex Hern, 'Google Maps Russia claims Crimea for the federation', *Guardian*, 22 April 2014; and Lorenzo Franceschi-Bicchierai, 'Russia's Yandex Is Removing Borders from Its Maps App', *Vice*, 10 June 2022.

PART THREE: EXTERNALITIES

A Brief History of the Prime Meridian: YouGov's tracker poll of 'The most famous US presidents' can be found on its website. (At the time of writing, Donald Trump ranks eighth, beneath Obama, Washington, George W. Bush, Jefferson, Clinton and Kennedy, which must be driving him nuts.) The text of the International Conference Held at Washington for the Purpose of Fixing a Prime Meridian and a Universal Day can be read online at Project Gutenberg. 'Why the Greenwich meridian moved' was explained by Stephen Malys et al. in the *Journal of Geodesy*, 1 August 2015. The description of Greenwich as a 'dingy London suburb' was printed in the *Louisville Courier-Journal* in June 1884.

Some Notes on Time Zones: Assorted articles on the (fascinating, if you're into that kind of thing) TimeAndDate.com website were useful in understanding the history and current status of time zones. In addition: '"Eradicating Ideological Viruses": China's Campaign of Repression Against Xinjiang's Muslims', Human Rights Watch, 9 September 2018; Michael A. Lombardi, 'Why is a minute divided into 60 seconds, an hour into 60 minutes, yet there are only 24 hours in a day?', *Scientific American*, 5 March 2007; Joseph Stromberg, 'Sandford Fleming Sets the World's Clock', *Smithsonian Magazine*, 18 November 2011; 'When Scotland and England had different time zones', *Scotsman*, 27 January 2017; Adam Taylor, 'The brief history of North Korea's time zone', *Washington Post*, 4 May 2018; Laurie Clarke,

'What would happen if we abolished time zones altogether?', *Wired*, 20 October 2019.

A Brief History of the International Date Line: The main source for this chapter was Robert H. van Gent's 'A History of the International Date Line', found on his website. Others include: Sarah Laskow, 'In 1844, the Philippines Skipped a Day, And It Took Decades for the Rest of the World to Notice', *Atlas Obscura*, 30 December 2015; Associated Press, 'Samoa loses a day and jumps forward in time', *Guardian*, 30 December 2011.

Of Maritime Boundaries, and the Law of the Sea: The text of UNCLOS can be read online on the UN Digital Library, if that's your bag. The story of the North Sea's borders was found in Professor Philip Steinberg's 'Borders Research in a Shifting Landscape', a 2021 lecture available on YouTube. Other sources included: Yukie Yoshikawa, 'The US–Japan–China Mistrust Spiral and Okinotorishima', *Asia-Pacific Journal*, 1 October 2007; Justin McCurry, 'Japan to spend millions on tiny islands 1,000 miles south of Tokyo', *Guardian*, 3 February 2016; Rahul Srivastava and Amit Kumar Akela, 'Why India Needs to Be on the International Continental Shelf Commission', *The Wire (India)*, 23 May 2017.

Some Notes on Landlocked Countries: This one began as an article on my Substack, *The Newsletter of (Not Quite) Everything*, and was included in the book at the suggestion of my agent, Antony Topping. Other sources: Rory Carroll and Andres Schipani, 'Bolivia's landlocked sailors pine for the high seas', *Guardian*, 28 August 2008; Dickens Olewe, 'Why landlocked Ethiopia wants to launch a navy', BBC News, 14 June 2018; Kyle Younker, 'Falklands war 30 years on: Will a vote solve the dispute?', *Christian Science Monitor*, 14 June 2012.

How the World Froze Territorial Claims in Antarctica: The Antarctic Treaty too can be read online. Other key sources: *In Our Time: Antarctica*, BBC Radio 4, 24 June 2010; David Adam, 'How do you claim land in Antarctica?', *Guardian*, 18 October 2007; Tao Tao Holmes, 'How a Baby Staked Argentina's Claim on Antarctica', *Atlas Obscura*, 25 February 2016; Klaus Dodds, 'In 30 years the Antarctic

Treaty becomes modifiable, and the fate of a continent could hang in the balance', *The Conversation*, 12 July 2018; Matthew Taylor, 'Antarctic's future in doubt after plan for world's biggest marine reserve is blocked', *Guardian*, 2 November 2018. A record of the decades-long attempt to locate Ernest Shackleton's famous but possibly fictional advert can be found on Antarctic-Circle.org.

The Other, Bigger, More Musical Europe: Another piece that originated in a post on *The Newsletter of (Not Quite) Everything*, based on Eurovision's unique map of Europe, plus a certain amount of trawling of the Eurovision and EBU websites. Another valuable source was Siobhán Doyle, '8 Eurovision controversies you probably didn't know about', RTE, 9 May 2023. Thanks to Tyron Wilson for his almost infinite Eurovision knowledge.

Boundaries in the Air: Theo Deutinger's map of flight information regions was invaluable, as were the websites of Skybrary, the NATS and ICAO. FlightAware's passenger statistics were reported by sources including Mary Kekatos, 'The great getaway begins: 6.4 MILLION travelers set off for the holidays as incredible flight tracker map shows how busy the skies are above the US', *DailyMail.com*, 23 December 2017. Other sources were 'The battle for the sky', *Economist*, 13 May 2014; Luke Harding, 'Russia and Norway resolve Arctic border dispute', *Guardian*, 15 September 2010; and Mark Vanhoenacker's 'View from the Cockpit' column, especially 'Flying in the far north: a story of magnetism and magic', *Financial Times*, 16 December 2021.

The Final Frontier: This idea of this being the final entry in the book came from my sometime collaborator Tom Phillips; the result was generously fact-checked by Kate Arkless Gray. The work of Tim Marshall was invaluable, especially 'The battle for space is about to heat up', *Prospect*, 23 April 2021; and *The Power of Geography*, Scribner, 2021. The paper 'Where is Space? And Why Does That Matter?' was written by Bhavya Lal and Emily Nightingale of the Science and Technology Policy Institution, for the 2014 Space Traffic Management conference. Other sources included Nadia Drake, 'Where, exactly, is the edge of space? It depends on who you ask', *National Geographic*, 20 December 2018; Marina Koren, 'Jeff Bezos Is Ready to Cross a Cosmically Controversial Line', *Atlantic*, 19 July 2021; Eric Betz, 'The Kármán Line: Where does space begin?', Astronomy.com, 5 March 2021; Elliot Ji, Michael B. Cerny and Raphael J. Piliero, 'What Does China Think About NASA's Artemis Accords?', *The Diplomat*, 17 September 2020; and Deng Xiaoci, 'Trump administration's "Artemis Accords" expose political agenda of moon colonization, show Cold War mentality against space rivals: observers', *Global Times*, 7 May 2020.

Conclusion: The End of the Line: Argentine Defence Minister Jorge Taiana's claim that the Falkland Islands would be Argentinian again sooner rather than later can be found, among rather a lot of other places, at 'Malvinas to be returned to Argentina soon, says Argentine Defense Minister', MercoPress, 9 February 2023. Both Vladimir Putin's July 2021 essay 'On the Historical Unity of Russians and Ukrainians', and his February 2022 address which immediately preceded the invasion, can be found on the Kremlin's website – if, for some reason, you wanted to read them.

Acknowledgments

There are two people in particular without whom I would never have written this book: my grandfather, Wally Horsey, who encouraged my interests in history, geography and absurdity alike; and my beloved fiancée, Agnes Frimston, who pointed out that there was a book in these interests, and who helped shaped the results. Neither, sadly, are with us any longer – Agnes died, with shocking suddenness and timing that would feel a bit too on the nose in a novel, just hours after I finished the first draft in June 2023. I miss her more than I can say. I suspect I always will.

The team who actually turned the bizarre and random contents of my brain into a coherent book include my wonderful and patient editor, Lindsay Davies; Tim Peters who provided the maps; Liz Marvin for the copy editing; Matthew Burne for the cover art; the team at Wildfire, especially Alex Clarke and Federica Trogu; and my agent, Antony Topping of Greene and Heaton.

A number of historians were kind enough to read chunks of the manuscript, to help me avoid howlers: Kevin Feeney, Rhiannon Garth Jones and my dear friend Matt Symonds. Others who offered insight and advice at various crucial points in the process include Alex Von Tunzelmann; Duncan Weldon; Dr Megan Barford of the Royal Museums Greenwich; Professor Philip Steinberg, Director of the International Boundaries Research Unit at the University of Durham; Jim Caruth, formerly the lead curator of maps at the British Library; and Lewis Baston, whose own very different book about borders, called *Borderlines*, is published shortly after this one, and which you should all purchase immediately.

I should also thank a number of others without whom I am not sure I would still be standing, let alone finishing books: my mother and stepfather, Kim and Alan; my aunts Jennifer and Leila, and uncle David; and the team at Podmasters' *Paper Cuts* podcast, including Andrew Harrison, Miranda Sawyer, Jason Hazeley, Gráinne Maguire, Liam Tait, Jess Harpin, Jacob Jarvis and Adam Wright (God, I've missed having colleagues). I should thank, too, the bafflingly sizable number of people who subscribe to my Substack, *The Newsletter of (Not Quite) Everything*, whose interest and support has enabled me to write full-time.

Last, but very far from least, there are so many friends to whom I owe a great deal these last few months that I'm terrified I might miss one out. Their names include but are not limited to Scot Fisher, Manu Ekanayake, Brad Curtis, Rachel Nekanda-Trepka, Larissa Fischer, Jasper Jackson, James Ball, Frankie Goodway, Marie Le Conte, Tom Phillips, Luke McGee, Holly Thomas, Ava Evans, Sarah Duggers, Andrew Swan, Harriet Tyce, Kate Arkless Gray, Matt Drinkwater, Anne-Marie Conneally, Aaron Lovell, Rachel Cunliffe, Pete Mitchell, Jim Cooray-Smith, Catherine Owen, Neil Atkinson and Henry Scampi, who remains, reassuringly, the best dog in the world. My heart is filled with love for every one of you.

Index

Page numbers in *italics* refer to maps.

About the Author

JONN ELLEDGE's previous books include *The Compendium of (Not Quite) Everything* and *Conspiracy: A History of Boll*cks Theories, and How Not to Fall for Them*. At the *New Statesman*, he created and ran its urbanism-focused CityMetric site, spending six happy years writing about cities, maps, and borders. He lives in London.

jonn.substack.com | @JonnElledge | JonnElledge